Contents

Preface

Christine Gruber and Helga Stefanov

Interpreting the causes of social problems, developing strategies for dealing with difficult life situations and providing social or social work services are all influenced by gender-specific perceptions and differences. Reflecting on gender differences and the analysis of gender-relationships should therefore permeate all fields of contemporary social work and should therefore also be part of social work training.

To date very few social work training programmes in Europe incorporate a systematic reflection and analysis of the impact of gender.

Reference to differences between women and men should not, however, cause us to overlook the sometimes very significant differences between members of the 'same' gender. Such differences are not only the results of social and cultural origin, sexual orientation, physique, education, and age, but also stem from individual development. Social work therefore considers it a particular challenge to perceive the individuality and the development potential of each human being and to include into the analysis of the respective social problems an analysis of the differing power structure relationships which apply (though to different degrees) to all members of a – discriminated – group.

It is the objective of this book, to bring about the integration of the analysis of gender relationships into social work theory, methods, and practice. We, the editors, are aware of the fact that the topics covered represent only part of relevant social work issues. This book is designed as a textbook and a workbook. The teaching suggestions at the end of most chapters are meant to facilitate addressing gender-specific aspects of social work during the teaching process.

We hope that the individual contributions will motivate the reader towards theoretical and personal reflections on gender roles and thereby contribute towards gender equality.

Acknowledgements

This publication is based on an inter-university co-operation project under Socrates-Erasmus for the development of the European Module 'Gender Aspects in Social Work' from 1997 to 2000.

A European Module consists of the development of new teaching contents to be integrated into training programmes of the participating universities.

We thank the European Commission for its approval and basic funding of the Module and the Office of European Educational Co-operation in Vienna, and the Austrian Ministry for Education, Science and Cultural Affairs for co-funding the project.

The positive response by the social work profession and by academic training institutions to the first publication of the results, 'Gender-Aspekte in der Sozialen Arbeit' (C. Gruber/E. Fröschl, Eds. (2001), Vienna) and their continuing interest provided the motivation for translation and preparation of an edition in English.

In particular we thank Geoffrey Mann of RHP and Professor Neil Thompson for their support in making this publication possible.

The Editors
Vienna, January 2002

About the Editors and Authors

The Editors

Gruber, Christine Mag. Dr: Head of the department for part-time studies and programme director at the Bundesakademie für Sozialarbeit, Vienna. Research and publications on sociology and the economics of social work; sociology of the family; curriculum development for social work training.

Stefanov, Helga Mag.: Lecturer at the Bundesakademie für Sozialarbeit, Vienna, Austria. Research and professional focus: comparative linguistics in the social sciences; comparative social work; social work as a human rights profession.

The Authors

Bates, John: Field leader, Social Studies, North East Wales Institute, UK. Research and publications on men and social work; the use of information technology in social work; and child protection.

Brunnberg, Elinor: Centre for Public Sector Research CEFOS at the University of Gothenburg, Sweden. Research focus: International comparisons of social work with children.

Brückner, Margrit Dr: Professor at the Fachhochschule Frankfurt a. Main, Germany; research and numerous publications on violence against women and gender relations.

Fröschl, Elfriede Mag.: Lecturer at the Bundesakademie für Sozialarbeit, Vienna, Austria. Founding member of the first women's refuge in Austria. Research and publications on legal and sociological aspects of violence against women.

Holwerda, Obertha Drs: Lecturer at the Hogeschool de Horst, Driebergen, Netherlands. Professional focus and publications: gender and diversity in social work.

Kullberg, Christian Ph.D.: Assistant Professor at the University of Örebro/Sweden. Research and publications on gender and social work, equal pay policy implementation, social work evaluation and inter-organisational co-operation.

Thompson, Neil Ph.D.: Independent consultant and author; Visiting Professor at the University of Liverpool, UK. Research and publications in anti-discriminatory practice; stress and staff care; integrating theory and practice; and loss and grief.

Vogt, Irmgard Dr: Professor at the Fachhochschule Frankfurt a. Main, Germany. Research focus and publications on gender and addictive substances, substance abuse, female health and illness, gender dynamics.

Zartler, Ulrike Mag. Dr: Lecturer at the Bundesakademie für Sozialarbeit, Vienna, Austria. Research focus and publications on childhood sociology, family sociology, violence against children and adolescents, schools and the community, and qualitative research methods.

1. Gender as a Structural Category: Its Significance in Social Work

Margrit Brückner

On the difficulty of having a gender and being human

Or is it the other way round? Does the difficulty lie in being human and having a gender?

Possibly there might also be another alternative: either being human **or** having a gender. These are questions with a highly explosive potential in our society, as demonstrated by the fact that in our training institutions as well as in social work practice such deliberations are often considered impertinent. At any rate, the concept of being human bears aspects of being tendentially sublime (which is the reason why specific groups of fellow human beings are time and again excluded) and reference to gender and sex is seen as something low and animalistic (Brückner, 1994). Bluntly expressed, talk about gender and sex is never relaxed, instead it opens a vast field of feelings and emotions. When women and men deal with this subject there are always strong dynamics. Women are irritated about gender-specific discrimination and demand inclusion; men take a defensive attitude or retreat to the safe havens of their 'old boys' networks'.

Social science research and practice does not take place in a vacuum but within a specific historical and social context. Their subjects and objects are human beings whose very existence is tied to their bodies. These social and corporeal factors, which bear a strong gender-specific connotation in our society, become part of any theoretical or practical undertaking, whether noticed or unnoticed. They influence the perspective, emotions, attitude and stance we take towards the world. We therefore must admit to this subjective and objective entanglement; admitting these facts is part of finding the 'truth'.

There is obviously an offensive element attached to human gender, something that has to be overcome and which stems from the recognition of one's own deficiencies and the fundamental dependence on the other gender. Gender in this connection means: the cultural interpretation of the often suppressed physical fact of belonging to one and only one gender (Becker-Schmidt (1993) *Eine differenzierte Analyse des Begriffs Geschlecht*). The widely prevailing ignorance among men regarding their being part of the male gender and the existence of another 'second' gender (Beauvoir) for instance when dealing with 'work' or 'youth', permits men to take a 'general' perspective and thus the main-stream becomes the male-stream. Men also develop assumptions about women, but mainly without leaving their male-centred positions (e.g. with regard to the role women play in educating young people against violence). The current emphasis on the 'female' in women and the need for a female perspective in theory and practice must therefore be seen as a consequence stemming from the fact that women have been 'forgotten' and structurally disadvantaged.

The male presumption of representing humankind as the 'first' gender has not only permitted men to camouflage discrimination of women, but also freed men of their own sexuality, without depriving them of it. Women, on the other hand, who laid claim to their part in humanity by taking 'male' positions, were simply denied any sexuality and treated as neuter.

The complexity of these issues and the continuous sublime gender-specific attributions on the basis of physical characteristics is clearly demonstrated by the American researcher Sandra Harding: 'When a woman enters a room, sex comes in and when a black person enters a room, race comes in.' (lecture at Frankfurt University, 28 November 1991). 'White' is accordingly not perceived as an ethnic 'colour', just as 'man' does not equate to sexuality and gender.

What I find disturbing about the New Women's Movement and gender research making gender and sexuality an issue is that it reminds women and men of the fact that they belong to a particular sex and that this fact has a significant impact on their opportunities for development in our societies. Raising such awareness often results in feelings of shame, as it draws our attention to parts of our personality which are taboo, in other words brings our 'private parts' into the spotlight. It is therefore disencumbering to present oneself as a sexually neutral human being. As a theoretician or a practitioner (male or female) I am an autonomous individual, independent of my body, and I will be judged – or judge myself – as to whether I am 'neutral' in this regard. The more profitable it appears (or is) to rise above one's sexuality or to ignore it, the more aggressive one tends to be towards anyone who points out the gender-relatedness of societal structures and patterns of interpretation as well as to the male determined construction of the autonomous individual.

All this explains why even women who fear for their traditional place in society or women who have invaded male bastions 'through their own power', fervently oppose the notion of 'sex' as an indicator of societal position. The latter, in particular, fear to be reduced to their being female, a shackle of which they had hoped to rid themselves, in order to become 'autonomous human beings' and to take up positions reserved for such beings (Flaake, 1993; Brückner, 1991; Rohde-Dachser, 1991).

The extreme emotional character of sex and gender can be seen from the embittered fight for female word forms and endings in linguistic contexts. In many cases this has become a 'question of religion' requiring professional avowal one way or the other, and provoking, depending on the individual personality, either allegiance or dissent. In German speaking countries gender-specific language has the advantage that it makes women visible and demonstrates that women no longer accept 'being implied'. The disadvantage lies in relating that statement to the gender-specific aspect only and thus reinforcing cultural gender

patterns. Gender-specific language as such does not denote progress but may, as in traditional societies, lend expression to the polarisation of gender-specific roles. Consideration needs to be given whether this is desirable. It is important, however, to raise awareness of linguistic formulations chosen by women and men, because they reflect gender relations.

The theoretical relevance of gender as a structural category

The development of gender-sensitive theory and research highlights the fundamental significance of individual gender structures for the understanding of social phenomena and supports gender-democratic ways of thinking.

The New Women's Movement and resultant women's research has made women and thus also men, visible with regard to structure and subject theories. It has raised awareness of gender-specific division of labour and power structures, traditionally ignored by scientists, and analyses them alongside the life situations and working potentials of women (Braun, 1995). The gender-neutral image of human beings, be it as 'free citizens', 'alienated production workers', or 'bourgeois individuals', as well as the purported gender neutrality of scientific analyses, have both turned out to be ideological constructs (Patzak, 1994; Nunner-Winkler, 1994). The hidden dual structure of western industrialised societies has become visible: although all human beings have been considered equal since the bourgeois revolution, inequality of women and men continued because they were seen as different from each other, and on different hierarchical levels with regard to their political, economic, social, and domestic positions (Metz-Göckel, 1993).

In the New Women's Movement women started to look at their life situation and arrived at new questions and issues for which they demanded scientific attention (Hagemann-White, 1991; Müller, 1994). There are two main issues: first, the conceptional reinterpretation of existing theoretical approaches, and second, taking up subjects hitherto considered taboo. The first includes a new definition of the concept of work, by integrating unpaid housework and care work, the second includes the issue of male violence against women and girls in so-called private spheres, at work, and in the prostitution business. According to Sandra Harding (1994) this change of perspective in the scientific field brings about increased knowledge and awareness in particular of the fact that women's work in the reproductive field had not been taken note of, as long as the children developed without problems and the man was freed to pursue his career. Such a change of perspective is also prerequisite to the perception of violence against women. Making rape among married partners an issue means, among other things, to take female desires equally seriously as a woman's 'no' in response to physical advances. It means, recognising women as human beings with their own desires and rights. Male sexual behaviour is interpreted differently depending on the image of women and the concept of 'justified' male claims to the female body are taken as the basis for such an interpretation. The private sphere is expected to provide room for the development and protection of civil individuality, free of any interference or control from outside; this protection at the same time serves to guarantee male predominance. Dealing with the current construction of privacy in women's research puts an end to the concept of autonomous, disembodied individuals, by raising awareness of the relevance of bodiliness, emotionality, and sociability and their gender specific attribution (Kerchner and Wilde, 1997).

In recent women's research the structural significance of gender is pegged to the dual role of women in society, on the one hand in the private reproductive sphere controlled by patriarchical power structures and on the other hand in the market-induced societal sphere under the control of the profit-oriented organisation of the production sphere (Metz-Göckel, 1993; Becker-Schmidt and Knapp, 1995). Due to the hierarchical gender relationship, male dominance controls both spheres. The reason is that the employment sphere, tailored to the standard male biography, is seen as superior to the family, deemed the central female life sphere; this also

has its impact on the structural principles of social politics. If gender research wants to understand the influence of gender in both spheres, it must deal, from the micro-sociological perspective, with gender as a social construct, and, from the macro-sociological perspective, with the socio-theoretical and socio-structural involvement of gender. The gender category is of structural significance for widely differing social phenomena (Becker-Schmidt and Knapp, 1995) particularly for:

- The social organisation of sexuality, the regulation of generatively and population politics.
- The division of labour and distribution of power within society.
- The cultural order.

In relation to inner psychic dynamics in individualisation and group processes, gender proves to be a collective category with regard to general norms and values, as well as a decisive factor of individual identity regarding the socialisation process (Adkins and Lury, 1995). If social and psychological processes are looked at together, the gender category is of high relevance on four different overlapping levels, each of which can be defined through approaches of development psychology, discourse theory, psychoanalysis, or power and structure theory (Flaake, 1996):

- The individual development in relationship to body images.
- Symbolical-cultural concepts of masculinity and femininity.
- The collective sub-conscious with its gender-anchored desires and fears.
- The socio-structural inequality of women and men.

The gender category highlights the synergies of the social situation, of cultural blue-printing and individual-social behaviour. Gender serves as the stencil through which vast spheres of human co-habitation are regulated and is, beyond all this, a factor in the standardisation of behaviour and action (Braun, 1995). Gender is, however, not a rigid classification characteristic, but part of social practice which develops interactively through everyday action (doing gender), requiring continual strife for meaning and definitions (Kahlert, 1995; Dölling and Krais, 1997). Whereas the constitutive elements of gender relations are of structural relevance and change only slowly (principles of production and confirmation; being a woman or a man), there are regulative standards which within the pre-determined framework of two genders permit a changeable spectrum of choices, such as hair-style, sports, and occupations (Hagemann-White, 1994).

At the beginning of women's research the 'subject woman' appeared as a homogeneous political actor. Today however, 'woman' is no longer understood as a **uniform** category but (in spite of all the differences) as a **unifying** category on the basis of gender-related definitions which hamper development (Maynard, 1995). The recognised guiding interest is not the solidification and entrenchment of gender images but making them visible. We are dealing here with constructed rather than essential differences; we are not interested in women 'being different' as an inherent feature but in revealing this 'being different' as a cultural construction (Thürmer-Rohr, 1995). The increasing awareness of the many facets of women and the differences between them is not only reflected in a new respect for differences but also in the perception of one's own intrinsic part in a dominant culture (c.f. the criticism of hegemonic claims of West German women towards East German women, Dölling, 1993). It is not only injustice experienced by oneself which needs to be probed, but also the injustice experienced by others and done unto others (Thürmer-Rohr, 1995). If gender loses its classifying relevance, the other in oneself, the non-identical becomes visible. Psychological processes of division can no longer find their individual and cultural expression in gender delineations and attributions. There is no longer unconditional understanding within a gender group, nor are there rigid groups but only temporary associations. The post-modern approach relativises the category 'gender' through differentiations within the category, by adding other categories such as class and ethnicity, and by challenging the differentiation between sex and gender. Katrin Braun (1995) sees the advantages of this relativisation in the fact that gender research no longer confirms the category 'woman' and ascribes women either the role of victims or that of the better human beings, but highlights their changeability. Nevertheless gender-related hierarchies within prevailing power structures still require research and change, but these should find their focus beyond the maxims of identity politics.

According to Regina Becker-Schmidt (1996) elements of resistance and reluctance in gender relations can only be researched by contextualising different levels of assumed gender differences, since only an analysis which is historically and socially precise, permits us to see existing gaps:

- Gender differences in sexuality relate to the interpretation of physical differences geared to meeting heterosexual male desires.
- Gender characters are seen as the result of socialisation-induced fixations on models of the same and the other sex.
- The social inequality of women and men is based on their belonging to different powerful groups, which, while in themselves not homogeneous, reflect significant differences with regard to life contexts.

In spite of the existing superior and inferior rankings and sectoral claims of hegemony the individual gender-specifically moulded social spheres are interdependent due to significant division of labour and need a relatively autonomous ability to function. The ensuing contradictions between participation and discrimination of women within and between these social spheres are reflected in the gender order, resulting on the one hand in the involvement of women in the social system, while letting them remain outsiders on the other hand. The latter generates the desire for change.

The societal construction of femininity and masculinity is subject to dynamic processes and according to Robert Connell (1995) it generates different patterns of masculinity through different 'gender regimes': the culturally significant hegemonic pattern (which need not necessarily be the most common one), as well as subordinate (e.g. gay) and marginalised forms of masculinity (e.g. of ethnically devalued groups). The main feature of these patterns is that they may be just as contradictory among themselves as the gender order *per se*. Therefore the fight among men for hegemony takes different forms and leads to the development of new masculinities, which give rise to further contradictions in the relationship between the genders.

Gender research aims to create awareness for the manifold impacts of gender and the gender order underlying societal structures. Gender specific discriminations are to be revealed and opportunities for change should be investigated by revealing contradictions. Gender research does not aim at creating new essentialist feminine and masculine attributions, but to resolve polarised concepts and polar thinking patterns, for gender should no longer remain the central principle of processes of social regulation (Krüger, 1994; Metz-Göckel, 1993). The fact that gender-sensitive research makes gender differences the centre of its attention thus involuntarily confirms it is a problem which cannot be resolved for the time being. In spite of all this, research on women and gender will be indispensable as long as gender remains the central criterion of power and socialisation.

Conclusions

Every human being in our society is attributed to a gender which is supposed to have or not to have certain properties and which has a high identity-forming significance for the individual. Acquiring a gender is on the one hand an individual socialisation-related process and on the other hand is influenced by living conditions which are socio-structurally and culturally determined. With gender having the character of a structural category in our society, 'doing gender' constitutes a significant factor of human life and existence, which, as long as this is still the case, must be adequately taken into account in research and practice. Gender interpretation is dependent on society and history and so is the development of categories and theories as well as the relevant pre-scientific assumptions. The methodological necessity being derived is therefore not so much the quest for the objective truth, but rather for the intersubjective testing of results and interpretations. The ethical context for this search is the social accountability of science and professional practice, including the awareness of the impact of one's own actions on gender relations.

References

Adkins, L. and Lury, C. (1995) Das Soziale in feministischen Theorien: Eine nützliche Analysekategorie? In: Armbruster, C., Müller, U. and Stein-Hilbers, M. (Eds.) *Neue Horizonte? Sozialwissenschaftliche Forschung über Geschlechter und Geschlechterverhältnisse*. Opladen, 41–60.

Becker-Schmidt, R. (1993) Geschlechterdifferenz-Geschlechterverhältnis: Soziale Dimensionen des Begriffs Geschlecht. *Zeitschrift für Frauenforschung*. 1, 2, 37–46.

Becker-Schmidt, R. (1996) Einheit-Zweiheit-Vielheit, identitätslogische Implikationen in feministischen Emanzipationskonzepten. *Zeitschrift für Frauenforschung*. 1, 2, 5–18.

Becker-Schmidt, R. and Knapp, G. (1995) Preface. In: Dies, (Ed.) *Das Geschlechterverhältnis als Gegenstand der Sozialwissenschaften*. Frankfurt/New York, 7–18.

Braun, K. (1995) Frauenforschung, Geschlechterforschung und feministische Politik. *Feministische Studien*. 2, 107–17.

Brückner, M. (1991) Von der Aneignung weiblicher Lebensräume oder Die Frau in der Tapete. *Kulturanalysen*. 1, 83–99.

Brückner, M. (1994) Geschlecht und Öffentlichkeit. In: Dies, and Meyer, B. (Eds.) *Die sichtbare Frau*. Freiburg, 19–56.

Connell, R. W. (1995) Neue Richtungen für Geschlechtertheorie, Männlichkeitsforschung und Geschlechterpolitik. In: Armbruster, C., Müller, U. and Stein-Hilbers, M. (Eds.) *Neue Horizonte? Sozialwissenschaftliche Forschung über Geschlechter und Geschlechterverhältnisse*. Opladen, 61–84.

Diezinger, A. et al. (Eds.) (1994) *Erfahrung mit Methode*. Freiburg.

Dölling, I. (1993) Aufschwung nach der Wende – Frauenforschung in der DDR und in den

Neuen Bundesländern. In: Helwig, G. and Nickel, H. M. (Eds.) *Frauen in Deutschland 1945–1992*. Bonn, 397–407.

Dölling, I. and Krais, B. (1997) Vorwort der Herausgeberinnen. In: Dies, (Ed.) *Ein alltägliches Spiel, Geschlechterkonstruktionen in der sozialen Praxis*. Frankfurt a.M., 7–16.

Flaake, K. (1993) Lieber schwach, aber gemeinsam als stark, aber einsam? In: Koppert, C. (Ed.) *Glück, Alltag und Desaster*. Berlin, 42–57.

Flaake, K. (1996) *Zusammenfassung der Diskussionen zum Seminar 'Soziale und psychische Bedeutung der Kategorie Geschlecht – feministische Perspektiven'*. Unpublished seminar paper.

Hagemann-White, C. (1991) Frauen fördern Wissenschaft. *Universität Osnabrück Magazin*. 7, 11–4.

Hagemann-White, C. (1994) Der Umgang mit Zweigeschlechtlichkeit als Forschungsaufgabe. In: Diezinger, A. et al. (Eds.) op. cit., 301–20

Harding, S. (1994) *Das Geschlecht des Wissens*. Frankfurt/New York.

Kahlert, H. (1995) Zweierlei Soziologien? *Soziologie*. 3, 23–31.

Kerchner, B. and Wilde, G. (1997) Preface. In: Dies, (Ed.) *Staat und Privatheit*. Opladen, 9–26.

Krüger, M. (1994) Methodologische und wissenschaftstheoretische Reflexionen über eine feministische Soziologie und Sozialforschung. In: Diezinger, A. et al. (Eds.) op. cit., 69–84.

Maynard, M. (1995) 'Das Verschwinden der Frau'. Geschlecht und Hierarchie in feministischen und sozialwissenschaftlichen Diskursen. In: Armbruster, C., Müller, U. and Stein-Hilbers, M. (Eds.) *Neue Horizonte? Sozialwissenschaftliche Forschung über Geschlechter und Geschlechterverhältnisse*. Opladen, 23–40.

Metz-Göckel, S. (1993) 'Permanenter Vorgriff auf die Gleichheit' -Frauenforschung in Westdeutschland. In: Helwig, G. and Nickel, H. M. (Eds.) *Frauen in Deutschland 1945–1992*. Bonn, 408–26.

Müller, U. (1994) Feminismus in der empirischen Forschung: Eine methodologische Bestandsaufnahme. In: Diezinger, A. et al. (Eds.) op. cit., 31–68.

Nunner-Winkler, G. (1994) Zur Definition von Frauenforschung. In: Deutsche Forschungsgemeinschaft (Ed.) *Sozialwissenschaftliche Frauenforschung in der BRD*. Berlin, 29–41.

Patzak, M. (1994) Paradigmenpromotor Frauenforschung? Methodologische und methodische Überlegungen zur Frauenforschung. *Soziologie*. 4, 7–26.

Rohde-Dachser, C. (1991) *Expeditionen in den dunklen Kontinent*. Berlin/Heidelberg/New York.

Thürmer-Rohr, C. (1995) Denken der Differenz. *Beiträge zur feministischen Theorie und Praxis*. 39, 87–97.

2. Poverty Risks and the Fight Against Poverty

Ulrike Zartler

Introduction

This chapter deals with poverty risks and the fight against poverty situations with the focus on the situation in central Europe. Four aspects of the comprehensive theme 'Poverty' will be considered under gender-specific aspects:

- **Part 1: What is poverty?** EUROSTAT publications list 57 million poor people in EU countries, with 6% to 26% of the population in the individual countries considered to be poor (Steiner and Giorgi, 1997, p178). Poverty therefore is not a negligible phenomenon regarding a dwindling minority or specific marginalised groups. More recent works discuss changes in the phenomenon poverty under the keyword 'New Poverty' (Bieback and Milz, 1995; Dietz, 1997; Eckardt, 1997). The first part of this chapter will describe the characteristics of 'new poverty' and will undertake to find an answer to the question 'what is poverty?' It will be shown that definition and measuring are not unproblematic and exert far reaching effects at varying levels.
- **Part 2: Female poverty – male poverty** Poverty in Europe is characterised by significant gender-specific differences: even in highly industrialised societies women still run a greater risk of poverty than men. Poverty and wealth always involve aspects of superiority and subordination as well as power relationships and are thus a classical component of gender research: 'The poverty of women relative to men is a manifestation of the unequal power relations between women and men, which have led to the development of economic, social, cultural, and political structures which discriminate against women and deny them the full expression of their social, political and economic rights.' (EAPN, 1997, p11). Part two will show why women are afflicted or threatened by poverty. Since

gender-specific poverty research has so far focussed on women and women certainly run a much higher risk of poverty, it will only be possible to touch on a few recent findings on the subject 'Men and poverty'.
- **Part 3: What are the effects of poverty?** Poverty and the risk of poverty affect various aspects of everyday life (e.g. consumer behaviour, health, social contacts). Some of these will be described in brief.
- **Part 4: Fighting and preventing poverty** This part describes measures which should be effectively introduced in order to reduce the vast differences in the prevalence of poverty along gender-specific lines.

What is poverty?

For decades poverty was seen as a phenomenon occurring only among marginal groups and specific population strata. More recent poverty research shows a shift in traditional markers of poverty, with the borderlines between poverty and non-poverty becoming more permeable and new types of poverty emerging. Although the 'old' type of poverty, *'eng und ausweglos mit materieller Knappheit, mit Schicht und kollektivem Schicksal, mit Stigma und Unentrinnbarkeit korreliert* (which closely and inevitably correlates with material want, with social strata and collective destiny, with stigma and inescapability)' (Bieback and Milz, 1995, p11) continues to exist, 'typical poverty' is on the decline, being replaced by numbers of different poverty life situations applying for periods of time. We can no longer generalise.

The key characteristics of 'new poverty' are (see among others Leisering, 1995, p68):

- **Temporal**: People who are affected by poverty do not necessarily remain poor throughout their lives. Rather, poverty becomes a patchwork of poverty phases, interruptions, recurrences, and partly total recovery.

- **Biography-related**: Biographic transitions (divorce, leaving home, transition between education and first job, birth of a child, job loss, death of the spouse, being pensioned off) are increasingly becoming the causes of poverty. The way in which the persons concerned cope with the situations depends also on how the poverty situation is biographically assessed. Poverty, however, is also becoming more and more 'privatised': collective risks are reinterpreted as personal fate, and not seen as a communal problem, but rather as an individual's personal destiny.

- **Transcending social borders**: Poverty is no longer restricted to specific 'traditional' poverty groups but it can hit every member of society. It invades social groups which used to be at comparatively low-risk with regard to poverty. This socially non-stratified widely scattered poverty is more difficult to perceive; something which also has political consequences.

Political and scientific discussions make use of different poverty concepts. The most common types are (see Steiner and Giorgi, 1997, p178; Wallner, 1999):

- **Absolute poverty** (physical subsistence level): A person is considered absolutely poor if they do not have sufficient material or immaterial means (resources) to meet basic needs.

- **Relative income poverty** (socio-cultural subsistence level): A person is considered relatively poor, if they must make do with resource levels lower than those of a reference group (usually the population of a region or a country). A household is assumed to be in a precarious situation if it falls below a certain average (weighted) per-capita-income level.

- **Relative spending poverty**: A person is considered poor, if their consumption level is below a certain percentage of the average consumption level of the reference group.

- **Social exclusion**: The yardstick for gauging poverty is the lack of participation in various economic, social and legal activities of a

society. Changes in participation, over time, are taken into account, as well as social indicators such as housing, health and participation in social activities.

There is general agreement on the fact that none of these definitions by themselves permit a comprehensive definition of poverty. In Europe we deal almost exclusively with a relative poverty concept (Hauser and Neumann, 1992). This is reflected in the definition of the Council of the European Union (1984) which states that individuals, families, and groups of persons may be considered poor whose disposable means (material, cultural, and social) are so minimal that they are excluded from participating in life-styles which are considered as the minimum acceptable in the individual member state in which they live.

Measuring poverty is a very sensitive matter, since the definition of poverty lines has an immediate impact on the poverty rates; the lower the line is, the lower the poverty rates (the poverty lines used in different research reports lie between 40 and 60 per cent, i.e. a person is considered poor if their income is less than 40, 50, or 60 percent of the average per capita income). In the European Union the poverty line is as a rule defined at half of the average net per capita income (50 per cent line).

The poverty risk thresholds calculated from the individual national averages vary widely among the EU countries; being generally significantly higher in most central, western, and northern European countries than in the EU countries of the south. The monthly poverty risk thresholds for individuals are very similar in Germany, the United Kingdom, France, Belgium, Denmark, the Netherlands, and Austria. They vary between ATS 7 700 and ATS 8 800. In Italy, Ireland and Spain the poverty thresholds lie between ATS 5 600 and ATS 6 200, and in Greece and Portugal they are below ATS 5 000 (Steiner and Giorgi, 1997, p178).

The practice of assessing poverty and the concept of relative income poverty are not generally accepted. Among others the following items of criticism have been raised (see Pfaff, 1992; Steiner and Giorgi, 1997; Wallner, 1999):

- Income disparity as a poverty indicator does not provide any information on the actual living conditions of the socially weak, but only informs us of the fact that there is a certain disparity of incomes in a society. If the disparity decreases, poverty would, according to this definition, decrease as well, no matter whether the living conditions of the socially poor have improved.

- Poverty need not necessarily be caused by incomes which are too low, but may depend on infra-structural and regional factors, such as e.g. services needed in case of illness or permanent care.
- Most studies are based on the income at the time of the survey (cross sectional studies). It is however of significant importance for the situation of a particular household, whether a low income situation is only temporary or of longer duration.
- The structure of the poor population differs whether we look at the income or at the expenditures. Older people often live in 'low-expenditure' households, whereas younger persons tend to live more often in 'low-income' households.
- The poverty risk thresholds are subject to political decision making. If income thresholds are not automatically adjusted, but are consciously adjusted either more slowly or more quickly than developments in general income, then the numbers of (relatively) poor persons are raised or lowered.
- The higher the percentage of public real transfer services – i.e. for health, education, public transport, cultural and sports facilities – the less significant the actual income is in monetary terms for the definition of poverty; and the less income can be seen as an indicator of the actual supply situation.
- There are considerable differences with regard to the use of weighting factors for the individual members of the household (equivalence scales). Weighting involves assumptions on the amount of per-capita savings a multi-person household can achieve in comparison to a single person household if housing, consumer goods etc. are shared. In Austria the first adult in each household is assigned the factor 1, every other adult 0.7, and each child 0.5 (Giorgi and Steiner, 1998, p120). EUROSTAT uses smaller weighting factors in rating members

of a common household (first adult = 1, further adults 0.5 each, children 0.3 each), which means that poverty risk thresholds become higher for single-person households and lower for multi-person households. The different scales have a clear impact on the groups identified as poor: the poverty level as well as the structure of the poverty population depend on these scales (see Sorensen, 1992).

- If the household income is used to determine the poverty status we must be aware of two hidden basic assumptions: it is taken for granted (1) that all members of the household contribute their total income to the household and (2) that the resources are distributed among the members according to need. These assumptions are not generally accepted and are a central issue in gender-specific poverty research: men and women living in the same household would accordingly share the same economic well-being and run the same poverty risks. Empirical studies give the impression that the quoted assumptions appear to be valid in richer societies. In poor societies, however, household resource distribution definitely favours men and boys. If resources are unequally distributed in households in richer societies, this applies particularly to poor households and those at risk of poverty. If women in such households have lower resources than men, the assumption of an equal distribution in the household would result in underestimating the poverty rates for women compared to men (see Sorensen, 1992). Sorensen (1992, p362) also shows that the poverty status of a person depends considerably on the income of other members of the household and on the effects of economies of sharing in larger households, which applies to women to a much larger extent than to men. It is the tendency that women avoid poverty by living together with a partner.

In order to assess poverty in a more appropriate and satisfactory way, complex multidimensional and longitudinal concepts of assessment would be needed.

Female poverty – male poverty

Gender-specific aspects of poverty

The distribution of poverty is characterised by vast gender-specific differences: more than 70 per cent of the estimated 1.3 billion people living in poverty world-wide are women (Notz, 1997). Over the past years the number of women living in poverty has risen disproportionally compared to men. Women do two thirds of the work world-wide but earn only one tenth of the total income and own less than one hundredth of the world's wealth (Der Standard, 15 October 1998, quoting UN statistics).

Although the economic situation of women, as well as their opportunities on the labour market and their income situation have significantly improved in Europe during the second half of the 20th century and although their economic dependence on the institution of marriage has decreased, there is the tendency of women running a higher risk of poverty than men: in all age groups (except children and adolescents) income poverty occurs far more frequently among women than among men (Pfaff, 1995, p39; Wallner, 1995).

Poverty among women is to a high degree the poverty of the family. This is particularly so for single mothers, but also affects couples with children. In addition, single women who live alone often have relatively insufficient (pension) incomes. The main groups of women in poverty and women at risk of poverty are single mothers, unemployed women, women of unemployed men with children, and old women.

Poverty among women and families usually also means poverty among children. Children and adolescents are a rapidly growing new segment among the population of the poor. Poverty of children is mainly linked to families with many children and single mothers. Lack of space prevents me from elaborating on this important subject in more detail here, but reference is made to the increasing body of research in recent years (e.g. Mansel and Brinkhoff, 1998; Mansel, Neubauer and Otto, 1997).

The 'feminisation of poverty' in advanced industrial societies has become a widely discussed topic, starting in the United States and moving on to Europe (Notz, 1997; Sorensen, 1992). The poverty of men, however, has so far only rarely been the explicit topic of empirical or theoretical discussion. Partly because of research bias but also particularly because of their quantitatively higher representation this paper will also focus on the female side of poverty.

Causes of female poverty

Women become poor because they are discriminated against on the labour market

Even when women are integrated into the labour market they are not protected against poverty or the risk of poverty, because they are still discriminated against. This applies among others to the following spheres:

Labour force participation

Although the orientation of women towards paid work and income has increased significantly over the last decades (in particular among married women and mothers), paid work still isn't the rule. The participation rate of women, which are traditionally assigned the role of family workers, is lower than that of men (this applies to southern and central Europe; in the Scandinavian countries the employment rates of women are more and more approaching those of men).

Expectations and attitudes with regard to women in employment have changed due to the increasing participation of women in the labour market; these changes have been partly an advantage, partly a disadvantage for women (Pfaff, 1995, p48). On one hand the acceptance of the participation of women in the labour market (if they are also mothers) has increased, leading to increased employment and income opportunities and better opportunities for returning to the labour market. On the other hand unmarried women (even if they have relatively small children) are expected to participate in the labour market and provide for themselves, their social security and their retirement pensions, without having the chance to do this in practice.

Income levels

Even if women have work and an income this does not guarantee that their income is adequate. Wages paid to women are below those of men due to high part time rates, wage discrimination, and vertical and horizontal labour market segregation. Women are still considered to be 'earning some extra money'. Women are found to a disproportionally high degree, in the lower wage groups. They work more frequently in low-wage industries (textiles, retail, low-status services), and the average income of women in full employment remains about one third lower than for men in the same job classes (Pfaff, 1992, p428; Notz, 1997, p9). According to the European Commission 33% of all women in full employment receive wages below the threshold which is considered 'fair wages' (the European Commission defines 'fair' wages as those which are above 68% of the national average) (Breiter, 1998). Too low incomes of women in most European countries are the beginning of a poverty spiral which continues into old age in the form of low pensions.

Precarious forms of employment

Just as the labour market opportunities, are unevenly distributed between men and women so too the labour market risks. Precarious forms of employment which do not permit independent subsistence and which provide little or no social security and harbour the risks of impoverishment, are more common among women than among men (Notz, 1997, p8). Women therefore also account for the greater part of the 'working poor', i.e. working persons with an income below the subsistence level.

Part-time employment

The labour market participation of women is characterised by a strong increase in part-time work. In 1994 in Germany 36% of all working women worked part-time, as opposed to 4% of the men (Rudolph, 1994, p24). In a society with insufficient day-care facilities for children, part-time employment enables mothers to participate in the work force, even though they have children. The income from such part-time work, however, is so low that very few women could provide for themselves on this basis, let alone for one or more children, if there were not an additional source of income (e.g. a comparatively well-paid 'bread-winner') in the same household. Part time work is also a

disadvantage with regard to providing for old age (Pfaff, 1995, p48).

Duration of participation in the labour market

The duration of women's participation in the labour market is shorter than for men. Women's employment is often interrupted, thus it is discontinuous, which has a negative effect on the height of their pensions.

Overall it becomes clear that women are more limited in their opportunities of avoiding poverty through paid work than men.

We shouldn't forget to mention here that the integration into the labour market not only has material aspects but that immaterial benefits can also be drawn from paid work, which may counteract social exclusion as one facet of poverty. Participation in the labour market, gives meaning to a person's life, structures the day, widens the horizon, creates commonality and allocates social status. It thus contributes to the development of the social identity (Jahoda, 1983, p136).

Women become poor because they have no job

Unemployment, in particular long-term unemployment, is among the main causes of poverty. The risk of unemployment is definitely higher for persons in 'marginal' employment with low incomes (Pfaff, 1992, p431).

Compared to their participation in the labour market the proportion of unemployed women is significantly higher. This applies in particular to long-term and multiple unemployment cases (Danneberg, 1997, p18; Wallner, 1995, p49). After longer periods of interruption in paid employment, usually due to custodial duties, the chances of returning to the labour market, even for women in their thirties, are significantly reduced. In 1997 twice as many unemployed women than men in Austria were listed difficult to place. The reason is mainly 'limited mobility', which means, no day-care for children (Breitner, 1998). The reasons given for the high unemployment rate among women are mainly the increase in the female working potential as well as competitive disadvantages deriving from custodial care duties. But these reasons suggest that, to a large extent, it is women's own 'fault' that they are unemployed and thus at risk of poverty.

In most cases women are listed as long-term unemployed persons for a significantly shorter period of time than men. Rather involuntarily they leave the labour market permanently, withdrawing into the household and family sphere. These women who basically want paid work but have not managed to return to the labour market, are referred to as 'silent reserve' (Appelt et al., 1987). The true scope of female unemployment is underestimated.

Women become poor because they bear the main burden of family work

The traditional structure of female poverty is changing: it has been possible to reduce the traditional poverty among elderly women to a degree (Pfaff, 1995). Instead, female poverty today means family poverty, and in particular the poverty of larger families and lone mothers, in short 'motherhood makes one poor' (Bieback and Milz, 1995, p15).

Female poverty results among others, from the uneven distribution of paid and unpaid work between men and women (gender-hierarchical distribution of work). Men are still automatically associated with participation in the labour market. Women are considered 'responsible' for reproductive and family work and at best as 'additional sources of income'. These are the reasons why it is difficult for women, in particular mothers, to take up paid employment: their 'responsibility' for family work means they can only temporarily participate in the labour market or do so in part-time form. In addition to the fact that they bear the main burden of bringing up children, they are also confronted with the problem of insufficient day-care services which makes it difficult for them to enter employment.

Starting a family still means for women that they partly or completely, temporarily or permanently give up their own income (Weidacher, 1995). The need to reconcile work and family is still seen primarily or totally as a women's problem. The results are not only disadvantages in the labour market, but also disadvantages with regard to retirement pensions, because they lack a continuous career. Riedmüller (1987) refers in this connection to the 'social risk of family work'.

Women become poor because they are not (or no longer) married

The percentage of women who subsist mainly through relatives (in particular husbands) is more and more on the decrease. Family or marriage as a 'subsistence guarantee' is no longer reliable (Ostner and Voges, 1995), but the social framework in most cases doesn't offer equivalent alternative guarantees through the labour market. Marriage is still the generally accepted and government-supported standard of living together, even though this no longer corresponds to reality. Deviations from this norm lead to poverty.

New poverty mainly develops when marriage and family no longer function. It often affects women (and also men) after divorce or after the death of a partner in old age (Pfaff, 1995, p54). In addition to the 'crisis of the standard employment situation' and the significance of labour-market related factors as risks for poverty, the 'crisis of the standard marriage' (increasing divorce rates, increasing numbers of lone mothers) is also a cause for poverty among women.

There is a higher probability that households of divorced or single-parenting women are income-poor, than of households with a male or two working adults. Custodial care duties force 'households headed by women' to have only limited opportunities to improve their situation through paid work (Voges and Ostner, 1995). In contrast, poverty is less frequent among women living in stable marriages (Krause 1993, according to Ostner and Voges, 1995, p99).

Women become poor because they are lone parents

Motherhood is particularly prone to make women poor, unmarried or divorced young women bear the main responsibility for caring for and bringing up their children and thus hardly have the opportunity to participate in the labour force on a continuous basis. The large numbers of lone mothers and their children are an increasing sector within the poor among families, women and children. In 1994 15.1% of all families with under age children in Western Germany were single-parent families, 24.5% in the former German Democratic Republic and 13% in Austria. Approximately 85% of single parents are women (Notz, 1997, p10). The majority of single parents today are divorced women (Napp-Peters, 1995; Voges and Ostner, 1995).

A comparatively high percentage of these families is unable to finance a living standard above the poverty line, with one of the main causes being the problems with regard to the reconciliation of work and family. In Austria 12% of single-parent households can be referred to as 'poor'. The poverty rate is thus twice as high as in the total population (Steiner and Giorgi, 1997, p187). Napp-Peters (1995) found out for Germany that one quarter of single-parents and their children live under the poverty line. The poorest group are women with children under three years of age (Notz, 1997, p10).

Lone mothers are often unable to make claims for support payments or what they get is not enough. Therefore these women, in particular, are in need of additional help. 85% of the household income of the lowest quarter of the Austrian single-parent households consists of social welfare payments (Steiner and Giorgi, 1997, p187). However German surveys show that many lone mothers are only temporarily in need of welfare support (Napp-Peters, 1995; Voges and Ostner, 1995, p136). In old age many former lone mothers are dependent on government transfer payments, because they did not pay social insurance contributions for long enough to be eligible for a sufficient pension.

Income poverty, however, is not the only aspect of poverty, which hits lone parents to a higher degree. Additional aspects are significantly reduced consumer activities, indebtedness, lack of time, and restricted social contacts (Napp-Peters, 1995).

The poverty risk among lone parents is considerable although they participate in the labour market to a much higher degree than married mothers, but working causes increased financial stress and time burdens because of the need to organise child care and household duties. Countries which provide incentives for married mothers to either leave the labour market or work only part time (through fiscal, social, or labour policies) aggravate conditions for lone mothers on the labour market.

Women become poor because they live with violent partners

Unemployment, poverty and the experience of violence are often closely linked (see EAPN, 1997). A survey made by the organisation 'Frauen beraten Frauen (Women counselling women)' (1997) in Vienna showed that 82.5% of the female clients at the counselling centre for women who had participated in a project against poverty and social exclusion in 1996 had experienced violence at some point in their lives.

Increased housing costs, the danger of unemployment and reduced social benefits are contributory factors why women cite financial reasons for staying with abusive partners. On the other hand the experience of violence increases physical and emotional stress, social isolation and the risk of job loss and thus contributes to the perpetuation of the situation.

Women become poor, because the social security system ignores the reality of their lives

Existing social security systems are based on continuous paid work and thus oriented along traditional male work biographies. Sufficient income security in old age, in case of illness and unemployment is only guaranteed through uninterrupted full-time work and an average income. The care work done by women is either totally neglected or taken into account only to a limited extent.

Women are structurally disadvantaged by the social security system because the criteria for eligibility and benefits do not correspond to their actual lives (see Braun and Jung, 1997; Dietz, 1997; Leitner, 1998). Their family obligations mean they are unable to adapt their life course to the standard male biography. Interruptions in working life caused by motherhood, child care, and family work are not taken into account by the transfer structure of the welfare state, which means that women are not sufficiently provided for by the system. This affects particularly divorced, single and older women, who, if the need arises, cannot resort to a 'bread-winner'. Interruptions of working life not only cause temporary loss of income but ensue further income loss which would also have to be compensated for (Pfaff, 1995, p42).

Old age poverty as a result of low social security contributions is not only caused by insufficient participation in the labour market but also by low wages over long contributory periods (Leitner, 1998). The average pensions of women are still very low, but gradually more and more women at least have a small pension of their own (Pfaff, 1992, p431). In spite of the existing discriminating structure the development of social systems in Europe can provide women with an opportunity for individual freedom. Women are therefore often in a position that they defend a system of which they are basically very critical (Braun and Jung, 1997, p9).

Male poverty

The group of poor men or those at risk of poverty has only been marginally studied by researchers. Therefore only a few tendencies can be pointed out here.

Male standard biographies are increasingly no longer the general norm either. Larger and larger population segments (i.e. men as well) are affected by what used to be considered 'typically female' labour market risks: they must interrupt paid work over longer periods of time, re-integrate themselves into the labour market through part-time work or work in insecure employment conditions. Continuous full-time employment is no longer a realistic perspective for a large number of male workers in industrialised countries. Men, too, will in future be increasingly forced to accept precarious employment conditions (Braun and Jung, 1997). If this 'feminising of working conditions' continues to increase, more and more men will be affected by poverty risks which so far had been limited to women.

Biographic milestones such as the end or premature end of education and training, starting a family, separation, divorce, birth of a child, illness or other impairment of working capacity, job loss, death within the family, all these are central factors in triggering poverty situations for men.

Young male adults are a group with a particularly high poverty risk. Although they have completed compulsory education and vocational training more often than comparable women of the same age group, they are at risk when entering the labour market as well as of being forced into long-term unemployment.

Poor men are very reluctant to seek help and often negate social problems over a longer period of time. Two thirds of the clients of Caritas Austria are women; a fact which cannot only be explained by the high percentage of lone mothers. As there are very few empirical findings on the subject of male poverty, we will present here some results of a nation-wide Austrian survey among clients of the social care agencies of Caritas which in problem situations provide stopgap relief (Wallner, 1999).

A total of 72% of men seeking help live without other family members, in comparison to only 24% of women help seekers. It was found that women in crisis often bear responsibility for several other persons as well, in particular their children, whereas social crises in the case of men are mostly linked to loneliness and a certain degree of isolation.

While women frequently manage to at least temporarily escape a poverty situation by entering a new partnership or have new perspectives open to them as a result, men often find it difficult to make any contacts at all. This attempt at resolving problem situations by entering into a partnership must be considered a highly problematic strategy. The situation of single men living in poverty is therefore often characterised by 'loneliness', and, over time, also with the loss of social skills and increasing neglect. They are perhaps the group which is materially, institutionally, and socially at greatest risk of social exclusion.' (Wallner, 1999, p89)

The predominant causal factor of poverty situations is loss of paid work: 70% of male Caritas clients are jobless. Loss of employment is – particularly for men – because of gender-specific attributions closely linked to questions of the sense of life and one's residual position in society.

Approximately one fifth of the cases have an at least partly impaired working capacity because of illness. 10% of clients are persons released from prison. Substance abuse is a severe problem for 15% (it is a predominant factor in the counselling process in one out of five cases, whereas this factor doesn't play a significant role with women), and 12% are about to be or have already been evicted from their homes. Approximately a quarter have alimony responsibilities which often aggravate their problem situation in particular when linked to income garnisheeing and prison terms.

What are the effects of poverty?

Poverty in Europe is different from, for example, poverty in India. Poverty in Europe means not enough money for housing, education, or recreation. It means financial problems in case of household repairs or replacement of appliances, payment for school ski weeks for the children, or with electricity bills. Poverty in Europe does not mean going hungry but it means being ashamed of being unable to afford things which are standard in our society, and it means enormous stress in coping with everyday life (ÖGB Frauen, 1997).

It may take a while until poverty becomes visible. Many persons living in poverty try to keep up the appearance of a 'normal' life because they are ashamed. Poverty is still a taboo and hides from the public view as 'ashamed' (Wallner, 1999) and 'socially invisible' poverty (Chassé et al., 1992). The de facto situation is that poor people are largely excluded from social life (further education, cultural events, cinema, restaurants, holidays and so on) in our society and very often they are virtually unable to change this situation for themselves (Breiter, 1998).

In a situation characterised by poverty or risk of poverty it is important to develop new competencies: vocational qualifications become less important and every day life skills become decisive for coping (finding shopping bargains, dealing with authorities, tapping financial resources).

A central effect is the **reduction of consumer spending**. In Austria, for instance, the per capita spending of the socially weakest in the fields of home-furnishing, private and public transport, leisure, cultural and sports activities, education, is in total three quarters lower than for average households. Meeting basic needs is also subject to limitations: households at risk of poverty show a per-capita spending on food which is approximately one third lower and on housing and heating about half as high as for average households. However, the percentage of these vital expenditures as a share of the total household budget is 59%, which is considerably higher than the average (39%) (see Steiner and Giorgi, 1997, p193).

Indebtedness is often a partial or contributory factor in the development of a poverty situation, with recent tendencies showing an increase of consumer loans and a decrease of mortgage debts (Mooslechner and Brandner, 1992; Wallner, 1995).

There is a close correlation between **poverty and health**. Poverty usually means worse living, working, and housing conditions, which in turn result in a worse state of health. Austria reports that low-income groups of all ages experience a greater impairment of their health than the population not living in poverty: 12% of non-poor adults refer to their state of health as 'bad', as opposed to 25% of the poor population, but in spite of this, socially weaker persons do not see their doctor more frequently (Giorgi and Steiner, 1998, p124).

In addition severe financial strain on poor households has an inhibiting effect on **social contacts**, which becomes obvious from the fact that they invite friends to their homes less frequently, are less frequently members in clubs or associations, and also have fewer contacts with neighbours. In Austria almost one out of two (48%) poor households stated that friends wouldn't be invited because of the costs involved. This percentage is almost seven (!) times higher than is the case for non-poor households (Giorgi and Steiner, 1998, p125).

Loss of home may be the effect of continuing poverty situations or also the beginning of a poverty spiral, because the lack of a place of residence can be considered an indicator of poverty and usually also has an effect on the working life (Mutschler, 1995; Wallner, 1995). A survey of homeless persons in Vienna (Scharinger, 1993) showed that the risks which lead to homelessness are largely the same as the poverty risks, which seems to indicate that homelessness is a radicalised form of poverty. The causes differ by gender. For women the end of a relationship and the loss of the economic protection linked to it is the most frequent cause for losing their homes. Many women return to their partners, from whom they have fled because of massive conflicts or violence, because they are in financial need and homeless. Some proceed from one abusive partnership to the next, because they precipitously move in with a new partner (Notz, 1997). In the case of homeless men their homelessness is not only caused by problems in the family but frequently also by unemployment, imprisonment, or stays in other institutions (Scharinger, 1993).

Fighting and preventing poverty

Changes in the poverty structure ('new poverty') have made it more difficult to assess and perceive poverty and it has also become more difficult to fight poverty with political measures.

The fight against poverty can only be successful today, if it is fought at different levels with the co-operation of different sectors. In addition to social and employment policies, educational, family, housing, and fiscal policies are among those bearing responsibility. These government sectors must be complemented and supported by the economy (Steiner and Wolf, 1996).

Particularly with a view to a gender-specific poverty discussion it would be useful to include indicators into economic analyses which take into account the unpaid work performed by women (EAPN, 1997). At present women have two options to provide for their social security (see Dietz, 1997, p148):

1. Housework, which is unpaid and leaves a woman dependent on her husband, even after his death, by being dependent on a widow's pension.
2. Paid work, impaired by the unfavourable conditions mentioned above.

A successful protection against poverty would have to improve the existing system, which is based on the general recognition of 'standard employment' and lasting marriages. So far it has been assumed that the majority of citizens enjoy sufficient social security either on the basis of paid work or as a family member of a bread-winner who is guaranteed social security through a continuous, permanent job. This will not suffice in the future. The social

system ought to guarantee an income above the poverty line for women (and children) even when they do not have, or do not want to have, a husband, or paying father who pays for their living either in part or in full (Pfaff, 1992, p441).

With regard to fighting poverty the following spheres are of central significance (see Steiner and Giorgi, 1997; Steiner and Wolf, 1996):

The opportunity to work and earn an income Avoiding poverty depends to a very large degree on the opportunity and possibility to participate in the labour market, to find a job, earn an adequate income, and also acquire eligibility for adequate benefits in old age (Pfaff, 1995, p43). Lack of job opportunities leads most people sooner or later into poverty or at least leads as a consequence to poverty in old age. This means that politicians should strive to either provide adequate job and income opportunities for everyone, including women, or to provide adequate transfer payments for those who cannot participate in the labour market.

A special problem are the inadequate job and income opportunities for mothers. Better job opportunities and a higher participation rate of women are not only an effective tool against family poverty and poverty among children, they are also a precondition for the better social security position of elderly women. This is the reason why attempts must be made to enable women to participate in the labour market and to bring about a better reconciliation of child care and work. Such measures for the reconciliation of family and work would have to include different components:

–Fair and just sharing of housework between women and men.
–More and qualitatively better child care facilities.
–Working hours which permit the better reconciliation of family and work.
–More attractive models for part time work.
–More flexibility of working hours in cases of illness of a family member.

Apart from the opportunity to find a job, women should have the chance to make an income which is high enough to live above the poverty line. Income opportunities of women are significantly lower than those of men. In order to avoid income poverty the following changes would be required (Pfaff, 1992, p441; Steiner and Wolf, 1996):

- –Redistribution of job opportunities among men and women.
- –Higher increase of minimum wages.
- –Changes in the horizontal and vertical income distribution.
- –Income re-distribution over the life cycle.
- –New distribution of the financing burdens of family tasks.
- –Supplementing the market income through a demand-oriented basic income in specific life phases.

Because of the increased poverty risk of long-term unemployed persons this group would require a substantial expansion of retraining and job programmes. The group of lone parents which is particularly susceptible to poverty risks would require a well targeted social policy, starting with the classical instruments of income and subsistence guarantees for groups which are permanently affected by poverty, in particular young lone parents and lone parents with several children. These instruments would have to be complemented by integrated labour market policy measures and child care provisions, since the period of care and family work results in career breaks and deprives many mothers of the opportunity of developing positions and careers in the labour market or to maintain their qualifications.

The number of insecure, poorly paid jobs, which are not at all or insufficiently protected by labour and social legislation is on the increase. If someone has only the opportunity to get such a precarious job there is a very high probability of poverty, even though the person works. This may be for various reasons: lack of qualifications, individual performance impairment, family obligations, legal provisions, regional conditions. This trend should be counterbalanced by legislative provisions and measures in the industrial relations sector.

Education and training systems
Access to the labour market and thus to employment and income opportunities is significantly controlled by the education and training system. Over the past decades the percentage of unskilled persons has decreased considerably and the level of education of men and women has become more and more equal.

Better education means more options. Educational barriers, however, lead to massive competitive disadvantages on the job market. Lack of education or insufficient education is linked to social exclusion in a threefold way:

1. It reduces, in particular for women, access to the labour market and thus the opportunity to reduce the financial stress in low-income households.
2. The risk of unemployment is much higher for unskilled persons and has a causal link to the risk of poverty.
3. The income of unskilled workers is considerably below that of the average population.

The direct correlation between education and opportunities in life will increase in importance in future because of the changes in the world of work. It must therefore be an objective of the fight against poverty, to enable all adolescents to get an adequate education and training and for all adults, who are willing to work, to receive adequate retraining and further training opportunities. This applies in particular for women and girls. Discriminatory factors in schools and training systems must be eliminated in order to reduce the 'inheritance of poverty' from (poorly trained) parents to their children in the lower social strata.

Financial benefits for persons without job opportunities
The fight against poverty has been quite successful over the last decades in the field of social security (e.g. the reduction of poverty in old age). Nevertheless the social security system still contains considerable disadvantages for women, because this system orients itself along high employment rates, ongoing continuous employment of single (male) income families, and life-long marriages. In this system women are attributed the role of housewife, child-minder, and (in case of labour market shortages) of a flexible, cheap labour force reserve. Providing independently for their subsistence is very difficult for women with children in particular in old age.

In addition to de-coupling the transfer benefits of the welfare state from a person's participation in the labour market, the equality of all family forms, or the reduction of the advantages for marriages and married parenthood, are important prerequisites for future social justice concepts (Braun and Jung, 1997; Sorensen, 1992; 1993).

When discussing a basic income for everyone, including social security, independent of the participation in the labour force, we are faced with the issue of an adequate balance between 'justice based on performance' and 'justice based on need' (Nullmeier and Vobruba, 1994, p13). The question is, whether social benefits and services should be linked more closely to the status as a member of the labour force or the status as a citizen, and whether social security 'exists within a certain framework on the basis of what a person is or of what they do' (German original, Wallner, 1999, p32).

Social and care services
In addition to an adequate material security sufficient social and care services are necessary in order to meet the needs of persons requiring help and care or of their carers who are often family members.

Housing
The supply of low-cost housing up to current standards for socially weak households is inadequate. It would be necessary to increase the volume of social housing projects and to provide more support in the housing sector to socially disadvantaged groups.

Summary

Poverty is no longer a phenomenon relating to marginalised groups but occurs, in the guise of 'new poverty' in many forms which can no longer be seen as typical or be generalised. Special characteristics of this 'new poverty' are that it is often of a temporary nature, that it is linked to a person's biography, and social marginalisation.

European research uses mainly the not uncontroversial concept of relative income poverty and sets the poverty line at half of the average per capita net income.

Although economic conditions have improved considerably over the past decades, women in Europe are at a much higher risk of poverty than men, which means that we may talk about the 'feminisation of poverty'. The poverty of women also means poverty of families and of children.

Causes for the high poverty rates among women include, among others:
- Discrimination in the labour market (employment participation, wage discrimination, precarious jobs).
- Unemployment.
- Unfair distribution of family work between the sexes.
- Lack of government provisions to enable women to engage in paid work (day care for children and dependants).
- End of a relationship (divorce, separation, death of spouse).
- Sole responsibility for bringing up children (lone mothers).
- Living together with violent partners.
- Discrimination by a social security system which orients itself on the male standard biography.

Poor men and men at risk of poverty have only marginally been the subject of research. But the poverty ratio among men will probably increase proportionally to the changes in the standard biographies of men ('feminisation of employment', interruptions in the biography). In the case of men poverty situations are frequently linked to social isolation.

Poverty affects different spheres of life. There is a drastic reduction of consumer spending but also a strong correlation between the state of health and social contacts.

A successful fight against (gender-specific) poverty must take place at different political *and* economic levels. Measures in the areas of job and income opportunities, education and training, monetary provisions and welfare state transfers, social and care services, as well as measures on the housing market are all of central significance.

The following literature is recommended as an introduction:

Bieback, K-J. and Milz, H. (1995) Zur Einführung: Armut in Zeiten des modernen Strukturwandels. In: Bieback, K-J. and Milz, H. (Eds.) *Neue Armut*. Frankfurt/New York. 7–27.

Notz, G. (1997) Die Feminisierung der Armut. In: GB Frauen (Ed.) *Arbeit, die sich 'LOHNt'. Eine Auseinandersetzung mit der Frage, wie es in Europa dazu Kommt, daß Armut Weiblich ist.* Dokumentation der VI. österreichischen ArbeitnehmerInnentagung der ÖGB-Frauen vom 18. Oktober 1997, Vienna.

References

Appelt, E., Lösch, A. and Prost, E. (Eds.) (1987) *Stille Reserve? Erwerbslose Frauen in Österreich.* Vienna.

Bauer, M. and Kronsteiner, C. (1997) Statistische Beiträge zur Armut, Armutsgefährdung und Sozialer Ausgrenzung. In: *ÖSTAT, Statistische Nachrichten.* 10/1997, 844–52.

Bieback, K-J. and Milz, H. (1995) Zur Einführung: Armut in Zeiten des modernen Strukturwandels. In: Bieback, K-J. and Milz, H. (Eds.) *Neue Armut.* Frankfurt/New York, 7–27.

Braun, H. and Jung, D. (1997) Globale Gerechtigkeit? Feministische Debatte zur Krise des Sozialstaats, In: Braun, H. and Jung, D. (Eds.) *Globale Gerechtigkeit? Feministische Debatte zur Krise des Sozialstaats.* Hamburg, 7–21.

Breiter, M. (1998) *Warum ist Armut weiblich? Warum sind in Österreich besonders Frauen arm oder armutsgefährdet?* Frauen Beraten Frauen. Vienna.

Chassé, K., Drygala, A. and Schmidt-Noerr, A. (Eds.) (1992) *Randgruppen 2000. Analysen zu Randgruppen und zur Randgruppenarbeit.* Bielefeld.

Danneberg, B. (1997) Armut im Überfluß. *an.schläge* 4/1997, 16–21

Dietz, B. (1997) *Soziologie der Armut: eine Einführung.* Frankfurt am Main/New York.

EAPN (European Anti-Poverty Network) (1997) *Women, Violence and Poverty,* Seminar report.

Eckardt, T. (1997) *Arm in Deutschland: eine sozialpolitische Bestandsaufnahme.* Landsberg am Lech.

Frauen Beraten Frauen (1997) *Still und leise in die Unsichtbarkeit? Gegen Armut und Soziale Ausgrenzung von Frauen.* Vienna.

Hanesch, W. (1994) *Armut in Deutschland.* Armutsbericht des DGB und des Paritätischen Wohlfahrtsverbandes, Reinbek bei Hamburg.

Hauser, R. and Neumann, U. (1992) Armut in der Bundesrepublik Deutschland. Die sozialwissenschaftliche Thematisierung nach dem Zweiten Weltkrieg, In: Leibfried, S. and Voges, W. (Eds.) *Armut im modernen Wohlfahrtsstaat, Sonderheft der KZfSS.* Opladen, 237–70.

Giorgi, L. and Steiner, H. (1998) Armutsgefährdung und Armut in Österreich. In: Bundesministerium für Arbeit, Gesundheit und Soziales (Eds.) (1998) *Bericht über die soziale Lage 1997.* Vienna, 119–26.

Jahoda, M. (1983) *Wieviel Arbeit braucht der Mensch?* Weinheim.

Kulawik, T. (1989) Auf unsicheren Wegen. Perspektiven der sozialen Sicherung von Frauen, In: Riedmüller, B. and Rodenstein, M. (Eds.) *Wie sicher ist die Soziale Sicherung?* Frankfurt, 241–65.

Leisering, L. (1995) Zweidrittelgesellschaft oder Risikogesellschaft? Zur gesellschaftlichen Verortung der neuen Armut in der Bundesrepublik Deutschland. In: Bieback, K-J. and Milz, H. (Eds.) *Neue Armut.* Frankfurt/New York, 58–92.

Leitner, S. (1998) *Geschlechterdifferenz als (diskriminierendes) Gestaltungsprinzip materieller Sicherung. Analyse der Alterssicherungssysteme in den USA, in Österreich und in Schweden.* Vienna, Institut für Höhere Studien, Political Science Series No. 57.

Mansel, J. and Brinkhoff, K-P. (Eds.) (1998) *Armut im Jugendalter. Soziale Ungleichheit, Gettoisierung und die psychosozialen Folgen.* Weinheim und Munich.

Mansel, J. and Neubauer, G. (1998) *Armut und soziale Ungleichheit bei Kindern. Über die veränderten Bedingungen des Aufwachsens.* Opladen.

Mooslechner, P. and Brandner, P. (1992) *Ökonomische Aspekte der Verschuldung privater Haushalte.* Österreichisches Institut für Wirtschaftsforschung. Vienna.

Mutschler, R. (1995) Wohnungsnot und Armut. In: Bieback, K-J. and Milz, H. (Eds.) *Neue Armut.* Frankfurt/New York: Campus, 235–59.

Notz, G. (1997) Die Feminisierung der Armut. In: ÖGB Frauen (Ed.) *Arbeit, die sich 'LOHNt'.*

Eine Auseinandersetzung mit der Frage, wie es in Europa dazu kommt, daß Armut weiblich ist. Dokumentation der VI. österreichischen ArbeitnehmerInnentagung der ÖGB-Frauen vom 18. Oktober 1997. Vienna.

Nullmeier, F. and Vobruba, G. (1994) Gerechtigkeit im sozialpolitischen Diskurs. In: Döring, F. et al. *Gerechtigkeit im Wohlfahrtsstaat.* Marburg, 11–66.

ÖGB Frauen (Ed.) (1997) *Arbeit, die sich 'LOHNt'. Eine Auseinandersetzung mit der Frage, wie es in Europa dazu kommt, daß Armut weiblich ist*, Dokumentation der VI. österreichischen ArbeitnehmerInnentagung der ÖGB-Frauen vom 18. Oktober 1997. Vienna.

Ostner, I. and Voges, W. (1995) Verschwindet der Ernährer-Ehemann? Wandel der Familienformen und soziale Sicherung der Frau, In: Bieback, K-J. Milz, H. (Eds.) *Neue Armut.* Frankfurt/New York, 93–106.

Otto, U. (Ed.) (1997) *Aufwachsen in Armut. Erfahrungswelten und soziale Lagen von Kindern armer Familien.* Opladen.

Pearce, D. (1978) The Feminization of Poverty: Women, Work and Welfare. *Urban and Social Change Review.* 11, 28–36.

Pfaff, A. B. (1992) Feminisierung der Armut durch den Sozialstaat? In: Leibfried, S. and Voges, W. (Eds.) *Armut im modernen Wohlfahrtsstaat. Sonderheft der KZfSS.* Opladen, 421–45.

Pfaff, A. B. (1995) Was ist das Neue an der neuen Armut? In: Bieback, K-J. Milz, H. (Eds.) *Neue Armut.* Frankfurt/New York, 28–57.

Riedmüller, B. (1987) Familienarbeit als soziales Risiko. *Widersprüche.* 2.

Rudolph, H. (1995) Strukturwandel des Arbeitsmarktes: Chancen und Risiken für Frauen. Presentation at the conference *Frauen und Arbeitsmarkt: Neue Wege -Neue Instrumente*, 15th December 1994, Munich.

Scharinger, C. (1993) 'Du wülst wissn, wo i schlof?' Zur sozialen Situation von akut Obdachlosen in Wien. In: Interdisziplinäres Forschungszentrum Sozialwissenschaften (IFS) (Ed.) *Final report.* Vienna.

Sørensen, A. (1992) Zur geschlechtsspezifischen Struktur von Armut. In: Leibfried, S. and Voges, W. (Eds.) *Armut im modernen Wohlfahrtsstaat. Sonderheft der KZfSS.* Opladen, 345–66.

Sørensen, A. (1993) Unterschiede im Lebenslauf von Frauen und Männern. In: Mayer, K. U. (Ed.) *Lebensverläufe und sozialer Wandel. Sonderheft 31 der Kölner Zeitschrift für Soziologie und Sozialpsychologie.* Opladen, 304–21.

Steiner, H. and Giorgi, L. (1997) Armut und Armutsbekämpfung in Österreich. In: Bundesministerium für Arbeit, Gesundheit und Soziales. (Ed.) (1997) *Bericht über die soziale Lage.* 1996. Vienna, 178–205.

Steiner, H. and Wolf, W. (1996) *Armutsgefährdung in Österreich.* Vienna, Bundesministerium für Arbeit und Soziales.

Voges, W. and Ostner, I. (1995) Wie arm sind alleinerziehende Frauen? In: Bieback, K-J. Milz, H. (Eds.) *Neue Armut.* Frankfurt/New York, 122–47.

Wallner, S. (1995) *Verarmungsrisiken im Wohlfahrtsstaat. Situationsanalyse und Problemkatalog zur sozialen Lage in Österreich.* Forschungsbericht der Julius Raab-Stiftung. Vienna.

Wallner-Ewald, S. (1999) *Verarmungsrisiken im Wohlfahrtsstaat II.* Leben am Rande des Sozialsystems. Die Klientinnen und Klienten der Sozialberatungsstellen der Caritas Österreich. Forschungsbericht der Julius Raab-Stiftung. Vienna.

Weidacher, A. (1995) Einkommenslagen in Familien ohne Kinder und mit Kindern. In: Bieback, K-J. Milz, H. (Eds.) *Neue Armut.* Frankfurt/New York, 148–80.

3. Family and Family Policies: Aspects of an Equality-oriented Family Policy

Christine Gruber

In considering the significance of family for women as well as for men, this chapter will demonstrate the unequal role distribution within the family, and the consequences thereof.

The effects of an unequal division of labour within the family involve both the micro and the macro spheres, particularly where no basic social security system exists, and social security depends on the employment system.

One of the most important structural changes in the past decades has been the increased presence of women in the labour market. Differences in the employment rates of women in the various European countries show the effect of social, ideological, and political frameworks.

Discussions differ throughout Europe regarding reconciliation of work and family life. Differences in national legislation on parental leave and parental allowances as well as the availability of 'public' support in the form of child care facilities make visible the differences of how egalitarian concepts determine family policy and politics in the individual EU countries.

It is the objective of this article to make clear that gender equality is feasible in all spheres of life and that such a development is a socio-political responsibility.

This review of gender differences touches on the personal as well as the professional life situation of women and men, with special reference to the work context of female and male social workers, since social work in many of its aspects involves work with difficult family situations and the social problems arising out of these situations.

The meaning of family

In all European countries family is the most important life sphere for women and men alike, more important than work (mean value men and women: family 1.19, work 1.55; measured on a 4 point scale from 1 = very important to 4 = not important at all) (see: Denz, H. (2002), special evaluation). Table 1 shows for which percentage of female and male respondents 'family' and/or 'work' are 'very important' and reveals that 'family' is slightly more important for women than for men.

For more than 90 per cent of women in 12 of the countries in which the survey was carried out (Great Britain, Sweden, France, Northern Ireland, Ireland, Denmark, Italy, Austria, Belgium, the Czech Republic, Hungary, and Poland) the family is the most important sphere of life, with the women in Sweden attributing the greatest significance to family (96%). For women in Finland and West Germany the family is slightly less important. 85 per cent of women in all other European countries (Spain, the Netherlands, Portugal, Greece, Bulgaria, Romania, and Slovenia) indicated the family as their most important sphere of life.

A comparison of the studies on European values in 1990 (see special evaluation in Gruber, 2001) and 1999 shows that in most European countries the significance of family increased among men as well as women in the ensuing decade.

We do not know the concept of family behind these answers. Family reality in Austria and Germany differs widely from that in Sweden or Italy. Whereas in the Northern European countries non-marital partnerships are on the increase, this form of living together is virtually non-existent in Italy. Traditions and standards of specific cultures, due, for instance, to the specific influence of the church in some countries, might provide explanations for these differences (see Cyprian and Vaskovics, 1997, p225).

Table 1   Significance of family and work (1999)

| | Family | | Work | |
	Women	Men	Women	Men
France	92.46	84.35	70.14	69.15
Germany (West)	83.84	78.45	33.46	51.65
Germany (East)	81.31	73.90	58.81	66.81
Austria	92.78	84.95	63.95	68.05
Italy	92.57	87.27	57.43	66.32
Spain	87.82	83.53	60.59	65.52
Portugal	85.34	83.17	56.10	59.02
Greece	87.24	83.56	58.59	57.07
Netherlands	85.17	75.98	41.37	53.55
Belgium	91.20	84.45	62.79	66.69
Luxembourg	89.42	86.32	51.33	54.09
Denmark	92.87	81.11	34.34	44.96
Sweden	95.77	83.33	58.00	50.72
Finland	83.46	76.45	53.75	50.08
Great Britain	92.70	85.26	32.60	50.44
Northern Ireland	92.65	87.86	37.62	47.38
Ireland	91.92	91.19	41.59	60.87
Hungary	91.88	85.16	55.70	58.08
Poland	91.96	91.68	75.05	81.46
Czech Republic	91.03	78.08	52.25	53.87
Slovenia	86.63	76.97	63.80	59.17
Bulgaria	85.44	80.06	60.29	62.84
Romania	86.82	83.21	69.28	72.07

There are a vast number of scientific definitions for 'family'. Most definitions relate to the generation aspect, in which one generation provides for the other (see Nave-Herz, 1997, p37) In reality there are different types of familial cohabitation: nuclear family, step family, single parent family, non-marital partnership, etc.

In parallel to the plurality of family types the following demographic trends have been observed in most western European countries (see Europäische Beobachtungsstelle für nationale Familienpolitiken, 1998):

- Increased numbers of single-parent families (in particular lone mothers).
- Continuous decrease in family size.
- Increased numbers of non-marital partnerships.
- Increased numbers of single households.
- Long-term drop in birth rates (there has been a slight increase in recent years but relative to significantly lower starting points).

Analyses of families carried out in different European countries usually also include studies on the roles of women and men and on the division of labour between men and women, the forms of living together, the role and function of children, etc. and highlight the influence of ideological positions and value systems in regard to the goals and targets of family policies.

Role allocation and division of labour within the family and their effects

From the societal point of view families fulfil important functions which are often cited to justify family policies (see: Badelt and Österle, 1998, p134):

- generative function (continuation of society)
- household function (fulfilling basic human needs such as clothing, food, and shelter)
- socialising function (raising children)
- placing function (providing for schooling and vocational training of children)
- recreational function (recovery from everyday strain, reproductive function)
- solidarity function (strengthening solidarity among generations)
- economic function (the household as a producer)

The question is in how far these functions correspond to tasks which are allocated to the role of a particular family member – the woman. Family work (raising children, caring for family members, taking care of the household) is often described in an idealising way but receives little or no recognition from society. The gender-specific division of labour still exists in our households to a varying degree. In the vast majority of partnerships in central Europe housework and caring for children are tasks performed mainly by women (see Famann et al., 1995; Garhammer, 1996; Keddi and Seidenspinner, 1991; Mikula, 1994). Men are traditionally seen in the role of breadwinner. The percentage of men with children, who do not share in the housework in the twelve EU countries – before the entry of Sweden, Finland, and Austria – dropped from 65 per cent in 1970 to 45 per cent in 1990 (see Künzler, 1995, p128).

The percentage of women who cook, clean, or do the laundry is three times as high as that of men. The situation is similar when it comes to caring for children. Women are responsible for taking care of the children and also for their development and their educational achievements. Fathers usually play with their children and share their leisure activities (see Faßmann et al., 1995, p37). It shows very clearly: the 'less pleasant' a task is, the lower the involvement of fathers and men.

The 'time-available' hypothesis, which links the amount of time spent in income-generating activities by each of the partners to the extent to which they engage in housework, can be considered refuted: the main responsibility for household and children still remains with the women, even if they are employed outside the home (see Faßmann et al., 1995, p45; Peuckert, 1996, p206). In such cases women first reduce their own needs, such as recreation, sleep, and personal care, in order to reconcile both work and family (see Bertram, 1997, p137). Although greater economic independence of working women does not lead to the elimination of the traditional division of housework, there are studies which indicate that partners of highly educated women who work full-time are more likely to share the housework than partners of women who are

'only' housewives or only work part-time (see Bacher and Wilk, 1996; Gershuny, 1994).

The time women spend on unpaid work is more or less the same in all countries (between 27 and 33 hours per week) (see Juster and Stafford, 1991 as quoted by Plantenga, 1997). The time men spend on unpaid work varies considerably (from 3.5 hours in Japan to 18 hours in Sweden). In summary it can be said that men in most European countries haven't changed significantly. They leave unpaid care and house work mainly to the women. There is still a vast discrepancy between the normative ideals of a family built on equality and partnership and the reality in society. The male household revolution has not happened yet. Doing unpaid housework has caused women to also become discriminated against in the working world. Equal sharing of unpaid housework is a prerequisite to the reconciliation of work and family.

Under these aspects the family is a source of discrimination for women. The unequal distribution of work within the family is the cause for more stress, less prosperity, and lower income. This discrimination is also the reason why women have less power, for instance with regard to participation in making consumer decisions (see Kirchler, 1989).

The respective authorities of partners in a marriage are – in line with resource theory – derived from their positions in the world of work: the partner with the higher earning status or the higher income has more power in the relationship and can therefore more easily achieve his or her interests. A differentiation between 'external' resources of income-generating work and 'internal' resources of services and production within the household allocates a certain amount of power to housewives, which however never matches the value of male resources. In contrast to this view feminist theorists see the household as a negative resource, because it prevents women from societal participation and because housework tends generally to be allocated to the powerless partner in a relationship (see Ferree, 1991).

According to this assumption, women increase their marital decision-making power if they have their own income. The power a woman can achieve however depends largely on the value attributed to her work by the couple (see Gather, 1996). If both partners are not (or no longer) employed in income-generating activities, the status of their previous employment, as well as, in the case of women, the duration of such past employment, plays a significant role in determining current status. For the man retirement means the loss of an essential social role, the role of breadwinner. This loss may lead to the lowering of his status within the family and to a possible shift or reversal of the gender relationship in favour of the woman, after retirement (see Gutman, 1987).

Outside the family this uneven distribution leads to uneven risks and discrimination. The long-term effect of inequality shows in the social safeguarding of women. Retirement pensions drawn by women are not only significantly lower than those of men because of their lower incomes, but also because of shorter contribution periods. Among the 15 per cent of pensioners in Austria, who receive an 'Ausgleichszulage' (a supplement paid to persons whose total pension is less than 582 Euros, which amounts to the difference between the pension and this threshold) almost three quarters (72%) are women (see Bundesministerium für Arbeit, Gesundheit und Soziales, 1998, p61). The consequences are even more striking for women who because of divorce do not qualify for any social security benefits. Society reacts to these problems in varying ways. Some feel that the work done in the interest of society should be remunerated and these persons therefore advocate benefits for eldercare and childcare (see Stolz-Willig and Veil, 1999, p94) as well as the splitting of retirement pensions. Others consider the equal distribution of family work between genders as the sustainable implementation of the legal equality of men and women within the family.

The participation of women in the labour market

One of the most significant structural changes in gender relations in most countries is the continuous increase in the number of women in the labour market. This phenomenon has

resulted in far reaching changes in the employment sector as well as in the family. Employment has become a decisive factor in life and family planning for women. The rate at which these changes take place and the extent of gender equality differs among European countries.

Employment rates of women in the European Union have risen constantly in the past years (see Rubery and Fagan, 1998, p4?) The employment rates of women between 15 and 64 years of age vary across the European countries. Whereas in Sweden and Denmark more than two thirds of working-age women are engaged in income-generating employment, the figures for Greece, Italy, Spain, and Luxembourg are below 40 per cent (see Figure 1).

Employment rates for men are higher in all European countries than those of women. The gender gap differs from country to country. A comparison of full-time employment rates for men and full-time employment rates for women shows an even wider gap. Scandinavia, the former GDR, and Portugal have the highest full-time employment rate at approximately 40 per cent, in the other countries it is between 31 and 37 per cent and only in Spain it is lower (27%). An analysis of the employment rates by age and motherhood, shows significant national differences with regard to full-time and part-time work (see Figure 2).

In eight of the 15 countries overall employment rates for women aged 20 to 49 years with no dependent children (see Figure 2) exceed 70 per cent, in the other countries they lie between 55 and 70 per cent. With the exception of the Netherlands it is mostly full-time employment. An analysis of the employment rates for women aged 20 to 49 with children shows the following results: in Germany, Austria, Finland, and Portugal it is approximately 65 per cent, in Spain, Ireland, Greece, Italy, and Luxembourg it is under 50 per cent.

Women of all ages, but particularly women of reproductive age, show continually rising labour-market participation. An analysis of the percentage of women among the working population according to part-time and full-time employment and according to the number of

Figure 1 Labour market status of men and women of working age, 1996

| | Women | | | | | | Men | | | | | |
| | Employment rate | | | Non-employment rate | | | Employment rate | | | Non-employment rate | | |
	Full time	Part time	All	Unemployed	Inactive	All	Full time	Part time	All	Unemployed	Inactive	All
Sweden	40%	28%	68%	7%	26%	32%	65%	6%	70%	9%	21%	30%
Denmark	44%	23%	67%	6%	27%	33%	72%	8%	81%	5%	15%	19%
UK	35%	28%	62%	4%	34%	38%	70%	5%	75%	8%	17%	25%
Austria	42%	17%	59%	3%	38%	42%	73%	3%	76%	4%	20%	24%
Finland	49%	9%	58%	11%	31%	42%	58%	5%	62%	12%	26%	38%
Germany (East)	44%	12%	56%	13%	31%	45%	68%	1%	69%	9%	22%	31%
Germany (West)	36%	20%	55%	5%	40%	45%	71%	3%	73%	6%	21%	27%
Netherlands	17%	37%	55%	5%	40%	45%	63%	12%	76%	4%	20%	24%
Portugal	48%	6%	54%	5%	41%	46%	69%	2%	71%	5%	24%	29%
France	37%	15%	52%	9%	39%	48%	64%	3%	67%	8%	25%	33%
Belgium	32%	14%	46%	7%	48%	55%	65%	2%	67%	5%	28%	33%
Ireland	33%	9%	43%	6%	51%	57%	64%	3%	67%	9%	24%	33%
Greece	35%	3%	39%	7%	54%	61%	71%	2%	73%	5%	23%	27%
Italy	32%	5%	36%	7%	57%	64%	63%	2%	65%	7%	28%	35%
Luxembourg	29%	7%	35%	2%	63%	65%	63%	1%	64%	2%	35%	36%
Spain	27%	5%	32%	14%	54%	68%	60%	2%	61%	13%	25%	39%
E15	34%	16%	50%	7%	43%	50%	66%	4%	70%	8%	23%	30%

Note: The percentages have been rounded and so do not add up to exactly 100 in some instances.
Source: European Labour Force Survey, 1996.
From Rubery and Fagan, 1998, p42.

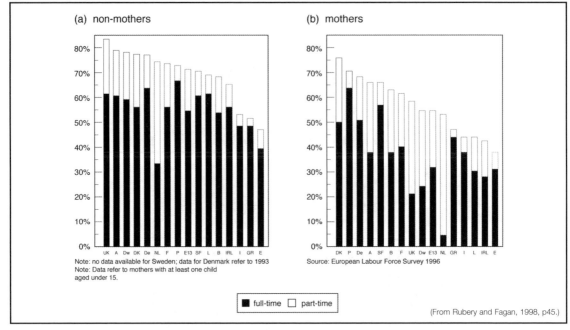

Figure 2 Full and part-time employment rates of mothers and non-mothers aged 20–49, 1996

children shows the following national differences:

- Part-time employment prevails in the Netherlands and in the UK.
- In Finland, Portugal and Denmark full-time employment is more common.
- In countries with low unemployment rates for women, such as Greece, Ireland, Spain and Italy, the age of the child has no effect on maternal employment rates.
- In countries such as France and Belgium, where the percentages of full-time and part-time employment are almost equal there is hardly any difference in full-time or part-time employment rates for women with or without children.
- Germany and Austria adhere to the breadwinner model, which means that following an interruption of employment for the birth of a child, a subsequent return to the labour market takes place only at a later point in time and usually for part-time employment.

Women's levels of qualification are another key characteristic which is strongly coupled with their employment rates, increasing with increased qualification levels. This pattern is particularly accentuated for mothers with

dependent children. A higher level of qualifications is also associated with the expression of more egalitarian sex role attitudes and a rejection of the traditional breadwinner model, and with modest modifications of the distribution of domestic work in the home. Since access to active labour market policy is linked to unemployment status, women are under-represented, since they often are not listed as unemployed in statistics (see Equal Opportunities and Employment in the European Union, 1998, p42).

The significant role which public opinion plays in women's employment rates shouldn't be disregarded. Bradshaw et al. (1998) have tried to classify different expectations with regard to the role of women and in particular of mothers in society.

On the basis of data gathered in 20 countries three groups of countries were identified with reference to the extent of socio-cultural support for the employment of mothers:

1. Sweden is among those countries in which the socio-cultural environment provides intensive support for the employment of mothers. National opinion polls show that mothers who are 'only' housewives have a

low status in society and also show that childcare outside the family to facilitate the employment of mothers of pre-school children is considered totally acceptable.

2. The Netherlands are part of the second group of countries. Reports on Dutch society and culture show that attitudes have changed with regard to reversed roles in the family and sharing of domestic work by the partners, but that childcare outside of the family is not widely accepted.

3. Germany is the country in which the employment of mothers finds little support in the socio-cultural environment. Surveys have shown that the traditional role patterns are widely accepted. Employment of mothers is generally considered a disadvantage for pre-school children. Only a few respondents said a mother with one child should be part of the work force. The opinion that a mother's place is in the home even when the youngest child has entered school, is still as common as the idea that the only acceptable employment at this time would be part-time employment. The only phase during the cycle of motherhood where maternal employment is considered acceptable is after the children have left home, and even then about half of the respondents advocated part-time work, the other half full-time employment. Similar results were found in Austria, Spain, and Italy (see Bradshaw et al., 1996).

Parental leave and compensation

The motives for the introduction of parental leave regulations throughout Europe were as follows: protecting the health of mother and child, relieving poverty of families with small children, growth in women's employment, improved quality of life of working parents by granting them free time as well as equality measures and a reduction of unemployment by replacing parents on leave by new employees.

As shown below there is a complex array of rights and financial benefits for parents. Most European countries have established some form of parental leave, with only Ireland, Great Britain, and Luxembourg lagging behind. The Dutch system of part-time work is also

comparatively minimalistic. Countries such as Belgium and Denmark have integrated their parental leave provisions into complex packages of measures, originally intended as a strategy for fighting unemployment. Eligible persons are usually female employees with minimum contributory times; universal eligibility as provided for under Swedish law is rare. In most countries parental leave is accompanied by a modest flat-rate income or even by a proportional substitute income. Only in the Mediterranean countries, Greece, Spain and Portugal are unpaid parental leave provisions still rudimentary.

Overview: Parental Leave and Parental Benefits

(Maternity leave and benefits; child care leave and benefits)

Belgium

Instead of extended maternity leave beyond the legal maternity leave, 'leave for family reasons' for 3–12 months following maternity leave; flat rate benefits: maximum 272 Euros.

Denmark

28 weeks including maternity leave, thereof four weeks before delivery and 14 weeks after delivery, 10 weeks child-care leave (legal right) for either the mother and/or the father (3% of fathers make use of this possibility). Minimum benefit 353 Euros/per week.

Thereafter, six months per parent, maximum of 12 months of leave until the child is nine years of age; benefit: 60% of unemployment benefit, approx. 212 Euros.

Germany

Child care leave until the child is three years of age. Child care benefit for 24 months (includes provision permitting working for up to 19 hours/week), maximum: 318 Euro (depending on income, the child's age and the number of children)

Finland

After maternity leave 6½ months leave for either the mother or the father. Child care benefit: 66% of the wages, minimum 259 Euros, followed by child care leave (mother or father) until the child is three years of age. Child care supplement: 259 Euros, extra supplements for siblings or in case of need.

France

One year parental leave, for either the mother or the father, may be extended to 36 months. Child care benefit only for the second child upward, 454 Euros/month.

Greece

Limited group of persons eligible for parental leave; no financial compensation.

Ireland

No legal right to child care leave or financial compensation.

Italy

Child care leave until the child is three years of age; fathers are also eligible; child care benefit: 30% of the prior income for six months.

Luxembourg

Father or mother eligible for child care leave of six months (prerequisite: 1 year of employment). The first six months following maternity leave, the other six months until the child is five years of age; financial compensation: 1492 Euros/per month.

Child care benefit/supplement: 410 Euros/month until the child is two years of age, starting with the third child until the youngest child is four years of age, if only one parent is employed.

Netherlands

Legal right to unpaid child care leave, either three months full time or six months part time until the child is eight years old. Financial compensation currently under discussion.

Austria

As of 1 January 2002 child care benefits are set at 436 Euros/per month, with the possibility of a supplement of 182 Euros/month for single mothers and economically disadvantaged families; eligibility for family allowance is a prerequisite to be eligible for child care benefits; employment prior to birth not a prerequisite.

Maximum duration is 36 months, six months of which is paid to the 'other' parent only, if the 'other' parent takes over the care of the child for this duration.

This change of system did not entail an extension of child care leave which remains at 24 months, six months thereof for the 'other' parent only.

Portugal

Child care leave: six months, unpaid, may be extended in six month increments up to a maximum of 24 months until the child is three years old.

Sweden

Each parent is entitled to 180 days of full-time leave, of which each parent has to take at least one month ('Papa-month'; one third to two fifths of all fathers take this month), five months can be transferred to the mother, if she agrees; parental leave can be taken until the child is eight years old. Parental benefit is seen as a compensation for lost earnings; it amounts to 75% of the income, maximum: 2640 Euros/month.

Spain

Right to a maximum of 36 months of child care leave; no compensation.

United Kingdom

Right to parental leave for a maximum of 10 months, without pay.

The provision of adequate childcare facilities offers an alternative to long parental leave. The availability of adequate childcare facilities is crucial to the extent to which mothers seek employment. In Finland this option is expressly part of provisions which either guarantee a place in a public child care facility or financial compensation to pay for child care in the home. In other countries parental leave and child care complement each other with child care provided after the period of paid parental leave.

Family politics in the EU member countries differ mainly with regard to the promotion of the integration of mothers in the labour market, the provision of childcare facilities, provisions regarding maternity/parental leave and financial compensation. In countries where options for leave are not supported by the provision of childcare facilities the system often indirectly serves to make mothers leave the labour market instead of supporting them in their return into employment. This is the situation in Germany. A study by Landenberger (1991) shows for Germany that extended parental leave provisions have not led to any improvements with regard to the employment of women. Only about half of the women return to the labour market during the leave period; the others remain outside the employment market for a longer period, or stay away permanently. 'Extended parental leave turns out to be the financially cushioned expulsion of women from the labour market rather than a strategy for supporting their return to the labour market.' (German original, Mayer, 1991, pVII)

In all countries parental leave is taken primarily by women, even where provisions exist for both men and women. Sweden has by far the highest male take-up rate (33–40%). For a long time Sweden was the only country where part of parental leave is lost if not used by the father. (There are now similar provisions in Austria.) At the same time the parental leave compensation in Sweden is relatively high. Men don't take parental leave if it is linked to relatively low financial compensation, as is the case in Austria, even if several months of leave are lost.

Reconciliation of employment and family

Family life and working life have different structural effects on the biographies of men and women. In the lives of men, family life and working life complement each other, in the lives of women they are a potential source of conflict. Career breaks usually mean that future employment and career opportunities are at least impaired. Measures which serve the reconciliation of family and employment strongly reflect prevailing ideologies.

The successful sequential and simultaneous reconciliation of family and employment exists only in Sweden and in France. In Sweden nine in ten young women are employed. In other countries the traditional 'Breadwinner/ Homemaker' family is still the recognised family model in government family policy, particularly in Ireland, Switzerland, Italy, Germany, and Austria. Women's social security coverage is

mostly linked to the husband, which means that divorce carries great social risks. Gornick (1997) created an indicator for job security taking into account the age of the child, the obligatory school age and the availability of child care. The purpose of this indicator is to evaluate the effectiveness of political measures with regard to providing child care services in order to facilitate employment. The higher the value reached by a country, the better the support structure provided for mothers in employment. Gornick arrived at the conclusion that Finland, Denmark, Sweden, Belgium, and France have the most comprehensive provisions for families with children and also the most generous support services for pre-school children. The United Kingdom is at the other end of the spectrum. In Italy there are considerable services for pre-school children but very restrictive provisions regarding parental leave are aggravated by an inadequate number of childcare facilities for children under three years of age. This last aspect was also found in France in spite of a very high level of services, whereas Finnish mothers appear to receive less support from the government the older the children are. With the exception of Sweden and Denmark, government support services end more or less with the beginning of school age. This is the point in time when the United Kingdom assumes the top position because of the traditionally long periods of time children spend in school, per day and over the year. Countries such as Germany, Austria, or the Netherlands hold middle positions. Main points of criticism are the opening hours of childcare facilities and the inadequate services offered outside of the schools, which constitute a problem with regard to the working hours of parents (Gornick, 1997).

Profiles of family policy

The European Union has no authority with regard to family policy. Family policy is left to the member states, which are free to organise family policy in ways they consider desirable. Nevertheless the European Union plays an important role in the field of family politics. Its task is to facilitate the exchange of information and best practice among member countries.

Economic intervention	Ecological intervention	
	Support of the employment of both parents through child care	*Constraint* of the employment of both parents through lack of child care
Support Assistance to families minimal economic necessity for both parents to be gainfully employed	Case A + +	Case B + −
Constraint Economic necessity for both parents to be gainfully employed	Case C − +	Case D − −

Source: Gauthier, 1991.

Figure 3   Profiles of family policy

Gauthier (1991) developed a grid which permits the classification of family policy in the OECD countries with regard to support for women's employment and cash benefits for families (see Figure 3).

Case A: Transfer payments support the family; gainful employment of both parents is not an economic necessity. Childcare facilities are readily available if needed. These two factors permit high flexibility in everyday life of the families (Denmark and France).

Case B: Financial support payments guarantee a defined minimum level of income; deficits with regard to the reconciliation of family and employment are a structural obstacle to the employment of both parents (Germany, Austria).

Case C: Family policy does not provide adequate compensation for the economic burdens of the family; therefore families with only one income are disadvantaged compared to the national standard; the services offered for the reconciliation of family and employment facilitate the employment of both parents (Sweden and the Netherlands are at the threshold from B to C).

Case D: Family policy does not compensate the economic burdens of the family, nor does it provide services to permit reconciling family with employment (United Kingdom and Italy).

Outlook

The interdependence of policies on women, families, and social, and labour markets become obvious through a comparison of EU countries with regard to the indicators: women's employment, gender specific income differences, percentage of women in political representative bodies, and fertility rate: (see Rosenberger, 1998, p73):

- Countries such as Sweden, Denmark and Finland have relatively high employment rates for women, relatively low gender specific income differences, relatively high percentages of women in politics, and comparatively high birth rates.
- Countries such as Italy, Spain, Portugal and Greece have relatively low employment rates for women, relatively high gender specific income differences, a low percentage of women in politics and low birth rates.

These results indicate that it is not the fact that women bear children which is the cause for the discrimination against women, but that their discrimination is a consequence of cultural norms and political strategies. If equality and equal opportunities are seen as political issues in the sense of costs, benefit, and interests, it goes without saying that men must give up something. Gender equality requires men to share socially desirable assets and advantages, such as higher income, better jobs, and career opportunities. They would also have to give up the advantage of placing certain burdens on women, and enjoying personal care and services rendered to them by women.

Gender differences are to be seen as a distribution conflict; if this is not the case we downplay their importance or even deny them politically. The goal is to equalise gender roles by equalising the division of labour. What is needed are provisions for the simultaneous reconciliation of work and family for men and women, which will eventually lead to the redistribution of unpaid work. Political and economic measures for the support and promotion of women are short-term requirements. Intensified measures providing for equality would improve opportunities for mothers to reconcile employment and family. Including fathers to an increasing degree into care and housework would probably have stronger effects than all social, family, and labour market measures together. In parallel, equality with regard to income and career opportunities would have to be guaranteed. Before this level of equality is achieved government measures such as provision of special training programmes, wage subsidies and subsidies of incremental costs, as well as improved childcare and more flexible working hours will be required. The problem of reconciling family with work only confronts individuals, particularly women, in its well-known everyday form because societal institutions have brought about a separation of these two spheres of life. Their reconciliation is left to individuals, mainly the women only, as their private problem, although their incompatibility has been brought about by society.

Didactic/methodological assignments

Individual work, possibly to be followed by group work or work in the plenary

Answer the first question in the 'Europäische Wertestudie' (Study of European Values) and then discuss it in your group.

1. I have here a list of different life spheres and would like to know how important they are in your life. Please, tell me for each sphere whether it is very important, rather important, not very important, or not important.

1 = very important ... 2 ... 3 ... 4 = not important

Spheres:

- work
- family
- friends
- free or leisure time
- politics
- religion

Group work

Analyse the provisions on parental leave and parental benefits of the country in which you live, under the aspects of gender equality and possibilities of reconciling work and family.

Group work with two different questions:

(a) Discuss parental benefits for all mothers (and fathers) **independent** of prior employment.

- Personal position:
  Reasoning
- Position(s) espoused in women's politics:
  Reasoning
- Position(s) espoused in family politics:
  Reasoning
- Socio-political position:
  Reasoning
- What is the level of parental benefits ?

(b) Discuss parental benefits for all mothers (and fathers) **dependent on** prior employment.

- Personal position:
  Reasoning
- Position(s) espoused in women's politics:
  Reasoning
- Position(s) espoused in family politics:
  Reasoning
- Socio-political position:
  Reasoning
- What is the level of parental benefits?

References

Bacher, J. and Wilk, L. (1996) Geschlechtsspezifische Arbeitsteilung – Ausmaß und Bedingungen männlicher Mitarbeit im Haushalt. In: Haller, M. et al. (Eds.) *Österreich im Wandel. Werte, Lebensformen und Lebensqualität 1986 bis 1993*, Munich -Oldenburg, 165–87.

Badelt, C. and Österle, A. (1998) *Grundzüge der Sozialpolitik*, special section, Vienna.

Bertram, H. Familienleben (1997) *Neue Wege zur Gestaltung von Lebenszeit, Arbeitszeit und Familienzeit*, Gütersloh.

Bundesministerium für Arbeit, Gesundheit und Soziales (Ed.) (1998) *Soziales Österreich: Sicherungssysteme im Überblick*. Vienna.

Bundesministerium für Frauenangelegenheiten (Ed.) (1995) *Bericht über die Situation der Frauen in Österreich, Frauenbericht*. Vienna.

Cyprian, G. and Vaskovics L. A. (1997) Ergebnisse der vergleichenden Familienforschung in Europa (Einführung) In: Vaskovics, L.A. (Ed.) *Familienleitbilder und Familienrealitäten*, Opladen, 224–8.

Denz, H. (Ed.) (2002) *Die europäische Seele, Leben und Glauben in Europa*. Vienna.

Europäische Beobachtungsstelle für Nationale Familienpolitiken, Europäische Kommission (Ed.) (1998) *Entwicklungen der Nationalen Familienpolitik im Jahre 1996*. West Yorkshire.

Europäische Beobachtungsstelle für Nationale Familienpolitiken, Europäische Kommission (Ed.) (1998) *Eine Synthese Nationaler Familienpolitiken*. 1996. West Yorkshire.

Faßmann, H. et al. Weibliche Lebensformen, In: Bundesministerium für Frauenangelegenheiten (Ed.) (1995) *Bericht über die Situation der Frauen in Österreich, Frauenbericht*. Vienna, 21–125.

Ferre, M. M. (1991) The Gender Division of Labour in Two-earner Marriages. *Journal of Family Issues*. 158–80.

Garhammer, M. (1996) Auf dem Weg zu egalitären Geschlechtsrollen ? Familiale Arbeitsteilung im Wandel, In: Buba, H. P. and Schneider, N.F. (Eds.) *Familie zwischen gesellschaftlicher Prägung und individuellem Design*. Opladen, 319–36.

Gather, C. (1996) Geschlechterkonstruktionen bei Paaren im Übergang in den Ruhestand. Zum Problem des Zusammenhanges von Geschlecht, Macht und Erwerbsarbeit. *Soziale Welt*. 223–49.

Gauthier, A.H. (1991) *The Western European Governments, Attitudes and Responses to the Demographic and Family Question*. Paper presented at the European Science Foundation Conference, St. Martin.

Gauthier, A. H. (1996) *The State and the Family, A Comparative Analysis of Family Policies in Industrialised Countries*. Oxford.

Gershuny, J., Godwin, M. and Jones, S. (1994) The Domestic Labour Revolution: A Process of Lagged Adoption, In: Anderson, M. et al. (Eds.) *The Social and Political Economy of Household*. Oxford.

Gornick, J. C. (1997) Supporting the Employment of Mothers: Policy Variation Across Fourteen Welfare States. *Journal of European Social Policy*, 1/1997, 45–70.

Gruber, G. and Fröschl, E. (Eds.) (2001) *Gender-Aspekte in der Sozialen Arbeit*. Vienna.

Gutman, D. (1987) *Reclaimed Powers*. New York.

Keddi, B. and Seidenspinner, G. (1991) Arbeitsteilung und Partnerschaft, In: Bertram, H. (Ed.) *Die Familie in Westdeutschland, Stabilität und Wandel familialer Lebensformen*. Opladen, 159ff.

Kirchler, E. (1989) *Kaufentscheidungen im privaten Haushalt*. Göttingen.

Künzler, J. (1995) Geschlechtsspezifische Arbeitsteilung: Die Beteiligung von Männern im Haushalt im internationalen Vergleich, *Zeitschrift für Frauenforschung des Instituts Frau und Gesellschaft*. 115–33.

Landenberger, M. (1991) Erziehungsurlaub: Arbeitsmarktpolitisches Instrument zur selektiven Ausgliederung und Wiedereingliederung. In: Mayer, K.U. et al. (Eds.) *Vom Regen in die Traufe: Frauen zwischen Beruf und Familie*. Frankfurt, 262–88.

Mayer, K.U. (1991) Einleitung, in Mayer, K.U. et al. (Eds.) *Vom Regen in die Traufe: Frauen zwischen Beruf und Familie*. Frankfurt S. VII–XXI.

Mikula, G. Gerechtigkeit und Ungerechtigkeit in der Familie: Ein Beitrag aus sozialpsychologischer Sicht, In: Badelt, C. (Ed.) *Familien zwischen Gerechtigkeitsidealen und Benachteiligung*. Vienna, 29–51.

Millar, J. and Warman, A. (1996) *Family Obligations in Europe*. London, Family Policy Studies Centre.

Nave-Herz, R. (1997) Pluralisierung familialer Lebensformen – ein Konstrukt der Wissenschaft? In: Vaskovics, L.A. (Ed.) *Familienleitbilder und Familienrealitäten*. Opladen, 36–49.

Peuckert, R. (1996) *Familienformen im sozialen Wandel*. Opladen.

Plantenga, J. (1997) European Constants and National Particularities: The Position of Women in the EU Labour Market, In: Geske Dijkstra, A. and Plantenga, J. *Gender and Economics: A European Perspective.* London.

Rosenberger, S. K. (1998) Chancengleichheit und Frauenförderung. Möglichkeiten und Modelle inner -und überbehördlicher Interessenvertretung, In: Bundesministerium für Arbeit, Gesundheit und Soziales (Ed.) *Goldmarie.* Vienna, 73–87.

Rubery, J. and Fagan, C. (1998) *Chancengleichheit und Beschäftigung in der Europäischen Union.* Bundesministerium für Arbeit, Gesundheit und Soziales and Bundesministerium für Frauenangelegenheiten und Verbraucherschutz. Vienna.

Stolz-Willig, B. and Veil, M. (Eds.) (1999) *Es rettet uns kein höh'res Wesen. Feministische Perspektiven der Arbeitsgesellschaft.* Hamburg.

Tölke, A. (1995) Geschlechtsspezifische Aspekte der Berufs -und Familienentwicklung in Nauck, B. and Onnen-Isemann, C. (Eds.) *Familie im Brennpunkt von Wissenschaft und Forschung.* Neuwied, 489–504.

Vaskovics, L.A. (Ed.) (1997) *Familienleitbilder und Familienrealitäten.* Opladen.

Zulehner, P.M. and Denz, H. (1993) *Wie Europa lebt und glaubt: Europäische Wertestudie.* Düsseldorf.

4. Care and Work

Margrit Brückner

It is the objective of this chapter to raise awareness of the inequality inherent in the division of labour along gender lines in societal required fields of care, which necessitate special policies for women in order to advance the general democratisation of society. Questions as to the focus these analyses should have and which policies are best suited to help us come closer to this goal must be an integral part of ongoing debate in society. This is because only theoretical and political openness and the acceptance of a certain parallel state of uncertainty can meet the demands of the changing manifold living conditions of women and men and their widely differing needs and interests and can result in a new distribution of care responsibilities between genders in a form that no longer leaves these tasks to one gender only.

Basic assumptions and development tendencies in the care debate

This debate focuses on the redefinition of the concept of work, a more just distribution of care between genders and socio-political recognition of women's work in the field of care. The foremost goal is that women should receive full social rights (social citizenship) for their work. Furthermore there is the call for a women-oriented, i.e. gender-conscious, organisation, handling, and recognition of care as an equal contribution to the work required by society.

Care in its comprehensive meaning is more than just dealing with custodial and nursing activities throughout the life-cycle (childhood – old age, health – illness) in an informal manner professionally carried out more or less by women, but also encompasses socio-pedagogical and social work intervention in special life situations (educational support, vocational training projects, support for single parents, care in women's shelters, work with

migrants). The scope of care and the forms it takes are subject to social change as are the definition of its fields. Political decisions delineate public and private responsibilities and thus the extent and significance of training programmes and whether work is paid or unpaid (Fraser 1994a + b). The different motives for and organisational forms of care work can only be understood in their societal relevance when related to a common interpretation framework of socially required custodial and nursing activities. Focussing in an isolated way on single aspects means running the risk of underestimating the interdependences of different fields of care and insufficiently recognising care as a central societal task in all its facets and its full socio-political significance. Women have, as activists and scientists, successfully attempted to influence the field of informal care towards social justice as well as to initiate new types of services specifically geared to girls and women. But what does it mean for the development of gender relations, when gender-segregated fields and tasks are (though with good reason) strengthened? What sort of relationships will develop between state, social rights, and women, if autonomous female activities are realised, familial care work of women is recognised, but real inequality between genders is not overcome? Care is closely linked to questions of the political regulation of the relationship of paid work to unpaid work and wage substitutes, and points to the gender bias at the base of this relationship. Approaches in democracy-theory need to take into account how care work is organised, since justice and equality must also be demanded for this field of socially relevant activities. Whereas the debate on special care ethics with women, carried by American feminists (Gilligan, 1984) in the 1980s and early 1990s, was taken up, differentiated, and revised in many ways in the German speaking countries (e.g. Nunner-Winkler (eds.), 1993; Nagl-Docekal (eds.), 1993) the same does not apply to the Anglo-American and Scandinavian debate on care as a specific activity of women.

The starting point for all deliberations must be the concern of making the work of women in the field of care visible and ascribing value to it. This happens in different ways depending on the respective framework of interpretation. No matter what their differences, all theorists are eventually confronted with the same age old question which was already asked by the first women's movement, and which is referred to as 'Wollstonecraft's dilemma' (Pateman, 1989) in the English language debate. Is the objective equal opportunities for women and the fight to make their living situations as close as possible to those of men or do we need, in order to maintain women's roles in the family, special rights for women which relate to their role as mothers and care-givers. But first the most important aspects of the different views of care:

In the British debate, which originally saw care only as informal care giving within the family, Celia Davies (1994) has become the spearhead of a new comprehensive concept of care, which differentiates between different types of 'caring work' depending on the degree of formalisation:

- 'Care giving work' in private contexts, characterised by emotions (positive and negative ones) and ethics, with a lesser significance of 'skills'.
- 'Care work' as unskilled, paid work in informal and institutional contexts, again with low significance of 'skills'.
- 'Professional care' as a recognised activity with formal qualification requirements in social work or nursing.

Taking these definitions as a basis today's analyses include the following aspects (Graham, 1993; Ungerson, 1994):

- Differences among women as carers regarding class, ethnicity, and sexual orientation.
- The right to self-determination of persons needing help.
- The need for help among 'carers' (e.g., because of old age or disability).
- Informal rendering of services and domestic shadow work.

- Public and private, informal and institutional types of care.
- Residential care within the framework of social and welfare systems.

This British 'care' concept has come closer to the more general concept of care used by Scandinavian women researchers in terms of how it relates to private and public, institutional and informal care-work and points out the link between gender and social civil rights (Leira, 1994). Arnlaug Leira sees the advantage of such an overall view in the fact that the respective relationship between private obligations and public services becomes visible, just as it highlights the ratio of paid to unpaid work, its normative basis and the gender-bias which also exists even in Scandinavia. She interprets 'caring' in the light of the different forms of institutionalisation of care (familial, informal, formalised), with women walking the borderline between the private and public spheres, as, even in Scandinavia, a shift is taking place, away from state-provided types of institutionalised care.

The American debate not only deals with the relationship between the public and private sphere, particularly with the significant issue of overcoming this division, but also deals with the societal form of the interpretation of needs and the definition of dependency (Fraser and Gordon, 1994).

Care giving transcends the public and private spheres since women perform educational, custodial and nursing work in both spheres and move from one sphere to the other, maybe as paid 'caregivers' to meet their familial duties or as informal caregivers organising social services (Abel and Nelson, 1990). Changes in one sector lead to changes in another, and necessitate substituting measures to avoid a care deficit, as is currently the case in the United States. Care takes place in different contexts, which according to Abel and Nelson (1990) can be represented on three dimensions: the forms of relationship between 'caregiver' and 'care receiver', the issue of remuneration, and the location where the work is performed. They consider unaffiliated providers, who work in the growing field between formalised work in institutions and informal work in their own household to be particularly significant. The latter perform paid care work either in their own households or in other households and negotiate working conditions on a private basis. Specific problems of care giving in formal organisations are bureaucracy and standardisation, but the professional context permits distancing with regard to time and contents which in turn helps all those involved in the care process to maintain their independence. Informal care giving on the basis of personal relationships is considered the societal ideal in the United States. Isolation and a lack of social support are however overlooked for the sake of an assumed emotional gratification. Fisher and Tronto (1990) take this ideal and the tradition of caring as a female duty on the basis of dependency as the starting point for their discussions. Caring is seen as a social activity for insuring physical, personal and environmental survival, based on interactions and always containing potential for conflict as it calls for required resources. Issues of power, justice, and trust are part of caring, which therefore assumes a political dimension. The more asymmetry there is between responsibility for the caring process and power over the necessary resources, the greater is the danger of failure. This asymmetry, however, exists almost everywhere for women in traditional care settings, whether these are informal or professional. In particular in the professional context it is often an aggravating factor that care receivers too have little control over the care process, leading to inevitable misunderstandings and flaws in the interaction between caregivers and care receivers. As the feminist counter model Fisher and Tronto (1990) discuss the ideal of sisterhood as a form of equality-based care. This will be dealt with again later on, when discussing the projects for women and girls initiated by the women's movement.

Didactic assignments

Group discussion
Formulate and discuss the fundamental criticisms of the care debate relating to the societal attitude towards care. Summarise the different facets of care on the basis of the different authors.

Care in the framework of welfare state theories

In the modern western welfare state there are three sources of income for women: men, the labour market, and the state (Lewis 1997a). According to Jane Lewis the politically established relationship between unpaid work in the family and paid work provided by the market, as well as to the services of the welfare state are the decisive factors characterising the social policy of each country and is also of vital significance for gender relations. Every country and every era has a different type of mixed economy relating to the ways and means in which care is divided between the sectors family, informal sphere, market and state. In most cases the primarily unpaid care provided by women constitutes a constantly significant share. We realise how diverse women's relationships to the welfare state are, compared to the standard male biography, and how differentiated a gender-comprehensive analysis must be, when we consider that women on the one hand render a large proportion of direct welfare services, paid or unpaid, whereas women together with their children constitute the majority of clients of welfare services (Lewis, 1997b).

Major indicators of gender equality with regard to social security are independent access to the labour market for everyone and thus also for women (Marshall, 1992) as well as the degree of eligibility for social security services during times when not participating in the labour force (e.g. due to illness or old age) either through transfer benefits or access to help and support services (Esping-Andersen, 1990).

The British sociologist Thomas H. Marshall (1992) developed an approach at the end of the 1940s that is based on three dimensions, which are characteristic of full citizenship and include civil and social rights. If women perform tasks of social relevance, such as care, but are not granted full social citizenship because this work does not bestow upon them the same rights as full-time paid work we must ask by which form of gender equality one can bring about a link between care and social participation. The Swedish scientist Gösta Esping-Andersen

(1990) sees a central criterion for social security in the degree of de-commodification of the commodity 'labour'. He developed this concept for the degree of life-long security that is more independent of the risks of the labour market by reducing these risks, while retaining the concept of social services rights derived from the labour process as a yardstick for universal social participation. However, such an orientation of social security along the lines of the commodity 'labour' means for many women nothing else but the negation of their situation which is often only partly or not at all market dependent. De-commodification creates a higher degree of independence of the labour market for fully-employed men (and fully-employed women) by providing protection against illness, unemployment, old age, etc. but for the large group of women who are not fully employed it has the opposite effect, since the major share of de-commodified social duties is performed within the family (and mainly by women):

- Their dependence on the male breadwinner or on means-tested welfare payments becomes permanent and the share of unpaid work performed by women may even increase under such circumstances.
- Most social benefits are only available to these women in their role as family member (wife) and not as an individual. Traditional women's work within the family has only been commodified to a very limited extent and this non-commodified work has become the tacit prerequisite for commodification processes (development of paid work). Therefore shifts between commodified and de-commodified work as related to informal care work has a different meaning in this case than in the case of other paid activities.

Commodification of care work in the historical perspective has always given women more independence from familial constellations and the opportunity for paid work (Sauer, 1997; Chamberlayne, 1996; Ostner, 1995). Clare Ungerson (1997) takes a critical look at the commodification of informal care (remuneration through minor transfer payments or wages) that is taking place in many welfare states, a quasi-salary for domestic nursing and care with

gender-specific effects. Ungerson interprets this trend as the onset of a new welfare mix of professionalised and informal nursing and care work paralleled by the increasing significance of market and money-based social systems aimed at reducing costs as well as the danger of the development of a shadow labour market for the underprivileged. Marginal payments maintain the separation between public and private sphere and strengthen the gender hierarchy between paid work and familial work because they are not in conformity with the market. Commodification on the other hand raises the question of type and levels of payment and thus is supportive with regard to demands for 'full citizenship' for women. Such a restructuring of the relationship between paid work and care work shows two new perspectives (Fraser 1994c): universalising pay for work or making all care work equal.

The development of supportive systems to accompany public measures providing for universal nursing at home is of great social significances. Empirical studies have shown that many women are willing to do care work and that they need support in the form of remuneration or through social and nursing services (Lewis 1997a).

McLaughlin and Glendinning (1994) advocate diverse models according to the motto 'not de-commodification but de-familiarisation', which would take into account the positions of individual family members, make possible various patterns of agreeing on paid and unpaid work and permit other types of autonomy of women beyond paid work (Lewis, 1997b). If there is no choice for or against care, for or against paid work, there will be an increasing trend (just as in the United States) to promote the integration of women into the labour market; going so far as the obligation to work, paralleled by the reduction (downsizing) of support for informal care (e.g. for lone mothers) with the consequence of a devaluation of informal care (Fraser and Gordon, 1994).

For many feminist theorists care has become the core of the analysis of welfare states (Knijn and Kremer, 1997), since the type of organisation of care reveals the gender bias and raises the question of equal citizenship rights. Four unsolved problem levels are contained in the relationship between care and the changing welfare states. Care as:

- A public and private responsibility.
- Paid or unpaid work.
- The codification of dependency or the opportunity for independence.
- The right of the care givers or of the care receivers.

Trudie Knijn and Monique Kremer start their analysis from the demand for inclusive citizenship for women and men, based on the recognition of care as an essential dimension of citizenship, which would make care as well as citizenship lose their gender-specific character. Their central question is 'to what extent, at what costs, and on the basis of what assumptions and conditions is this responsibility undertaken' (Knijn and Kremer, 1997, p349). The unilateral link between care and dependency is misleading, since all human beings, in particular in societies characterised by strict division of labour, are structurally interdependent, only at different times and in different ways. It is therefore indispensable to re-establish necessary (as opposed to unnecessary) dependence as the human standard situation as well as to highlight the fictive nature of independence (Fraser and Gordon, 1994).

Recognising the interdependence between generations and genders necessitates a redefinition of rights and needs of care givers and care receivers through 'the citizenship right to time for care and the right to professional care' (Knijn and Kremer, 1997, p354). Prerequisites for due recognition of care are abandoning the dichotomy of dependence and independence, redefining the concept of work, and ridding care of the image of being non-work or work of low value.

Didactic assignments

Group discussion: which cornerstones for gender equality are brought up? Do you agree with them? Can you come up with further aspects or different ones?

Care from the perspective of action theory

In two decades of the British care debate, care has become a vital component of female

identity and a vehicle of far-reaching studies on gender and gender-specific identity, in particular in the domestic sphere (cf. Chamberlayne, 1996, p51). Initially care had been predominantly seen as a mixture of 'labour and love' and the innovative concept had been to understand it as work. Clare Ungerson (1994) relates care as 'labour and love' also to paid institutionalised care work since informal caring because of the component of love, would be considered to be better in comparison to paid care which would be seen as a lower quality surrogate.

The complexity and intangibility of care, even for 'professional care givers', has been illustrated by Celia Davies (1994), by taking female nurses as an example. These suffer from being unable to articulate their own work. Beyond the skills that are seen as instruments, there is no recognised form of public appreciation or esteem, which would reflect the multifaceted nature of care work with regard to the ability to be able to relate. This official inarticulateness is linked to the personal fear of losing inter-human care skills through instrumental training, a fear of loss which is reflected as love in the cultural standard of care and not as work and can be found as a golden thread linking all care professions (Rabe-Kleberg, 1993; Rommelspacher, 1992). According to Davis (1994) professional care denotes a synergy of formal knowledge and skills with an understanding of the overall situation, i.e. a combination of professional knowledge and general everyday know-how and the ability to build and maintain relationships (attention, dedication, creating a friendly atmosphere) qualities, which go unnoticed in the professional world because they are ascribed to the private sphere (Ostner and Beck-Gernsheim, 1979).

Contrary to the care debate in Britain, care, as a profession, has been the focus of attention in Germany since the seventies after only a relatively short debate on housework. The reason for this is that many feminists work in this field. The relationship between gender role and professional role drew much attention, in particular the fact that qualities derived from the female gender role are incorporated as quasi natural features into typically female professions, something which most feminists view in a rather ambivalent manner. Discussions at the theoretical level have focussed on the question whether there is anything like special female skills (Knapp, 1988) and at the practical level on how these should be seen; whether as unacceptable, unreasonable expectations or as valuable qualities. The self-image and professional image of the majority of feminists working in the social field have shown, and still show, elements of both features – contradictory as they are:

- Anger at the intrinsic exploitation, voiced as 'we don't want to do all the relationship work for you – abstract: for society, or concrete: for men – any longer' (Sozialarbeiterinnengruppe, Frankfurt, 1978).
- The positive awareness of 'other' support and relationship abilities which become mainly manifest for women and girls in political and professional work and are beginning to find their expression in politics (Brückner, 1996; Brückner and Holler, 1990). The skills resulting from the unreasonable expectations in the traditional role of women were transformed into specific female strengths through cooperation among women and feminist support for women and girls and were interpreted as a basis for empowerment; based on the awareness that 'women are different', namely that they have more empathy and more solidarity (Flaake, 1997; Fraser, 1994b).

At the theoretical level the controversy around the 'female work potential' (Ostner and Beck-Gernsheim, 1979) was a central issue which in many aspects was similar to the care debates and can be understood as a foil for debates on social work as relationship work. The starting point was the hypothesis 'what you do governs what you are' (Ostner, 1993, p110), i.e. socialisation of housework implies a certain type of work organisation (differentiated from paid work) and results in specific patterns determining relationships with other people. The heuristic concept of female working capacity, constructed in an ideally typified manner, originally served to analyse the disadvantaged status of women in the labour market, by highlighting anticipated interaction competences as qualifications, taking female nurses as an example. Transferring these extraprofessional competences from private activities to professional work in a suitable way is left to the women themselves – without any recognition. This very often leads to failures or at least discontent resulting from incorrect expectations. Whereas there are clear formalised specifications for the work of men, expectations regarding the occupational performance of women remain rather vague. On the one hand housework is delegated to women, on the other hand they are assigned invisible, housework-related tasks on the labour market. This type of 'care work turned into an occupation' (Ostner, 1993, p16) with its unstructured work patterns and its mix of tasks results in the lack of demarcation between occupation and person and in distancing problems with regard to occupational expectations (Gildemeister 1998). Ilona Ostner (1993) however assumes that this traditional form of female socialisation has become less prevalent in today's changed families and that person-oriented services have evolved, also for women, along hierarchical lines from highly professional to housework-like.

The strategic utilisation of the ideal of the female capacity to care is the basis for feminist approaches to work with women and girls, although its intrinsic hopes for joint liberalisation, later individual self-actualisation and mutual recognition have not been realised in many aspects (Brückner, 1996). Nevertheless it has been possible to take a positive view of women 'being different' and to use this as a basis for building an autonomous network of support for women and girls, expanding the public representation of women, and increasing women's self-esteem. In contrast to these positive conclusions Gudrun-Axeli Knapp (1988) highlights the problematic aspects of cementing differences and considers it a trap, when the patriarchal deficit definitions that are intrinsic to the low valuation of women's work are converted into positive definitions of female qualities. Ursula Rabe-Kleberg (1988) also points out the negative origins of a specific female work qualification, namely the exclusion of women from the 'general' public and thus from professional work. In 'typically female' occupations female qualifications are once more used against women, by forcing them to accept far worse conditions than men for the person-related services they carry out, namely in 'actual human' conditions as opposed to professionally defined conditions with binding structures with inherent distancing opportunities. Birgit Rommelspacher (1992) presents similar arguments by taking the link between neighbourly love and subjugation of women as well as societal powerlessness as the basis for specifically female care abilities. Fisher and Tronto (1990) differentiate between three ideals of feminist considerateness: motherliness, friendship, and sisterhood. They contrast the strengths of the first model, which they see as increasing the stature of mothers and the power vested in them, contrasted with grave risks: a hierarchical relationship to clients and the preservation of patriarchal structures with matriarchal symbols. The second model stresses friendship, equality, and closeness among women, but has the advantage that friendship implies voluntariness and choice and not necessarily caring. The greatest significance lies in the third model, sisterhood, which combines two moments: equality of all women (and of all human beings) and inequality with regard to different needs and obligations, which originally stems from the sequence of siblings. Women are different in many ways (from health to the access to power) but there is a mutual obligation for help among sisters, which may be able to mitigate these inequalities or even level them out, as the idea of equality and the concept of sisterhood ' ... bids us to look at specific caring activities in terms of power relationships and the possibility of minimising power inequalities' (Fisher and Tronto, 1990, p53).

Didactic assignments

Group discussion
Summarise the specific aspects of British, German and American care debates; discuss their commonalities and their differences.

The significance of feminist analyses of social policies for a new relationship between care and work

The starting point of feminist social politics is the analysis of the patriarchal sexual contract,

which explicitly or implicitly provides the basis for Western welfare regimes (Kurz-Scherf, 1997; Veil, 1996; Ostner, 1995). The close link between social benefits to paid work and the consequent low level of independent social security of women is particularly marked in Germany (similarly in the United Kingdom), whereas social security in other welfare states (in particular in Scandinavia) is seen as more closely linked to general civil rights than to one's position in the labour market. Due to the traditional differentiation between paid work and housework the German concept of social security is based on a gender-hierarchical, dualistic structure: persons performing work for pay are insured against social risks whereas women doing housework are either dependent on their husbands or can only resort to welfare. A redefinition of the concept of work and the redistribution of paid work and care work therefore constitute the centre of interest. The feminist concept of work includes housework because it is just as vital and life preserving as paid work. This concept exhibits a tendency towards eliminating the differentiation between paid and unpaid work (Kurz Scherf, 1997). The way society deals with working time in conjunction with a more equal distribution of social obligations is of extreme significance. Two social developments thus appear possible: a high volume of paid work coupled with a market-induced set of social activities or a society with a much lower share of paid work with low overall levels of earned income coupled with non-market-induced social services.

In a controversial paper the Dutch social scientist Selma Sevenhuijsen (1997) demonstrated how new principles of welfare can be developed by means of a care theory. She criticised the view of many feminists who see care merely as work and who strive for a gender-neutral equality of distribution. She contrasts these views with her own transformative strategy in which care is seen as a societal practice and is based on the concept that care-ethical rights are based on their being the basis for the universal well-being of all. She does not see citizenship so much as a construct of rights but as a form of acting on an ethical basis. Despite public responsibility for care Sevenhuijsen sees care as a female resource of acting and being expressed in commitment to social professions as well as in the informal practice of caring and to which she attributes positive value. Freedom and autonomy to her are not necessarily linked to paid work and participation in the labour market. The central difference between Sevenhuijsen's approach and most feminist care approaches lies in the fact that Sevenhuijsen aims at the strengthening of non-professional care fields whereas the politics of the 'Neue Frauenbewegung' (new women's movement) in Germany aims at professionalisation without considering paid work as the only way for all women. In Germany as well, different interest groups take their own approaches and have their own lobbies (e.g. the numerous centres for mothers).

In contrast to Sevenhuijsen, Renate Rampf (1997) considers care ethics an important welfare state complement, but not a substitute for a legal framework, since it is not care ethics that are indispensable for a democratic welfare state but rights in general.

If increasingly men, too, fail to fulfil the requirements (either for themselves or for their families) for social security based on the insurance principle, there will be increased opportunities for the development of social rights on the basis of social citizenship, e.g. through minimum security models (Veil 1997) as well as for a model of flexible reduction of working hours plus professionalisation of part of the currently unpaid and unqualified work carried out in private households ...' (Kurz Scherf, 1997, p47). For a number of years the European Union, for political reasons of employment as well as for reasons of social integration politics, has shown an increased interest in new forms of societal organisation to cope with responsibilities between market and state, which occur particularly frequently in the field of care (Evers, 1997). At times of an increased differentiation of life situations social relationships, which create abilities to act, such as for instance non-profit initiatives (public action groups) gain increasingly in socio-integrative importance. Through the interaction of the state, market, employer, and independent providers (welfare mix) such

initiatives not only fulfil a service function but also a democratic function by giving new issues societal relevance and by ensuring that these get the requisite support services. For several years the European Union has also dealt, at least on the level of research studies and concept development, with the socio-political responsibilities of private households and the financial recognition of informal services (Evers, Pijl and Ungerson (Eds), 1994). This shows the extent of the influence of feminist care analyses and care practices in Europe.

The care debates have so far been successful with regard to the following issues:

- They have contributed to a new definition of work by making women's work in the house visible, by developing new types of help and support for women and girls and by criticising the construction of social professions and the definition of their responsibilities.
- They have raised awareness of the gender-specific link between work and love, by drawing attention to the fact that labour and love, either love for the family or for the neighbour, are equated only for women.
- They have permanently challenged the current types of organisation of care in western welfare states.

Didactic assignments

Discussion rounds
Discuss the following questions, first in small gender-segregated groups, then in the plenary: which socio-political model of the distribution of care and paid work do you consider fair and appropriate? Refer to the models presented.

References

Abel, E.K. and Nelson, M.K. (1990) Circles of Care: An Introductory Essay. Dies, (Ed.) *Circles of Care: Work and Identity in Women's Lives.* Albany. 4–34.

Brückner, M. and Holler, S. (1990) *Frauenprojekte und soziale Arbeit*. Frankfurt.

Brückner, M. (1996) *Frauen- und Mädchenprojekte, von feministischen Gewissheiten zu neuen Suchbewegungen*. Opladen.

Chamberlayne, P. (1996) Fürsorge und Pflege in der britischen feministischen Diskussion. *Feministische Studien 2*. 47–60.

Davies, C. (1994) *Competence Versus Care? Gender and Caring Work Revisited*, Lecture presented to the Research Committee 19, 13th World Congress of Sociology, Bielefeld.

Esping-Andersen, G. (1990) *The Three Worlds of Welfare Capitalism*. Oxford.

Evers, A. (1997) Freie Wohlfahrtspflege und Europäische Integration. Der 'Dritte Sektor' im Geeinten Europa. *Zeitschrift für Sozialreform*, 43. Jg., H 3, 208–26.

Evers, A., Pijl, M. and Ungerson, C. (Eds.) (1994) *Payments for Care*. European Centre Vienna. Aldershot.

Flaake, K. (1997) Frauen in Arbeitszusammenhängen: Kooperation und Konkurrenz – unvereinbar? *Zeitschrift für Frauenforschung 15*. Jg., H1/2, 69–77.

Fisher, B. and Tronto, J. (1990) Toward a Feminist Theory of Care. In: Abel, E.K. and Nelson, M.K. (Eds.) *Circles of Care: work and identity in women's lives*. Albany, 35–62.

Fraser, N. (1994a) Die Frauen, die Wohlfahrt und die Politik der Bedürfnisinterpretation (1987). In: Dies, *Widerspenstige Praktiken: Macht, Diskurs, Geschlecht*. Frankfurt/Main, 222–48.

Fraser, N. (1994b) *Der Kampf um die Bedürfnisse: Entwurf für eine sozialistisch-feministische kritische Theorie der politischen Kultur im Spätkapitalismus* (1990) ibid. 249–91.

Fraser, N. (1994c) After the Family Wage: Gender Equity and the Welfare State. *Political Theory*. 22: 4, 591–618.

Fraser, N. and Gordon, L. (1994) 'Dependency' Demystified: Inscriptions of Power in a Keyword of the Welfare State. *Social Politics*. 1: 1, 4–31.

Gerhard, U. (1996) Feministische Sozialpolitik in vergleichender Perspektive. *Feministische Studien*. 2: 6–17.

Gerhard, U. (1997) Soziale Bürgerrechte – ein Konzept für Frauen? In: Behning, U. (Ed.) *Das Private ist ökonomisch*. Berlin, 23–40.

Gildemeister, R. (1998) Halbierte Arbeitswelten? Gefühlsarbeit und Geschlechterkonstrukte am Beispiel professionalisierter Berufe. *Supervision*. 33, 48–59.

Gilligan, C. (1984) *Die andere Stimme. Lebenskonflikte und Moral der Frau*. München.

Graham, H. (1993) Feminist Perspectives on Caring. In Bornat, J., Pereira, C., Pilgrim, D. and Williams, F. (Eds.) (1993) *Community Care: A Reader*. London, 124–33.

Knapp, G-A. (1988) Das Konzept weibliches Arbeitsvermögen – theoriegeleitete Zugänge, Irrwege, Perspektiven. *Frauenforschung* Jg.6, 4, 8–19.

Knijn, T. and Kremer, M. (1997) Gender and the Caring Dimension of Welfare States: Toward Inclusive Citizenship. *Social Politics*. 4: 3, 328–61.

Kurz-Scherf, I. (1997) Kopfkrise der Frauenforschung. *Die Frau in unserer Zeit*. 26. Jg., 4, 11–16.

Leira, A. (1994). *Caring and the Gendering of Citizenship*. Lecture presented to the Research Committee 19, 13th World Congress of Sociology, Bielefeld.

Lewis, J. (1997a) Bezahlte Arbeit, unbezahlte Arbeit und wohlfahrtsstaatliche Leistungen. In: Behning, U. (Ed.) *Das Private ist ökonomisch*. Berlin, 67–86.

Lewis, J. (1997b) Gender and Welfare Regimes: Further Thoughts. *Social Politics*. 4: 2, 160–77.

Marshall, T. H. (1992) *Bürgerrechte und soziale Klassen*. Frankfurt/Main.

McLaughlin, E. and Glendinning, C. (1994) Paying for Care in Europe. Is there a Feminist Approach? In: Hantrais, L. and Mangen, S. (Eds.) *Family Policy and the Welfare of Women*. University of Loughborogh, 52–69.

Nagl-Docekal, H. (Ed.) (1993) Jenseits der Geschlechtermoral. *Beiträge zur Feministischen Ethik*. Frankfurt/Main.

Nunner-Winkler, G. (Ed.) (1993) *Weibliche Moral: Die Kontroverse um eine geschlechtsspezifische Ethik*. Frankfurt am Main/New York.

Ostner, I. (1993) Zum letzten Male: Anmerkungen zum 'weiblichen Arbeitsvermögen'. In: Krell, G. and Osterloh, M. (Eds.) *Personalpolitik aus der Sicht von Frauen*. München/Mehring, 107–21.

Ostner, I. (1995) Arm ohne Ehemann? Sozialpolitische Regulierung von Lebenschancen für Frauen im internationalen

Vergleich. *Aus Politik und Zeitgeschichte, Beilage zur Wochenzeitung 'Das Parlament'*, B 36–37, 1.Sept., 3–12.

Ostner, I. and Beck-Gernsheim, E. (1979) *Mitmenschlichkeit als Beruf*. Frankfurt am Main/New York.

Pateman, C. (1989) *The Disorder of Women*. Cambridge.

Rabe-Kleberg, U. (1988) Weibliches Arbeitsvermögen und soziale Berufe – ein gutes Verhältnis? *Frauenforschung*. Jg. 6, 4, 28–31.

Rabe-Kleberg, U. (1993) *Verantwortlichkeit 'und Macht*. Bielefeld.

Rampf, R. (1997) Kann die Care-Perspektive auf sozialstaatliche Fragestellungen übertragen werden? Braun, H. and Jung, D. (Eds.) ibid. 96–112.

Rommelspacher, B. (1992) *Mitmenschlichkeit und Unterwerfung*. Frankfurt am Main/New York.

Sauer, B. (1997a) Krise des Wohlfahrtsstaats. Eine Männerinstitution unter Globalisierungsdruck? In: Braun, H. and Jung, D. (Eds.) ibid. 113–147.

Sevenhuijsen, S. (1997) Feministische Überlegungen zum Thema Care und Staatsbürgerschaft. In: Braun, H. and Jung, D (Eds.) ibid. 74–95.

Sozialarbeiterinnengruppe Frankfurt (1978) Gefühlsarbeit. *Sozialmagazin*. 9, 22–31.

Ungerson, C. (1994) The *Commodification of Care: Current Policies and Future Politics*. Lecture presented to the Research Committee 19, 13th World Congress of Sociology, Bielefeld.

Ungerson, C. (1997) Social Politics and the Commodification of Care. *Social Politics*. 4: 3, 362–81.

Veil, M. (1996) Debatten zur Zukunft des bundesdeutschen Sozialstaats -feministische Einwände. *Feministische Studien*. 2. 61–74.

Veil, M. (1997) Wie zukunftsweisend sind feministische Sozialpolitikentwürfe in der Krise des Sozialstaats? *Widersprüche*. 17. Jg., 66, 4, 189–96.

5. Love and Sexuality

Margrit Brückner

Each of the four fields is covered by (a) an introductory text and (b) didactic suggestions.

The subjects love and sexuality are of great significance, since they constitute basic human needs whose cultural and gender-specific formats often remain at unconscious levels. This lack of conscious awareness means that our own beliefs and attitudes become part of social work practice in an unchecked and untested form. Of equal significance is dealing with ethnic and social strata specific differences within a culture and a country, in order to take into proper account the concerns and living conditions of social work clients and addressees. Students should therefore be able to reflect theoretically and personally on gender roles in the areas of love and sexuality and they should be able to competently contribute to the equality of the sexes in love relationships.

The arrangement of gender relationships in love and sexuality

Female and male concepts of love

Female life concepts, as opposed to those of their male counterparts, are characterised by a special relationship between reality and fantasy. This is due to the fact that women are more strongly denied the possibility to act out their wishes than men. The result is a limited capacity to imagine one's own developmental capacities linked to the acceptance of a far-reaching male predominance in occupying social and physical space. These two factors both result in an excessive desire (fed by imposed or self-inflicted restrictions) for a man,

through whom a better opportunity for access to a fulfilled life appears to exist, than one's own strengths could provide. The success of the yellow press is proof thereof. It fulfils the desire for 'perfect happiness' and 'true love'. Even the failure of dream marriages, concluded in front of the whole world doesn't have a negative impact. The wishes are not affected, and their intensity may even be enhanced and own denials justified in retrospect, providing for a certain sense of satisfaction. Love stories published by the media cater to women not to men. The amount of comfort needed to derive from the world of fantasies depends on the degree of denial and sacrifice, which are characteristic of the female life situation. This specifically female interweaving of fantasy and reality contributes to the maintenance of traditional life situations: believing in the one big love on the one hand and settling without complaint into the daily routine of married life. This is particularly true for socially disadvantaged girls and women in the social work environment, who are the ones who reckon most with a happy life as a mother at the side of a husband, and who often don't believe in education or training for themselves.

It is quite irrelevant here, whether such marriages and relationships are love marriages or relationships or not, whoever would be able to determine that anyway. On the contrary and in contrast to general belief it appears to be rather rare that a woman lives with a man because she is specifically interested in him as a person. It is far more likely that she took him because he wanted it, because she was pregnant, or simply because he was 'there'. True choice would have meant testing and exploring together ideas of chances and limits of sharing everyday life and discussing mutual expectations of marriage. Very few women dare to undertake such explorations. And while men are often just as likely not to take such opportunities, the traditional power gradient has meant that they are culturally more likely to get their way. It is therefore not surprising to find that particularly violent men usually have very rigid and traditional concepts of typically male or female characteristics (Brockhaus and Kolshorn, 1993). Such men adhere particularly strongly to and do not accept challenges to concepts of male predominance and higher value.

Images of themselves created by men and women and shaping their attitudes are partially rooted in their cultural heritage but partly also something of their own as they have not only found these images and values passed on to them by tradition, but also actively internalised pictures on their own. Female self-images often focus on traditional female images of boundless motherhood and of being desperately needed on the basis of selflessness and 'being there' for others. Women share this cultural image of the ever giving never demanding being, which a woman is supposed to be, with their men. This is the basis for a common relationship pattern: the woman may voice her wishes with regard to marriage and family life, she may try to convince her husband of her ideas, or try to secretly get him to the point where he thinks they are his own ideas, but it is only the man who has the right to openly demand the implementation and fulfilment of his wishes with little regard to the objections of the woman. Nevertheless, both consider the woman responsible for the quality of their relationship; because a good wife must succeed in achieving congruence between his and her needs and thus create perfect harmony, even without contributions on his part. This may result in a continuous process wherein the man's need for total love turns into complete dominance and the woman's need for total love turns into complete dependence. Her selflessness and total self-sacrifice for husband and family are part of the prevailing ideology and Christian mythology (represented by the Virgin Mary), which both simply need to adopt.

Positive fantasies of women, tied to traditional male attributes of virility, power, strength, ability to prevail, fearlessness, and enterprise help to perpetuate the existing gender relationship and the complementary role of women. This male image is attractive for women because it helps in an indirect way to strengthen the self-esteem of women in traditional arrangements of the sexes: even though they may not bear these attributes themselves, attributes which are in fact hard to achieve, they can participate in them through identification. Women can also experience their own value in such arrangements in an indirect way, by feeling recognised as desirable women in their role as objects of male desire, achieving power through his need for her. The conventional tradition that men first have to 'court' and woo a woman before they 'win' her, nourishes fantasies in women as being the goddess of love who is free to either accept or reject the man to her feet, but on the other hand also the fantasy of male freedom of choice, independent of the woman's will, as he has to succeed in his attempt to win her because of the male right to predominance. Many traditionally thinking men have this feeling of there being a male 'right' beyond the woman's personality and individuality. In their perception, by making a woman the gift of their courtship, they have made a sufficient contribution to the relationship and have shown their love for all times. But women, too, consider the courtship of men, which flatters them, as something which becomes more and more binding, the longer it goes on.

Women clearly consider traditional forms of possessive virility not only as repulsive, but also as attractive, because it presents itself as attentiveness, interest and care, in particular during the phase of early love. At a much later point in time women become aware of the price they very often have to pay; when the demarcation between care and control becomes unclear and the possessive features become clearer and are felt more strongly.

Entering a relationship inevitably raises questions for both partners: how much of the own person and of one's own interests should be set back for the sake of the partner and for common causes, and how many rights and how much independence beyond the relationship do the two partners want to maintain. Our culture provides clear answers to these questions in traditional gender arrangements, and these differ considerably for men and women. For women the centre of life is expected to be their family, for which they should forgo their own needs, in particular if they have children, and considering social circumstances they must do so. The man, too, is expected to care for the family, but he is not only granted independent life spheres, but (in particular with regard to work and income) he is obliged to be successful in other spheres of life. On the other hand, if women take up paid work, this does not change the priority of their family obligations, neither in the eyes of society, nor in his eyes and little or not at all in her own eyes. Love, a relationship, children, this is what many women wish for. Very few women strive towards fulfilling these wishes permanently in a non-conformist way (homosexual love; frequently changing non-binding relationships; living or parenting alone, etc.). For quite a while most young women have wanted both, job and family, but have more or less been forced to accept that their own work and career must be subordinated to family obligations, or that they must live with a double or triple burden, or they divide their priorities, particularly in the lower classes. Choosing a partner does not take place on the basis of common attitudes towards the sharing of family obligations, but on congruence on the emotional level, which is unfortunately not a very reliable instrument for gauging the successful managing of joint everyday life, but more romantic and erotic, in line with our romantic model of love.

Establishing demarcations is an integral part of male identity, even if only for fear of losing one's identity. On the other hand the main focus of female identity is on eliminating borders, making the borders of the self permeable in search of becoming one with the partner. In view of this drastic schism between the sexes with regard to wishes for closeness and need for distance, men are attributed the desire for freedom and women the desire for bonding. At the same time each sex is to a large extent denied the emotional capability and social opportunity of the other. But, although men are because of the hierarchy of sexes permitted to use and exploit female capabilities in dealing with closeness directly for their purposes, women show a tendency towards admiring and supporting, secretly or openly, male independence and machismo attitudes, even when they are directed against themselves, as they hope for indirect participation. Social work with women should therefore always start from female strengths, i.e. from their abilities and the required next steps into a new future, in order to encourage and support them in their need for independence (Brückner, 1996).

Didactic assignments

1. Discussion about differences and commonalities between social work clients and social workers, with regard to their respective individual concepts of relationships and gender roles. Whereas the traditional concepts presented here are shared by many addressees, many social workers, and female ones in particular, reject the intrinsic expectations as unreasonable for women and consciously strive for different concepts of relationships, love and sexuality. Such efforts are often precarious because of one's own ambivalences and because of traditional behaviour patterns of many male partners. It is therefore necessary, when dealing with this subject that students learn to differentiate between their own wishes and concepts and those of the clients, even if it is difficult to accept their ways of life when these are contrary to one's own image of women and men. This is particularly true when encountering and working with women and men from other cultures. As we are not always aware of our own attitudes, wishes and fears, supervised and discussion sessions oriented towards self-awareness are of particular importance.

2. Audio-cassette: 'Verstrickungen im Liebeslabyrinth: Zwischen Selbstverwirklichung und Selbstverlust' (Entangled in the labyrinth of love: between self-realisation and loss of self), recording of a broadcast of a lecture for the 'Forum der Wissenschaft' (Science Forum), Radio Bremen 2, Germany, on 19 December 1996; rebroadcast 6 February 1997 in 'Studio 2 – Perspektiven' (Studio 2 – Perspectives), of 'Sender Freies Berlin', Germany, duration 60 minutes; followed by a discussion.

Reflections on desire, in particular female desire

Desire is the expression of one's own sexual wishes, which make us vulnerable, because they are directed towards another person, independent of the self, as desire always needs a counterpart, an object. Desire thus contains elements of self-realisation, of self-emergence, but at the same time also elements of self-loss, of self-elimination.

Lou Andreas-Salomé (1985) sees the greatest danger for the passion of love in giving up one's self; only those who preserve their self can in their living abundance symbolise life to the other, only they can be seen as the power of life (German original: Ibid. p70). Passion therefore does not mean giving oneself up for one another, but to discharge oneself through the other. Eroticism and sexuality are therefore borderline experiences, walks along the narrow line between self-realisation, self-preservation and self-loss, between taking possession and giving oneself up, between lust and harassment.

One aspect of why Eros is so dangerous lies in the desire for and the simultaneous fear of closeness and in the inability of most people to draw friendly borderlines (Moeller, 1989, p28) between themselves and the other person. The fear of becoming one leads to violent border setting if the wish for dependence and the wish for separation exist in irreconcilable juxtaposition. The self must be strong enough to protect itself at the same time as it loses itself; otherwise one's own ambivalence becomes unbearable and must be split into two opposite feelings, fighting against one another.

One's own desire evinces desire for another, which the latter can grant or refuse. This harbours a danger for the own self, which is prevented by the unilateral, legitimised right of the man to a woman's body. In the 'free power play' this greed-filled revelation of the needs of one's own body, the instinctive drive, appears equally frightening for both sexes. The prevailing construction of the relationship of the sexes serves the maintenance of male power, but also the down play of human instinctive drives, as there is either no counterpart or no desire on one's own part.

A prerequisite for desire is the positive connotation of one's own body, with the perception of 'bodiliness' being a truly cultural phenomenon. For women it is particularly important to acquire possession of the inner body space in order to develop a body concept which includes the sexual organs, because women cannot easily check the integrity of their genitals. Children perceive their external genitals in lustful play during the first and second years of life, if given the chance to do so. Such playfulness serves the development of a body concept and a self-image of the body.

'The concept of a body joined properly in all its parts, produces a body concept that is normally reliable (...). This concept, which forms the core of our body identity, is based on innumerable experiences of self-touching and being touched, of seeing and being seen, of feeling and comparing, that one can describe oneself and be described by others – as a whole and in all parts which permit the body to function.' (German original: Kestenberg, 1988, p350).

But it is this very security that many girls cannot acquire in our culture because parents or other adults create confusion on the subject of the female sexual organs or negate their existence. This has tremendously inhibiting results on the psychosexual development of girls.

During adolescence the negation of female sexual development continues, with menarche and menstruation still not bearing any positive connotation (Flaake, 1994). Although menarche marks the sexual maturity of a girl, her becoming a woman, it is not celebrated in our culture but remains a taboo associated with shame, with the effect that for many girls it bears implications of fear. If menstruation is seen as something dirty, which has to be hidden, the adolescent woman cannot develop pride in her body, but learns to despise it, with all the consequences such self-contempt has for future sexual experiences. For many boys, puberty is also a difficult life phase, characterised by insecurity with regard to what a 'real man' is, what he is supposed to become. The development of a firm psychosocial identity is often made even more difficult by the lack of male role models, since socialisation is often to a large extent or completely left to women. Therefore their concept of manhood remains abstract and is often shaped by idealised images. The sexual development of boys is not so much dominated by prohibitions but is characterised by demands for achievements that exert great pressures and can cause great stress and strain. In particular peer-groups in socially lower strata play significant roles in this connection.

Didactic assignments

Discuss ways of social work intervention on the basis of an example taken from the work in a social work agency. Initially male and female students should discuss the following example in separate groups and then together in a plenary:

A neighbourhood meeting with two social workers and a student on placement is supposed to deal with improving the living conditions in the neighbourhood. Some of the young men in the audience, however, disturb the meeting with loud, rude interjections: 'it's boring here ... I need a woman ... we'll be heading for the brothel shortly, at least we'll get some action there ... I need a woman, I can lay ... etc.'. Nobody reacts to these provocations but the senior social worker eventually gratefully takes up the suggestion of a participant to close the meeting as the situation has become increasingly unpleasant and communication amidst the noise has become almost impossible. Not only have the young men not got any reaction to their attempts to gain attention through sexualised interruptions but their comments about women remained unanswered, not responded to. The incident was not mentioned in the subsequent team meeting, and the placement student, who had felt very uncomfortable in this situation, only spoke about this experience in a subsequent supervision session at which only women were present.

Approaches to gender-democratic concepts of love

At present there are a number of empty spaces in the debates on the subject of love and lust between women and men. These should be filled. Although lesbian and homosexual lust are no longer taboo, which means that it has become easier to acknowledge homosexual relationship aspirations today, in the feminist movement for example, new taboos have developed about *heterosexual* desires. Even if it is of concern for many women and girls there is no room in feminism today for the topic of love and eroticism with men.

By placing male violence in the foreground of debate, the feminist movement and its theories are perceived as warning against or even forbidding, rather than supporting women and girls in their desires regarding men. This fact has its effects on feminist approaches to working with women and girls but also to gender conscious youth work, and should be reconsidered. A blueprint for a good life always includes erotic fulfilment and sexual self-determination – be it heterosexual or homosexual.

At the beginning of the second women's movement at the end of the 1960s the following emotions had equal weight:

- Anger towards selfish, hostile men and towards 'circumstances'.
- The desire to occupy one's own space and a lust for one's own body and its desires.

Since the 1970s when sexual liberation and the dissolution of the bourgeois nuclear family were the centre of attention, there have been no public debates led by men dealing with gender relationships related to love relationships. The men's movement and men's research haven't made heterosexual love relationships a central aspect of their deliberations. Utopias based on a different gender relationship, mutual wishes of the genders, blueprints for the cohabitation of generations and genders have disappeared from public debate just as has the debate on love, sexuality, eroticism, and desire between women and men, which had been taken up again in the 1970s. This is, however, the secret unchangeable perpetuation of the patriarchy with its specific gender arrangements. The harmonisation of needs and actions for emancipation on the one hand and lust for a relationship with a man on the other remains an unresolved problem which becomes insurmountable for many women and girls because of societal conditions as well as due to internal causes. What is called for here is innovative action for the sake of future-oriented, equal gender relationships as the basis for social work in coming years.

Didactic assignments

Open discussion of the topic: which sexual standards and attitudes do we, who work in the field of social work, want to pass on and where do we want to stand in the eyes of clients with regard to sexuality, love and desire?

Objectives:

- Reduction and elimination of prejudices.
- Realising one's own attitude to sexuality and one's own wishes regarding love as well as their significance for social work.
- Joint deliberations on which steps must be taken towards achieving gender-democratic relationships. Attitudes towards sexuality, which are significant from the professional point of view, cannot be imposed on anybody. Therefore this highly emotional and loaded topic requires sensitive guidance towards reflection.

Sexuality and love in gender-conscious youth work

Sexual change in the second half of the 20th century

To develop an approach to the question of what teachers of social work and social workers should convey to young women and men with regard to sexuality and eroticism and how they want to become active in this field we should take a brief look at different sexual epochs since the 1950s and 1960s in order to highlight the time-factor in sexuality. The sexually repressive climate of the early 1960s involved on the one hand enormous frustration but on the other hand it involved a certain degree of protection, in particular for young women. Both sexes were supposed to remain 'proper', a rule which was usually broken in small consecutive steps and was characterised by the fear of pregnancy and its social consequences for both partners.

Today, young women and girls probably have to fight much more on their own and depend to a much larger extent on their individual skills in arguing, convincing and succeeding, as the old sexual control mechanisms no longer exist. But what did the protective mantle of societal prudery far into the 1960s consist of? Fear of the final breaking of taboos, i.e. pre-marital sex, which was not at least socially secured by an

engagement, was so deeply rooted in many young women that it exceeded sexual desire and male courting. This fear was not only related to threats from the outside but to sexuality as such, which from early childhood on had been referred to as something forbidden. But young men weren't free of these taboos either which resulted in sexual inhibitions in particular towards 'untouched' young women. It is not a question of wishing those times back, but of drawing consequences from the liberalisation process, i.e. of educating young women and men towards a point, where they are able to become aware of their own wishes and to respect those of the partner.

A prerequisite is to know one's own needs, and to know about pregnancy and diseases, such as AIDS. Young women today, know so much more, but whether they know so much more about their own needs, remains in doubt. The sexual revolution of the students' movement led to a significant point of departure among young women and men towards new opportunities for sexual development, but also led to a certain pressure to dare it all. Many young women feared being too old for virginity and felt it necessary to actively look for a suitable partner. Some entered into more or less vague, limited relationships, which made their 'defloration' an event whose most important aspect besides the excitement was the fact that it had taken place at all. Maybe such a consciously staged calculated limit of a relationship does not make it less difficult and painful than failed hopes for true love. Whether sexuality should for reasons of convention be embedded in love, and most young women could not imagine sexuality in any other way, or whether tying sexuality to a love relationship corresponded to one's own wishes, may have differed from case to case.

The young women who helped carry the sexual revolution had grown up in a climate of an inseparable link between love and sexuality, at least for women. Breaking with this ideal therefore meant not only a new legitimacy of sexual desire outside long-term relationships, but also the end of a socially and emotionally supported sexuality promising emotional security. Young girls today should have the opportunity to learn, to make sure that the vulnerability created by desire and the explosiveness of one's own wishes and those of others is embedded into a situation which they themselves consider sufficiently supportive and loving. The young women who then had set out into new times had by no means been victims of their times, but had taken an active role. Sexuality played an important role but in a more far-reaching sense than today. There were seminars on sexuality, sexual liberation was an issue which was publicly discussed and also served to provoke.

Almost overnight sexuality was no longer taboo but an integral part of the liberation from traditional humanity. It was certainly women who experienced this curiosity, initially an exciting game. Later, having to accept that their boyfriend had spent the night elsewhere or that the partner of her night-time adventure showed nothing but indifference the morning after, exceeded her abilities to cope. The thrill and excitement consisted mainly in the breaking of taboos, in getting oneself into unknown exciting nocturnal situations, in living through and subsequently talking about these adventures and in setting off into anti-bourgeois worlds. What was important was mastering more or less self-chosen challenges, escaping depressingly narrow bourgeois confines. Sexuality probably did not play the most important role in all this. Testing and experimenting as such was already part of, maybe the most important part of, enjoyment. If all this is correct we should ask ourselves, what sexuality between young women and men means today, if it is no longer the breaking of taboos. Maybe it stands for the search for closeness and belonging, or for the substitute for closeness and belonging?

The beginning of the second women's movement led to the next step in sexual development. Sexuality now meant discovering one's self: self-examination groups were formed, more gentle methods of abortion and contraception were shared, along with more gentle methods of giving birth. It was then that women began to feel misunderstood and not recognised by men, sexually or as people. The growing anger of women stemmed from the frequent lack of sensitivity and respect of men,

but also from the increasingly exhibited cheekiness of sometimes rather brute attempts at sexual and personal self-liberalisation and maybe also from unconscious feelings of guilt resulting from breaking taboos and radically turning away from their family origin and its values.

The emerging question of whether love between women and men was possible (Alice Schwarzer coined the term 'Zwangsheterosexualität' – forced heterosexuality) was paralleled by the topic of love between women, and was declared the better alternative by some women. The clitoris was discovered as the locus of independent female lust and replaced the vagina in significance, the latter now being seen as the place of male penetration. Quite often the explosive question of sexual orientation for women appeared to define exclusion and inclusion, right and wrong. It appears difficult not to experience other orientations as an attack on one's own sexual identity and therefore to feel the need to put them down. There is now more caution in the public exchange on sexuality among women as well.

Today young women can only identify with the public image of women as sex objects or with the feminist image as being the victims of male violence. Sexual counterpoints are, unlike those in the times of sexual awakening, now only relevant for homosexually oriented women and girls. There has been no return to repression, but nevertheless there is no climate fostering self-assurance on ways of sexual development. The sexual eras described here, were a sequence of prohibition (1950s), awakening (late 1960s and early 1970s), and violence in the relationship of the sexes (1980s), which have formed today's middle aged adults.

An important prerequisite for reflected, pedagogical intervention is the ability to take a highly differentiated view of one's self and one's own emotions regarding sexuality. Without knowing one's own needs, wishes, limits, and spheres of modesty as closely as possible, an open view of the sexuality of young women and men, what they have in common and how they differ, is not possible. It will only be possible to decipher the conscious and unconscious messages which social workers convey when working with adolescents, when they can be perceived in their own right and are not filtered through one's own attitudes towards sexuality. Only then will it be possible to develop suitable approaches in practice. This is an example from work in a youth club as described by a young female staff member:

> *The boys are busy doing many things, such as playing football. The girls, however, are just hanging around, doing 'nothing'.*

A fact that irritated the staff member and made her wish for change. During supervision it turned out that 'nothing' was the worker's interpretation of the fact, which irritated her, that the girls were not active in ways she wanted them to be, but that they lived their form of femininity in ways which were in sharp contrast to emancipator's ideas. The girls were actually very busy doing what they were doing: making great efforts at presenting themselves – being attractive to the boys, vying for and catching their attention. Understanding this concept is a prerequisite for any further pedagogical considerations.

Didactic assignments

1. In order to create an understanding of the cultural roots of sexuality and differing sexual debates in different eras the following questions (suitable for discussion in small groups) should be elaborated (an alternative method would be brainstorming using flip-charts):

- What are your attitudes regarding individual cultural norms on what is right/wrong or good/bad and the changes these norms are undergoing?
- Which different socio-political attitudes towards sexuality are you aware of, relating to?
  –Who is allowed to have sex with whom?
  –Which forms of birth control are permitted for whom?
  –What is the definition of consenting and forced sex?

2. Discuss the results of the study on changes in the sexual behaviour of adolescents in: 'Das Parlament' (weekly press release periodical), for the week of 12–19 January 1996 (see Appendix).

Sexual values and standards in social work

Despite all social discussion on sexuality and sexual abuse so far there have been hardly any open professional discussions on how to deal with sexuality in social work. Two aspects need to be taken into account here: one, dealing with sexuality-related remarks on life by addressees and clients of social work, and the second being the development or clarification of political standards of the profession in social work in contact with addressees of either sex.

Basic to all decisions related to the first aspect should be the broadest possible acceptance of sexual relationships among clients, when both partners are equally able to make independent decisions which do not violate their self-esteem. Preventive strategies should be considered when there are great differences between the partners regarding their inner and external independence, and when there is a danger that the weaker partner will be abused. Other central issues focus on dealing with teenage pregnancies, abortion, and contraception.

With regard to the second aspect all sexual contacts between clients and social workers fall, ethically, under the rule of total abstinence, as long as a working relationship exists.

Didactic assignments

In this context guided seminar discussions, in a positive and accepting atmosphere, are required, dealing with the following issues:

- Acceptance, prohibition or prevention of sexual relationships among clients in different populations:
  –adolescents
  –aged persons
  –physically or mentally disabled persons
  –persons of the same sex

  Attention must be given to the respective legal provisions and the supervisory responsibilities of social workers.

- Discussion of the abstinence rule and discussion of possible seduction scenarios, as well as how to handle violations on the part of colleagues.

References

Brockhaus, U. and Kolshorn, M. (1993) *Sexuelle Gewalt gegen Mädchen und Jungen*. Frankfurt/New York.

Brückner, M. (1983) *Die Liebe der Frauen*. Frankfurt a.M.

Brückner, M. (1996) *Frauen und Mädchenprojekte, von feministischen Gewißheiten zu neuen Suchbewegungen*. Opladen.

Brückner, M. (1998) *Wege aus der Gewalt gegen Frauen und Mädchen.* Frankfurt a.M.

Flaake, K. (1994) Ein eigenes Begehren? In: Brückner, M. and Meyer, B. (Eds.) *Die sichtbare Frau*. Freiburg.

Kestenberg, J. (1988) Der komplexe Charakter weiblicher Identität. *Psyche. 42,* 349–64.

Lou, A-S. (1985). Die Erotik. In: Dies, *Die Erotik*. Frankfurt a.M/Berlin, Vier Aufsätze.

Moeller, M. L. (1989) Die große Einsamkeit zu zweit. *Psychologie Heute.* 16 (7), 20–8.

Bibliography

On love and sexuality in general

Beck, U. and Beck-Gernsheim, E. (1990) *Das ganz normale Chaos der Liebe*. Frankfurt a.M.

Benjamin, J. (1990) *Die Fesseln der Liebe: Psychoanalyse, Feminismus und das Problem der Macht*. Frankfurt a.M.

Brückner, M. (1988) Die Sehnsucht nach den Kugelmenschen oder vom Wunsch nach Aufhebung der Geschlechtertrennung. In: Hagemann-White, C. and Rerrich M. (Eds.) *Frauen Männer Bilder*. Bielefeld, 194–223.

Brückner, M. (1990) Von der Schwierigkeit weiblichen Begehrens. *Zeitschrift für Sexualforschung. 3.*

Brückner, M. (1994) Sexuelle Zeiten. In: Garbrecht, A. (Ed.) *Wer vor mir liegt ist ungewiß*. Hamburg, 95–111.

Brückner, M. (1984) Ariadne im Liebeslabyrinth. In: Heenen, S. (Ed.) *Frauenstrategien*. Frankfurt, 11–34.

Düring, S. and Hauch, M. (Eds.) (1995) *Heterosexuelle Verhältnisse*. Stuttgart.

Gambaroff, M. (1987) *Sag mir, wie sehr liebst du mich*. Reinbek.

Kernberg, O. (1995) Love Relations. *Normality and Pathology*. New Haven/London.

Lerner, H. G. (1990) *The Dance of Intimacy*. New York.

Norretranders, T. (Ed.) (1986) *Hingabe. Über den Orgasmus des Mannes*. Reinbek.

Schenk, H. (1991) *Die Befreiung des weiblichen Begehrens*. Köln.

Schmidt, G. (1995) Über den Wandel heterosexueller Beziehungen. *Zeitschrift für Sexualforschung.* 8, 1–11.

Weeks, J. (1995) *Invented Moralities. Sexual Values in an Age of Uncertainty*. Cambridge.

On love and sexuality of adolescents

Behnke, C. and Meuer, C. (1997) Zwischen aufgeklärter Doppelmoral und partnerschaftlicher Orientierung – Frauenbilder junger Männer. *Zeitschrift für Sexualforschung.* 10. 1–18.

Boeger, A. and Mantey, C. (1998) Sexuelle Erfahrungen und Einstellungen junger Erwachsener. *Zeitschrift für Sexualforschung.* 11, 130–48.

Düring, S. (1996) Manchmal wär ich gern ein bißchen geiler. Sexuell befreit und doch nicht glücklich? *Pro Familia Magazin.* 5, 8–10.

Flaake, K. (1996) Weibliche Adoleszenz, Körperlichkeit und Sexualität. *Zeitschrift für Sexualforschung.* 4, 303–14.

Furian, M. (1996) Liebeserziehung – Ausweg aus der gesellschaftlichen Beziehungskrise. *Kind, Jugend, Gesellschaft.* 1, 3–12.

Lauer, D. (1998) Kritik aus der Perspektive sexualpädagogischer Erfahrung. Zur Studie über Frauenbilder junger Männer von Cornelia Behnke und Michael Meuser. *Zeitschrift für Sexualforschung* 11, 54–8.

Schmidt, G., Klusmann, D. and Zeitzschel, U. (1992) Veränderungen der Jugendsexualität zwischen 1970 und 1990. *Zeitschrift für Sexualforschung.* 5, 191–218.

Schmidt, P., Plies, K. and Nickel, B. (1998) *Zwischen Lust und Frust -Jugendsexualität in den 90er Jahren*. Opladen.

Schmidt, R-B. (1997) Sexualkonzepte weiblicher und männlicher Jugendlicher. *Zeitschrift für Frauenforschung.* 1/2, 129–45.

Waldeck, R. (1998) Die Fesseln der Frau. Zur Psychoanalyse der weiblichen Adoleszenz. *Zeitschrift für Sexualforschung.* 11, 30–43.

Woollett, A. and Marshall, H. (1996) Reading the Body: Young Women's Accounts of the Meanings of the Body in Relation to Independence, Responsibility and Maturity. *The European Journal of Women's Studies.* 3, 199–214.

Wrede, B. and Hunfeld, M. (1997) *Sexualität – (k) ein Thema in der Hochschulausbildung? Hochschuldidaktisches Ausbildungskonzept für Sexualpädagogik*. Bielefeld.

6. Love and Sex: Homosexuality

Obertha Holwerda

Introduction

Even though the Universal Declaration of Human Rights does not allow discrimination on the basis of sex and sexual nature, discrimination still occurs. Therefore, and also because love and sex is associated with heterosexuality, the decision is justified to pay separate attention to love and homosexuality within the theme of love and sex.

Holland serves as the basis of this description, which means that in other countries different themes may be considered important, which also depends on the nation's history toward homosexuality, its political climate and perhaps also on some other matters.

This chapter has been written from my own 'socio-agogical' background and my own work experience and experience of life.

Before dwelling upon this subject, I will explain the meaning of the term *homosexuality*. Next I will give a brief history of homosexuality with emphasis on the history of lesbian women.

After the historical part the link between gender, identity and homosexuality will be made.

Definition of homosexuality

The Hungarian physician Kertbeny coined *homosexuality* in 1869. Of course, there had always been homosexuals, but they had been devoid of a term that was more or less objective to them. 'People who are like **that**', or prejudiced expressions such as 'sodomites' (from the Bible) were used.

A definition for homosexuality (De Horstink, *DIC,* folder 99) is:

Homosexuality is the emotional and sexual preference towards people of one's own sex.

This preference mostly is an integral part of one's personality.

Homosexuality is a contraction of the Greek *homos* (same) and the Latin *sexus*.

Homosexuality is an objective, scientific notation for sexuality aimed towards one's own sex. Some people prefer *homophile*, in which – *phile*, which originates from the Greek *philein* (to love), lays more emphasis on the loving element, which is more than the 'sexual nature'.

History (as seen from the Dutch situation)

Homosexuality has not always been a taboo subject. In Ancient Greece (600 BC) some forms of homosexuality were acknowledged and accepted. This era also spawned Sappho's poetry (a poetess living on the island of Lesbos, *lesbian* is derived from this name). Her poems are symbols of love relations between women.

In the Roman culture and within the Jewish-Christian tradition homosexuality was censored, and feminine behaviour on the part of men was regarded with hostility (feminine male behaviour was tagged homosexual). From the Middle Ages through the Second World War there were periods of tolerance and periods of fanatical oppression. For instance, during the Second World War homosexuals were deported to the death camps. In times of poverty homosexuality was sinful and women were sometimes tagged witches (and burnt or drowned).

If a person was caught in the act (or if there was a suspicion of homosexual acts), he or she was punished severely. Punishments varied from death to years of solitary incarceration for men. Women generally received milder punishment. They were not executed, nor were their periods of incarceration as long as that for men. Upon the French annexation of the Netherlands homosexuality ceased to be punishable by law. However, early in the twentieth century homosexual acts became punishable by law once again when Article 248bis came into effect (this Article made homosexual acts with minors punishable, which was not the case with regard to heterosexual acts).

Reportedly, only men were punishable in England. According to Queen Victoria, women did not experience sexual lust and therefore codification was unnecessary.

In the course of time there have been many opinions of how homosexuality grows on a person. They include:

- It is genetically determined (meaning it is innate).
- It is a disease.
- One is seduced into it.
- It is a neurological deviation.
- There is a so-called third sex.
- It is brought about by the upbringing by a dominant mother.
- It is hormonal.
- It is a matter of choice.

The above is a list of the most frequently heard opinions. The various opinions can be found in attempts to prove one's right in one's approach to homosexuality. There was no successful cure for the disease, a gene was looked for and 'something' was found. The neurological deviation was dismissed by psychiatrists, the dominant mother angle was investigated and found to be beside the truth, the hormonal opinion was not proved and it remains a question why it is so important to know why someone is homosexual. One may wonder why it should be so important to be able to answer this question. What is the possible threat?

Assignment in four sub-groups

- Find out your nation's history regarding homosexuality.
- Find out what discussions used to be important and what matters are being discussed now.
- Divide history into portions of fifty years and find out for each period if there used to be differences (or have been differences since then) in the positions of homosexual men and women.

Present your findings at a time to be agreed on.

Changing society: The 1960s

The 1960s was the age of 'flower power', democratisation, the second feminist wave, the age of tolerance, the age of experiment, the age of sexual freedom, everyone was allowed their position of choice.

The Universal Declaration of Human Rights was codified and signed by many countries. The Declaration includes many provisions against discrimination on the basis of sex and sexual nature.

Opinions on sexuality changed under the influence of contraceptives. Self-control mores, according to which sexuality was linked to marriage and reproduction, became less and less a dominant factor. Creative mores became dominant. The latter de-links sexuality from marriage and reproduction; sexuality means creating or shaping one's emotions and enjoying lust. The taboo surrounding homosexuality faded, tolerance gained ground. Sexuality was no longer linked to reproduction; lust and enjoyment were allowed (even though many churches were not in agreement).

Sex linked to enjoyment and lust diminished the taboo under which homosexuality suffered.

Lesbian women

As the history of lesbian women is 'special', it is dealt with separately.

Prior to the second feminist wave the butch–fem culture came into existence. It put the taboo on lesbian love on the agenda, it made autonomous sexuality and eroticism among women visible and, contrary to popular belief, it was certainly not meant to be a reproduction of heterosexual patterns.

To the outside world erotic relations among women were considered rebel acts, but for lesbian women they involved intimacy and sexuality. The butch-fem culture evoked much aggression from heterosexual cultures, but also from within homosexual cultures, in particular from those people who were afraid or expected trouble if they became 'visible'.

Among other things, the second feminist wave was preoccupied with inequality of power between men and women and the consequences of that inequality. In the late sixties the discussion about power relations between men and women and the liberation of sexuality erupted within the feminist movement. Women started to wonder whether cohabitation with men was no longer allowed, after all men represented 'the oppressors' and oppression had to be fought. A group of women chose to share all aspects of their lives with women, they called themselves **new lesbians**. They have since then represented the opinion that being lesbian is a political choice.

Within the 'old' lesbian movements all kinds of groups came into being. They included a group wishing to make visible the joys of a lesbian existence, another group wished to be visible in art, literature and music. Both old-style and new-style lesbian women began to explore the limits and pleasures of sexuality.

Assignment

Draw up an outlook of the future. First individually, then in groups of six: **homosexual life in the year 2020**. What will change and what is the basis for your expectations? Allow 45 minutes, to be followed by a plenary exchange of views with attention to be paid to agreements, differences and why they arise.

After this look at history a link is made between homosexuality and gender/identity.

Gender, identity and homosexuality

Gender can be divided into various interconnected and mutually reinforcing layers. The meaning of gender in this interconnection and reinforcement is of importance.

The layers are:

- **The nucleus-sex identity:** one learns from rules, regulations and behaviour how to behave as a man or a woman, one is socialised to be a man or a woman.

The socialisation process is dependent on:

- **The current and internalised beliefs about behaviour fit for men and women.**
  The beliefs differ for every:
  –Historic age.
  –Culture.
  –Social environment.

And are dependent on:

- **The social context:** which is expressed in:
  –The social positions of men and women.
  –The division of labour between men and women.
  –The division of care, money, power and status.
  –The current society.

Popular opinion about the development of gender/identity is based on the obviousness of heterosexuality; after all children are raised in a society in which heterosexuality is the norm; at school, in books, TV programmes and also with their peers they see mostly heterosexual examples. Children are raised to adopt sex-dependent social behaviour, the so-called sex-role behaviour. Girls learn to behave as girls and that later they will marry a husband. In this way men and women learn from early age that certain qualities, certain behaviour and role patterns are befitting of society and culture and that these qualities, role patterns and behaviour are predetermined for men and women. This learning process is called the socialisation process.

There is not full agreement in science and gender/women studies about the ways in which this process develops. I will dwell briefly on the effect education has on the behaviour of boys and girls, if raised within a husband-wife relationship (Chodorow, 1980). According to the object-relation theory that Chodorow describes, boys and girls develop sex-stereotyped behaviour since children are mainly raised by their mothers or some other woman and not by their (absent) father. Which is the reason why boys and girls develop in opposite directions? Since girls can identify with a woman, they develop strong relational skills, but less clear ego limitations. Since boys cannot identify with the person who cares for them, they develop a fear for independence and a tendency for autonomy. They identify with a father who mostly works somewhere else. Male social workers have analysed men's socialisation and drawn up a number of **male codes** (these are general guidelines identifying men's behaviour and experiences, v.d. Loo, 1997).

Female codes have been described by Gommers (1997). Note that the codes meet current norms, which gives them a hetero-typical and hetero-sexual bias. Men and women deviate from these codes.

Male codes are:

1. A man is a breadwinner for himself and his dependants.
2. Men experience intimacy through sexuality.
3. A man must perform sexually and father an heir.
4. Men have a bias to act and to perform.
5. Men are independent and omnipotent.
6. A man does not need help.
7. Men exercise self-control. They are not afraid and do not cry.
8. Men are aggressive; however, they know how to control themselves but are no walkovers.

Female codes are:

1. The family is priority number one. Paid work is extra.
2. Intimacy first, only then sexuality.
3. I will wait my turn.
4. Talking about it helps.
5. My responses are spontaneous and sensitive.
6. I care for the members of my family.
7. I am not angry, but sad and because of that I am entitled to consolation.
8. When I am hurt, I will withdraw.

Since the codes above have heterosexuality as their basis, it will be clear that the codes cannot be applied to homosexual men and women. They tend to review their coding and seek codes that meet their homosexual identity, which implies letting go of interiorised ideas belonging to the 'old' codes. They also develop a number of 'survival codes' (which is typical of oppressed and discriminated people and groups). Important survival codes are:

- I am strong, independent and cannot be hurt.
- Even though I am gay, I will remain in the closet for then I will not be burdened by discrimination.
- Who is to care what I am?
- I love to be gay.

Assignment

Do you recognise these 'survival codes'? Suppose that in your personal or professional life you come across someone who has developed a so-called survival code. How would you deal with it?

Discuss this in groups of six and report to the other groups how you would deal with this and motivate your ideas.

Allow 45 minutes for this assignment.

At what particular moment do homosexual men and women begin to review their 'coding'?

This happens as soon as somebody realises that they are not a heterosexual, but fall in love with someone of their own sex. They will start seeking their own identity. Various models of identity development have been described; I would like to present the phased model as described by Ponse (1978) showing the findings of a survey among women:

- Phase 1. Feelings of sexual-emotional attraction to members of one's own sex.
- Phase 2. Identification of these feelings as lesbian or homosexual.
- Phase 3. Acceptance of these feelings and their meaning for one's own identity.
- Phase 4. Seeking admittance to lesbian or homosexual subcultures.
- Phase 5. Enter into lesbian or homosexual relations.

Identity development need not proceed according to this phased model; the phases may assume a different order.

Back to the codes and in particular those codes that have to do with love and sex.

Just as heterosexual women, lesbian women link sexuality and intimacy; they value emotional commitment in sexual contacts. Many lesbian women want a monogamous sexual relationship – still, a fair number want an open sexual relationship (Califia, 1979) monogamous or not has nothing to do with one's satisfaction with sexuality (Peplau, 1978). As lesbian women have longer relationships, the frequency of sexual contacts diminishes; however, intimacy does not.

Although little research has been done into lesbian women and sexuality, the research does show (summarised by Schruers (1990) in *Vrouwen in lesbische relaties* (Women in Lesbian Relations), p35) that women in lesbian relationships are more satisfied with the sexual aspects of their relationship than heterosexual women.

Homosexual men do not link sexuality and intimacy as much. Sex and intimacy are more apart with them (Hedblom, 1973). Homosexual men appreciate fleeting contacts (Duffy and Rusbult, 1985, 1986). Within their relationship they share intimacy, whereas sex is not always shared with one's steady partner.

Finally, **gender, identity** and the development of **behaviour befitting for men and women** (the so-called sex-role behaviour). As noted before, female codes are no longer a matter of course for lesbian women. Which means that for instance the choice of profession will assume a different dimension; after all, one has to make one's own living in the future. And with this the choice of a career has assumed a different coding (satisfying work and a reasonable income have become of importance).

Having children is not necessarily obvious. If children are wanted, a choice will have to be made. Lesbian women will have to start a new quest for whatever behaviour befits them within their relationships. For instance taking the initiative, normally described as behaviour befitting for men, is important to them in the choice of a partner, in sexuality, in entertainment, etc. Since lesbian women assume public tasks and positions, they develop public skills.

This development is also applicable to homosexual men; they also seek behaviour that is befitting to them; they also develop emotions and intimacy within their relationships. For them fatherhood is usually unrealisable. For lesbian women as well as homosexual men the development of behaviour that is befitting to them belongs to identity development. Since many obvious things are no longer obvious and there are very few examples, this is usually a phase in the life of homosexual men and women during which they need help and support. This help and support may be in the form of counselling groups; however, more help may be necessary and social work looms in the background. For this kind of social work the knowledge and acceptance of homosexuality and an ability to work with gender, homosexuality, identity are indispensable.

Assignment

Pair work: think of two themes to be used in a counselling group for homosexual men and women. The group consists of young people who only recently discovered that they harbour homosexual feelings.

Put the themes in writing and compare them to the other pairs' themes and discover where the similarities and differences originate.

Allow an hour for this assignment.

Finally, I would like to dwell upon the present situation.

Discrimination on the basis of homosexuality is again on the agenda as a result of the arrival on these shores of people from other cultures and countries where homosexuality is a taboo subject. Therefore it has once again become necessary to discuss this subject, denounce religious matters and be informative on homosexuality.

The first group of homosexual men and women who come out of the closet have reached retirement age or the age to be admitted to a senior citizens' home. They do not want to live in a home with just heterosexual old people: they want a place for themselves. This has led a senior citizens' home to building semi autonomous care units for homosexuals.

Gay games, sports and dance – a group of gays who take pride in their homosexuality has come out.

Behavioural codes are subject to change, female–male macho behaviour is admissible for homosexual men as well as lesbian women. Legislation has been changed, homosexual men and women can register as partners, and they can adopt children (albeit under certain conditions). AIDS is no longer a disease ascribed solely to homosexuals.

The assignment

With reference to new developments you are to discuss the subject *Homosexuals and children* in groups of six.

What do you think of the development that homosexual men and women can adopt children? And what about the development when one of the two is the biological parent, the partner becomes co-parent?

Discuss this for about 45 minutes. The discussion should result in a statement that you are to present in the plenary group (you are to do this according to the statements game).

Overall time: about 1.5 hours.

With this assignment I would like to finish the chapter devoted to love and sex. This has been a brief encounter. Much has been written about this subject and for those of you who are interested it is recommended to find more texts in literature.

References

Califia, P, (1979) Lesbian Sexuality. *Journal of Homosexuality*. jrg 4: 3, 255–66.

Chodorow, N. (1978) *The Reproduction of Mothering. Psychoanalysis and Sociology of Gender.* University of California Press, Berkeleij.

Costera Meijer, I.E.A. (1991) *Over Normaal Gesproken.* Uitg. Schorer, Amsterdam.

Duffy, S.M. and Rusbult, C.E. (1985/86) Satisfaction and Commitment in Homosexual and Heterosexual Relationships. *Journal of Homosexuality*. jrg 12: 2, 1–23.

Gelauff, C. (1988) *Lust Last en Keuze, Denken over Lesbisch Bestaan*. Uitg. Schorer, Amsterdam.

Gommers, E. (1997) *Seksespecifieke Hulpverlening in het* A.M.W. Uitg. S.W.P., Utrecht.

Hansen, D. and Holwerda, O. (1994) *Lesbische Vrouwen en Welzijnswerk*. Reader Uitg. de Horst, Driebergen.

Hansen, D. and Holwerda, O. (1995) *Lesbische Vrouwen en Relatievormgeving.* Reader Uitg. de Horst, Driebergen.

Hansen, D. and Meulenbelt, A. (Ed.) (1992) *Werken met Liefde*. Uitg. Schorer, Amsterdam.

Hedblom, J.H. (1973) Dimensions of Lesbian Sexual Experience. *Archives of Sexual Behavior.* 2: 4, 329–41.

van Kooten, N. A. and Wijnmer, S. (1985) *Verkeerde Vriendschap*. Uitg. Sarah, Amsterdam.

v.d.Loo, J. (1997) Mannen en Intake, Uitg. Transact, Utrecht.

Loulan, J.A. (1992) *Lesben Liebe Leidenschaft*. Uitg. Orlanda Frauenverlag, Berlin.

Meulenbelt, (Ed.) (1998) *De Eerste Sekse -Meningen over Mannelijkheid*. Uitg. van Gennep, Amsterdam, 191–205.

v Oort, D. (1992) *Homostudies*. Rijksuniversiteit, Utrecht.

Ponse, B. (1978) *Identities in the Lesbian World. The Social Construction of Self*. Uitg. Greenwood, Westport.

Schreurs, K. (1986/87) Het is Maar Hoe je het Bekijkt. *Homostudies*. Rijksuniversiteit, Utrecht.

Schreurs, K. (1990) Vrouwen in Lesbische Relaties. *Homostudies*. Rijksuniversiteit, Utrecht.

Schuijf, J. (1994) *Een Stilzwijgende Samenzwering*. Uitg. Stichting beheer IISG, Amsterdam.

Sengers, W.J. (1969) *Homoseksualiteit als Klacht.* Uitg. Paul Brand, Bussum.

v Ussel, J. (1974) Afscheid van de Seksualiteit, Uitg. Loghum Slaterus, Deventer.

Warmerdam, H. en Koenders, P. (1987) *Cultuur en Ontspanning – het COC van 1946–1966*, Uitg. N.I.V.H. COC/Rijksuniversiteit, Utrecht.

7. Trafficking in Women

Elfriede Fröschl

Definition

'We talk of trafficking in women whenever women migrate on the basis of deception and false promises on the part of intermediaries, when they incur high debts for this purpose, and as a consequence are in a desperate situation in the target country. When women, because of this are forced to perform activities and render services against their will, forced into slavery-like exploitative work, or are deprived of their personal freedom and sexual integrity by husbands or employers.' (German original, LEFÖ, 1996, p20) 'Trafficking in women' is a relatively young term, which has given rise to criticism because it implies that women are passive objects and does not take into account the role of the consumers. As a consequence of the inflationary use of this term, female migrants from certain countries are as a matter of course viewed as victims of trafficking in women. However, because of its widespread use, for clarity, this term is also used in this article.

Trafficking in women is often equated to recruiting women as prostitutes for pimps or as workers in night clubs. In reality, however, these aspects account for only a part of trafficking activities. Women are also trafficked as domestic labour, for marriage, or for false adoptions (LEFÖ, 1996).

Past and present

In Europe the beginnings of trafficking in women go back to antiquity, in Latin America to the times of the Spanish conquest. At that time African women were brought to Latin America, not only as labourers, but also to serve the Spanish colonisers for sexual and child-bearing purposes. The more recent history of women trafficking and sex tourism is closely linked to the Vietnam War. So-called 'Rest and Recreation Centres' for American soldiers were established mainly in Thailand and in the Philippines and became the basis for the sex industry in these two countries.

Current target destinations are Western Europe, the United States, and Japan. The 'traded' women come from Asia, Africa, Latin America, and the countries of the former Eastern Bloc, where trafficking in women is drastically on the increase.

It is estimated that from Thailand alone 200,000 women have been trafficked to Europe, Australia, and Japan for exploitive purposes. A total of 500,000 women mainly from Asia, Africa, and Latin America are assumed to arrive in the European Union each year. Trafficking in women is a worldwide phenomenon, making use of well organised criminal networks. The legal situation in most European countries makes the fight against trafficking in women difficult, since the victims are usually forced to return to their countries of origin and are therefore not willing to testify or do not even turn to the police for help, for fear of deportation. Detailed information on the extent of trafficking in women and on the respective legal situations in individual countries can be obtained on the internet at: *http://www.uri.edu/artsci/wms/hughes/catw/factbook.htm*.

Migration as a 'free' decision of a woman

Within the women's movement there have been two controversial positions on prostitution for a long time. One says that prostitution may definitely be the result of a freely undertaken decision on the part of a woman. According to the other position prostitution is always the manifestation of a violence-based relationship.

Discussions on this subject restarted in 1995 at the United Nations World Conference on Women in Beijing. The final conference document states that only 'forced' prostitution can be considered violence against women. Opponents to this position say that prostitution is an extreme form of violence against women; that there is nothing like 'voluntary' prostitution and that recognizing prostitution as work would mean turning pimps into 'business managers' (Raymond, 1996). Advocates of the recognition of prostitution, on the other hand, say that the decriminalisation of prostitution would improve the social rights of prostitutes and reduce their dependence on pimps.

This discussion also includes the question of trafficking in women, as this is often equated to prostitution. The concept of differentiating between 'voluntary prostitution' and 'forced prostitution' and of granting women the 'freedom to choose' is strongly advocated by European and North American women. Representatives from the South have a very reserved position against this view: 'There is no freedom of choice for women who are forced into prostitution because of the prevailing power structures and poor living conditions. Western prostitutes have more options to choose which work they want to do, whereas prostitute migrants have no rights to any type of work in target countries. Female migrants therefore need more opportunities for working in Europe.' (German original, LEFÖ, 1996, p19).

More recent theoretical approaches see the central issue in the feminisation of migration. Women usually can only emigrate from their home countries or migrate into another country with the help of illegal international intermediaries and by adapting to the 'market' with its sexist and racist structures. 'Women are mainly sought in their reproductive capacity in sexual, emotional, and domestic spheres' (German original, Daumgartner, 1998, p113) Baumgartner criticises the term 'trafficking in women', because 'it supports the prevailing cliché according to which women are victims in need of protection. The concept of 'woman' as a 'commodity' which is implied by the term 'trafficking' degrades female migrants to dependent, obedient 'trading objects' and negates their existence as active subjects.' (German original, Baumgartner, 1998, p131) Considering the economic situation in the countries of origin the question whether women migrate or work as prostitutes voluntarily or involuntarily is of secondary importance 'since the majority of female migrants are in a

structural predicament and hope that working abroad will give them a life perspective which they could never attain in their home countries'. (German original, Baumgartner, 1998, p132).

Causes

The economic situation in the countries of origin

Migratory flows are basically the consequence of economic imbalance, i.e. of the existence of rich and poor countries. The high indebtedness of the countries of origin, together with high inflation rates causes a drop in real income. 'Since the 1980s enormous redistribution activities have been taking place between south and north. In 1960 the richest 20 per cent had an annual income which was 30 times higher than that of the poorest 20 per cent; today it is 60 times higher. Women are the ones who are most affected by this phenomenon' (German original, König, 1997, p54). The impoverished rural population in these countries, which migrates into the big cities where there is neither accommodation nor work is particularly hard hit by this development. The number of persons who live beneath the poverty line is continuously increasing. In Columbia, Brazil, and Peru, for example, nearly half of the population cannot satisfy their basic needs.

The special situation of women

Women account for half of the world's population. They do two thirds of the work, but receive only one tenth of the world's income and own less than one hundredth of the world's property. This was stated by the UN in 1980. It is estimated that at present 565 million women in the rural areas of the southern hemisphere live far below the poverty line (LEFÖ, 1996, p83). In many 'poor' countries women must provide for their families as heads of households and are therefore directly affected by economic crises. The poverty of women as a result of economic adjustment measures and their responsibilities for their families are seen as the main reasons why women migrate to big cities or to other countries. Very often the only work they can find is as prostitutes. 'In Thailand alone there are 60,000 brothels and 2 million prostitutes, 800,000 of whom are under 16 years of age.' (German original, LEFÖ, 1996, p84).

Tourism

'It is not a coincidence that the countries of origin of migrants who become victims of trafficking in women are identical with the countries which have recently seen a boom in tourism, such as the Caribbean countries or Thailand.' (German original, LEFÖ, 1996, p84). For most Caribbean islands tourism has become a vital source of foreign currency. Tourism brings the native population into contact with Western affluence and makes women hope to share in this affluence, through prostitution or by marrying a man from Western Europe or North America.

Militarism and the sex industry

The war in Vietnam has made visible the close link between military conflicts and an increase in prostitution and in the infrastructure required for this purpose and has also drawn worldwide attention to this issue. (German original, LEFÖ, 1996, p85).

In special 'Rest and Recreation Centres' native women were available for the sexual gratification of soldiers deployed in Vietnam. After the end of the Vietnam War these centres were adapted for mass tourism. A similar phenomenon was caused by the presence of US soldiers in Latin America.

Aspects of trafficking in women

It is impossible to describe the course of the numerous migration flows in detail. On the one hand women from the so-called Third World are taken to North America, Japan, Australia and the countries of the European Union. On the other hand, however, Thailand, for example, has become a target country itself because of its extensive sex industry. It is estimated that 50 percent of the prostitutes in Thailand come from Myanmar. Women who migrate to the European Union are mainly:

- Women from Southwest Asia, the Philippines, Thailand, and Indonesia. Some of these women already worked as prostitutes in their home countries. According to Tampep, an organisation offering support to the victims of trafficking, an estimated 20% of the women who come to Europe do not know that they will work as prostitutes.
- African women from Ghana, Zaire, Nigeria, and Ethiopia. They are often brought to Europe by relatives or friends who already live in Europe. It is not their intention to work as prostitutes but mostly there is no other way for them to make a living in Europe. In addition there are also numerous 'trading routes' within Africa as a result of the increase in sex tourism.
- Women from Latin America. Approximately 50,000 women alone come from the Dominican Republic to Spain, Italy, Austria, and the Netherlands each year. These women give their need to provide for children as the main reason for their migration. In Brazil there is not only a boom in trafficking in women but also in child prostitution. Brazil is the preferred destination for paedophiles from Europe and the United States.
- Prostitutes from Central and Eastern Europe (Poland, the countries of the former Soviet Union, the Czech Republic, Slovakia, Bulgaria, and former Yugoslavia). Whereas the number of women mentioned under items 1 to 3 is remaining stable, the number of women from the former Communist countries is rapidly increasing. According to estimates 500,000 prostitutes from Central and Eastern Europe work in the European Union. The 'business' is controlled by international gangs (e.g. Russian mafia). Because of the geographic proximity to the 'Golden West' and because of the lack of any perspectives for the future in their home countries, women from Eastern Europe are particularly at risk (Straßen und Grenzwege, 1996; http://www.uri.edu/artsci/wms/ hughes/catw/factbook.htm).

Social work models

Since trafficking in women is an international 'business' it can only be fought with the help of cross-border cooperation. This includes information campaigns for women in the countries of origin as well as awareness raising activities in the target countries. The need for social work with the victims has only been recognized in the last few years. Earlier the women had been expected to testify in court against the traffickers only to be subsequently (or often even prior to the trial) sent back to their home countries. In many cases women were deported by the police. It was only after women's organisations had begun to support these women and do intensive lobbying on their behalf that Europe became aware of the fact that it was necessary to cooperate with the victims and to provide them with options if trafficking was to be effectively counteracted. 'The Hague Ministerial Declaration on the European Guidelines for Effective Measures to Prevent and Combat Trafficking in Women for the Purposes of Sexual Exploitation states that advice and support for victims of trafficking not only serves to provide restitution for the victims but, by strengthening the position of women, contributes to the prevention of and fight against trafficking in women' (German original, Interventionsstelle für Betroffene des Frauenhandels, 1997, p2). The same Declaration says that trafficking in women is a gross violation of the human rights of women and that it can only be fought by coordinated and multi-disciplinary cooperation among various institutions. The European countries are encouraged to provide for 'adequate measures for the protection of victims, emergency shelters, medical and social support, and counselling in the victims' languages, as well as adequate financial support.' (German original, Interventionsstelle für Betroffene des Frauenhandels, 1997). The social work model introduced below starts with the needs of the prostitutes and is designed to gradually extend their scope of options, thus having an 'empowering' effect.

Street work at the border between Germany and Poland

As a reaction to the new dimensions of trafficking in women from Eastern Europe a pilot programme for HIV/Aids prevention among street prostitutes at the German-Polish and German-Czech borders was launched in 1994. The 'Bella Donna' women's centre in Frankfurt/Oder, Germany, undertook the task of offering street work.

It began with the distribution of condoms and information material in several languages. Pimps were included in the programme; otherwise there wouldn't have been a chance to get into contact with the prostitutes. Gradually it became possible to talk to the prostitutes alone. They started to talk about their life situation and how they were recruited. Even when women had been aware of the fact that they would be working as prostitutes they often had no idea of the conditions under which they would be working. It soon became clear that the pimps are the greatest health hazard for the women because they force women to make as much money as possible. Aids prevention therefore cannot take place in isolation from violence prevention.

After a year the street workers started to hold seminars right by the motorway. The topics they addressed were: problems at work, sexual practices, contraception, rates, experience with violent clients, etc. This exchange of information provided individual support to the women.

The experience gained in this way led to further projects:

- Developing a system of health care in cooperation with the public health offices in the region. A concrete result was that women can get anonymous and free treatment in nearly all public health centres.
- Cooperating with special units of the police which undertake raids, in order to make them aware of the special situation of these women.
- Providing emergency accommodation for abused victims.
- Establishing a meeting place for prostitutes, including the offer of language courses. Better knowledge of the local language enables the women to negotiate with their clients more professionally. The pimps were sceptical of this meeting place; they were, however, interested in the free-of-charge German courses.

According to the experience of the social workers it is very important not to take an ideological approach but to define on site which strategies serve to 'empower' the women, which strategies can be accepted. The basis for this work is to treat the women with respect.

The systematic prosecution of the smugglers instead of the women would be the starting point of stopping trafficking. This could be done by supporting rather than prosecuting the women, moving away from treating the real victims as criminals, by decriminalizing them. It would be necessary for these women to be tolerated by the immigration office and to be provided with options for the time thereafter. (German original, LEFÖ, 1996, p144).

On the basis of their practical experience the social workers have developed the following rules of conduct which are shared in seminars:

Goals of street work with prostitutes

- A woman's health is the first priority. For this purpose a woman working as a prostitute must develop a professional attitude. She must realize that her body is her capital, because then she will also know that health care and in particular the use of condoms is of vital importance and in her own interest.
- Giving women the opportunity for (anonymous and voluntary) medical examinations in health centres in the proximity of their place of work.
- Developing the professionalism of prostitutes (negotiations with clients, behaviour towards clients). The prostitutes must for instance realise that working without condoms does not automatically bring more clients but may deter those clients who want to make sure they are in no danger of an HIV infection.
- Concurrent work with pimps, owners of sex clubs etc. in order to make it clear to them that the women's health is also in their interest.

Rules for street work

- Accepting the women's choice of their occupation and life style.
- Personal contacts, intensive 'field work' and developing mutual trust are decisive – in the beginning it is enough to simply listen. Personal counselling with regard to medical, social, legal, and psychological problems is usually only the second step. But it is not enough to hand out information material and brochures.

- Reflection on one's own 'missionary' impulses (e.g. the wish to 'save' these women from prostitution).
- If a woman asks for assistance it is important to define together with her what she really wants and needs.
- No intervention or action without the consent or the cooperation of the woman concerned (the woman should be in control of the support process).
- Working with 'peer-educators'. Street workers could train experienced and respected prostitutes to pass on information to other prostitutes.
- Demonstrations of the correct use of condoms and providing information on lubricants should take place in the immediate vicinity of where the prostitutes work.
- Information on contracting the HIV virus or STDs and on reliable brands of condoms and lubricants should be available in written form and in several languages (adapted from: Straßen und Grenzwege, 1996, p115–7).

However, as long as the main causes for the migration of women – poverty in their home countries, high profits and patriarchal social structures, which give men the ideological basis for the purchase of women, continue to prevail, trafficking in women cannot be eliminated. Individual social work can at best only reduce women's problems. This is the reason why cooperation, particularly with women's organisations in their countries of origin, is vitally important. There are some isolated tendencies to prosecute not the illegal prostitutes but their clients. Whether such measures will actually result in a change of behaviour and in how far the women will actually benefit from them is hard to say, since economic dependence and power structures play an important role in connection with trafficking in women.

Didactic assignment

Aims: To provide information on the different aspects of trafficking in women, and to offer an opportunity for insights into the legal situation and into possibilities of empowering women.
Methods: work in small groups.

Use cases typical of the local situation; include different categories of cases, for instance women who are brought into a country:

- to work as prostitutes
- as domestic workers
- for marriage

What does 'empowerment' mean in these cases ?

References

Baumgartner, M.Le Breton (1998) Die Feminisierung der Migration. Eine Analyse im Kontext neoliberaler Arbeits- und Aufenthaltsverhältnisse. In: Klingebiel, R. and Shalini, R. (Eds.) *Globalisierung aus Frauensicht.* Bonn, 112–34.

Interventionsstelle für Betroffene des Frauenhandels (1997) *Conceptual Draft.* Vienna.

König, I. (1997) Diapositive der Macht – Bilder einer geteilten Gesellschaft. In: Verein Frauen Beraten Frauen (Ed.) *Still und leise in die Unsichtbarkeit? Gegen Armut und soziale Ausgrenzung von Frauen*, Conference Proceedings, Vienna, 53–60.

Krovinus, B. (1997) *Trafficking in Women.* Presentation given at the conference 'Police Combatting Violence against Women'.

LEFÖ (Lateinamerikanische exilierte Frauen in Österreich) (1996) *Frauenhandel. Frauenpolitische Perspektiven nach der Weltfrauenkonferenz' 95.* Bundesministerin für Frauenangelegenheiten, Vienna.

Raymond, J. (1996) *Trafficking and Prostitution: Beijing and its Aftermath.* Presentation at the conference 'Violence, Abuse and Women's Citizenship', Brighton.

Seager, J.and Olson, A. (1986) *Der Frauenatlas. Daten, Fakten und Informationen zur Lage der Frauen auf unserer Erde.* Frankfurt/Main.

Straßen und Grenzwege (1996*) Profem a Rozkos bez Rizika.* This brochure can be ordered from Rozkos bez Rizika, Bolzanova 1, 10100 Praha 1.

Internet

Facts and legal background information regarding trafficking in women for a large number of countries can be found under *http://www.uri.edu/artsci/wms/hughes/catw/factbook.htm*

8. Multi-culture and Gender

Obertha Holwerda

During the past few years societies in most European countries have experienced sweeping changes. People from other countries and continents-in particular refugees and migrant workers-have come in and continued their lives here. This resulted in society acquiring a multi-cultural character spawning problems in many ways.

In this chapter I will endeavour to describe the background to these problems and provide a basis for discussion. I would also like to incorporate the gender aspect.

The approach that I have chosen originates from my own professional and academic background, which is 'socio-agogical sciences' in the Netherlands focussing on the methodology of intervention.

The aims are:

- Starting to discuss the subject matter.
- Consciousness raising with regard to the changing society.
- Its implications for men and women.
- Consciousness raising with regard to the differences, analysing the differences relating to gender positions and being able to relate them to the positions in society.

Concepts

Multi-culture and gender

Multi-culture: literally this means having several cultural or ethnic groups within a society (*COD*).

According to Gommers, multi-culture linked to society is the mix of various cultural groups without any of them yielding their cultural identities. She calls it a society that allows space differentiation, even though the indigenous society is present; it is a society which she regards as enriching.

The groups forming part of such a multi-cultural society are:

- The original inhabitants (mostly called the indigenous population).
- Repatriates from (former) colonies.

- Migrants, the foreign workers with their families.
- Refugees.

The last three groups are often called ethnic groups, migrants or *allochtonen*. This terminology for the non-indigenous people is often used interchangeably. Multi-culture entails a pluriform society taking shape in more and more countries.

Gender

Anja Meulenbelt (in *The first sex*) describes gender as sex identity. Gender refers to the meaning given to the male and the female within certain historic, cultural and social contexts.

Gender can be described in various interrelating and mutually strengthening layers. These layers are:

- Nucleus gender identity: one learns through rules, regulations and behaviour how one is to behave as a man or a woman: one is socialised as a man or a woman. This so-called socialisation process is related to:
- The prevailing incorporated images of what is proper for a man or a woman. These images differ from one historic period to the next, among cultures and social strata, and relate to:
- the social context, which is expressed in:
  - The social positions of men and women.
  - The distribution of labour.
  - The distribution of care, money, power and status.
  - The society in which one lives.

Consolidation assignment with multi-culture

A 45-minute discussion in groups of four about the question:

Is there a multi-cultural society in the place where you live? If so, what are the positive influences? If not, why not? Prepare a survey of your findings and discuss them with the plenary group.

Time: about 1½ hours in total.

Consolidation assignment with gender

A 45-minute discussion in multi-facetted groups of three or four.

What behaviour is befitting to the present generation of men or women? Find examples.

What behaviour is befitting for men and women originating from another country?

What are the differences? Be prepared to present your opinion.

Present it in an appropriate form to the plenary group.

Time: about 1½ hours in total.

What is culture and how does culture come about?

And what about gender positions in these cultures?

Culture: what is it?

There are various definitions for *culture* and I will give a few:

1. Keesing in *Theory of Cultures* describes culture as a 'design for living' of socio-cultural systems emphasising the directional character of culture.
2. Pinto in *Interculturele Communicatie,* or Intercultural Communications, describes culture as an evolving system of rules handed down from generation to generation, which are adhered to, often subconsciously, by a group of people feeling themselves members of this group. Moreover, the set of rules determines the group's view of its environment and is the **frame of reference** of and for its behaviour.
3. Vermeulen in *Cultura* (a treatise on culture consciousness in the studies of non-indigenous ethical groups) says culture is the common world of experiences, values and knowledge characterising a certain social unit. It is a collective system of meanings that people have built up together over time.

Culture becomes visible in how people act, how they associate: it tells about their **frame of reference** (see Sanneke Bolhuis in *Leren en Veranderen bij Volwassenen*, or Teaching and Change with Adults). This frame of reference is the result of the total sum of the learning processes that one goes through: the sum of knowledge, skills and attitudes consciously or subconsciously entertained by an adult. The road to one's frame of reference is called one's learning history, which is influenced by three aspects:

- The personal aspect: talent, capabilities and interest.
- The situations and events that one experiences.
- The general social and historical context in which one's life takes place.

People react to the world around them from their own frame of reference: they have opinions about for instance how men and women should act, what is proper and what isn't.

People from different cultures depart from different frames of reference, they give different meanings to what surrounds them; just think about the meaning of snow to an Eskimo and the meaning of snow for a Moroccan.

When one considers culture as the common world of meanings of a certain social system, it will include the following (Tennekes and Hofstede):

- **Language**. Every social system has more or less its own language. Consider for instance jargon.
- **Knowledge.** This is the everyday knowledge of how things work; how one is expected to act. Consider the traffic code, the rights and duties of people, etc.
- **Norms and values.** What is considered normal and what is not?
- **Symbols, rituals and heroes**. Flags are symbols, status is a symbol. Rituals include how people greet each other. Heroes are people who are highly regarded.

These four elements are needed to go about one's life in a social system.

How then does culture arise? Considering each social system to be within a certain environment, the specific culture evolves from within communication among people and their environments. They develop common knowledge, opinions and values about their realities. In the course of time a culture will arise within a social system. This culture is unknown to newcomers and, if they want to be included in that social system they will have to familiarise themselves with it. People themselves give meaning to their environments. Different environments affect people, they develop differences in cultural values.

Condon and Yousef in *Uit Interculturele Gespreksvoering* (From Intercultural Conversation) (Edwin Hoffman, Willem Arts, p29-31) have developed a scheme for the **orientation of values** of the six universal human themes. These orientations of values are not linked to ethnic groups or countries; they are universal orientations of values valid for any person. They are:

One's own

Individualism as against mutual dependence; individualism, individuality, I and we.

Age: young, middle-aged, old.

Sex: male and female (equal), female (superior), male (superior).

Family

Dominating relational styles in families: individualist, lateral relations, linear relations.

Attitude towards authority: democracy, aimed at authority, authoritarian, strong man.

Family-linked role behaviour: open, more general role expectations, specific role expectations.

Family-linked individual social mobility: strong mobility, generation-phased mobility, weak mobility (if one was born poor, one will remain poor the rest of one's life).

Society

Supporting and aiding one another and committing oneself: independence, symmetrical commitments, and complementary commitments.

Opinions on membership: member of many groups, the group is subordinate, individuals and groups are important, member of few groups, group is important.

Intermediaries or not: no intermediary, only experts as intermediaries, intermediaries necessary.

Extent of formality: mostly informal, formal on occasion, formal as a rule.

Opinions relating to property: everything is privately owned, property is private and communal, all property is communal.

Human nature

Human understanding as compared to sensibility and urges: the human being is rational, the human being acts intuitively, and the human being is irrational.

Basically people tend towards the good, the good and evil, the evil.

What people look for and what they can achieve: the human being as investigator; there is an inextricable relation between good and bad luck; whatever the human being wants to achieve, life is mostly sadness.

Human fickleness: the human being changes, learns and grows, the human being grows slowly, the human being is incapable of change (aggression, egotism, etc.)

Nature

The relation between the human being and nature: the human being dominates nature, the human being lives in harmony with nature, nature dominates nature.

Methods to acquire knowledge about nature: from science, by reasoning, from specific experiences in nature.

The nature and being of nature: everything can be explained, spiritual, the human being and nature are embedded by the same spirit, organic, and the human being and nature are part of the same organism.

Time: people are aimed at the future, people are aimed at the present, and people are aimed at the past.

The supernatural

The relation between people and the supernatural: there is no God, every human being has something god-like, and the human being is subordinate to the supernatural.

The meaning of life: achieving material goals, enriching knowledge and science, the spiritual elevation of the mind.

The providential view: what is good in life is infinite when one makes a dedicated effort, there is a balance between prosperity and bad luck, what is good in life is limited.

Science of the cosmic order: this will be fathomed eventually, it is a mix of religion and science, the cosmic order is mysterious and beyond knowledge.

The above scheme is meant to show how different values ascribed to fundamental human themes can be. This scheme takes into account the gender aspect; it has been incorporated in the orientations of value.

Finally, I would like to proceed to Geert Hofstede, who has chosen a different angle: on the basis of four aspects. Hofstede drafts **a cultural profile** of a country or people. He has done this by cultural research in a great number of countries. The research showed that cultures do not differ at random. There are a number of common problems, problems to which different cultures gave different answers. The problems are called **cultural dimensions.** They are aspects that allow for comparison between a culture and other cultures – they are aspects that determine the cultural profile of a land or people.

The cultural dimensions are:

1. **Power distance** deals with the belief whether power differences in society are normal or not. In cultures with great power distance, power is a given thing. Power differences are a fact of life, they precede the choice between good and evil, every human being has his or her place. In cultures with minor power-distance the use of power is subordinate to good and evil, power differences should be as small as possible.
2. **Individualism versus collectivism** deals with the relation between I-we-they. In Collectivism the group interest precedes the individual interest. In Individualism this is reversed. In collectivist cultures it is important to maintain the harmony with your environment. Group opinion is more important than one's own. In collectivist cultures the word *no* is little used, it is an impolite word. In individualist cultures honesty is more important than politeness, handling conflicts should be learned. There is no collective embarrassment. The individual is important.

3. **Femininity versus masculinity** deals with the differences in roles ascribed to the sexes. It is about the appreciation of the so-called soft-care-characteristics as against so-called tough-competence-characteristics. It is about the question whether a society is more masculine or more feminine. In western society the so-called masculine characteristics of achievement, competence, and business-mindedness have high scores.
4. **Avoidance of uncertainty** deals with the extent to which one feels threatened by unfamiliar situations. Whenever a culture does not manage to deal with the unknown, fear of anything strange, deviating and unfamiliar will arise. Different ideas and behaviour are distrusted. Strict rules are developed.

In particular the third dimension, femininity versus masculinity, pays attention to the gender aspect of a culture.

- To be able to understand culture, one needs an understanding of the cultural dimensions.
- To be able to fathom the significance of culture for a social system one needs an understanding of the elements as described above.
- To understand a people's behaviour within a culture one needs knowledge of the place taken by the orientations of values (frame of reference).

Before proceeding with the elaboration of the gender-specific ingredients I will refer to the consequences of living in a country with a 'strange' culture.

Consolidation assignment

You are to deal with the following assignment in groups of four:

You are to consider orientation of values from your frame of reference. In what way does your frame of reference influence this? Having done this, you are to proceed to cultural dimensions: which dimension plays the dominant role in the country in which you live?

This part of the assignment takes about an hour. Then you write down your findings on a sheet of paper, you compare the findings of other groups, you pay attention to the differences and question the ideas supporting the differences.

Time: about 2 hours in total.

Multi-cultural co-habitation in one country

When people move from one culture to another and the latter differs in many aspects from the one they come from, these people may suffer a so-called culture shock. The world surrounding them may be incomprehensible, threatening and horrifying to them. Mostly they do not speak the language, their own frame of reference ceases to support their daily experiences, afterall, the frame of reference was shaped in their own culture. They have to adjust to the new situation. The frame of reference needs to be changed. The country in which they are staying expects the migrants to adapt to their new environment. They are a minority in their new country. The extent of difficulties encountered by these people depends on a number of factors:

- **The migration factor**. Whether they have come voluntarily or involuntarily, the extent of preparation for the future; if the stay is permanent or temporary.
- **The orientation of values**. Are there great differences between the former situation and the present? In many cases the values do not fit the present environment.
- **Is migration experienced as stressful?** This depends on the person and the circumstances: can they deal with stressful situations or does one experience difficulties? Migration can be considered as the discovery of many new things, but also as the loss of many old and familiar things. The reversibility of migration is a contributory factor. Is a return possible or out of the question?

A stress-enhancing factor is the minority status, which may have all kinds of consequences: discrimination on the basis of outward characteristics, social isolation (not speaking the language), isolation from faraway relatives and inadequate housing and working conditions.

A contributory stress factor is the pressure to integrate. There is pressure to adapt with

regard to various factors: language, clothing, schooling, social behaviour, etc.

Migration is a phased process. For a successful migration it is important to go through all its phases. The phases are:

Phase 1: preparation

Good preparation depends on the information received, is this information correct or is the country of choice presented as a paradise?

Phase 2: the actual move

Is the move successful or hampered by bureaucracy? It often happens that a man leaves his family to fend for themselves to prepare entry for the rest of the family in the country of choice. The man then lacks support and isolation may begin to play a role.

Phase 3: the first period

This is the period in which to get acquainted with the new country, expectations are often high. They are optimistic about possible achievements and confident about the future.

If many disappointments are met in this phase, symptoms of a problem migration will emerge, such as suspicion, fear, sleeplessness, stomach and intestinal complaints. It is important to refer to social workers for help in the earliest possible stage of such cases.

Phase 4: disillusionment

This is a difficult phase; what is important now is to face reality, to adjust expectations, to acquire a place in society and to ask the question will I be successful in this country? Do I want to stay? Can I stay? And what will happen if it goes wrong? In this phase too social-work support may be of paramount importance.

Phase 5: parting of the ways

Depending on the development in the preceding two phases, the question now arises if they will be able to find their balance in their 'new country'. Are they willing to integrate? Or do they choose to live among people from the country of their own origin?

The position of the migrant is not easy; it is a minority position, a position in which prejudice, discrimination and racism, neglect, inequality, etc. is met.

So far I have been discussing **migrants**, not **refugees**. Refugees have a different status, a different position. They are persecuted in their countries of origin and often have to fear death. They want to return to their countries whenever possible. They would rather not live in the country that has accepted them, but they have no choice but to stay. Their experiences were often traumatic and they need professional assistance to cope with these experiences.

Refugees are mostly educated people as opposed to most migrants, who are not.

Whenever people meet, they bring themselves. They express judgements and prejudices. They interpret their experiences from their own norms and values. One person may value the other highly, but there is the tendency to consider one's own culture superior to that of others. This is called ethnocentrism, which means that a different culture is explained from the point of view of one's own.

When considering the influence of the cultural dimensions, the frame of reference and the orientation to values to someone's well-being, it appears that it is important to know the cultural dimensions of other countries and groups, since these frames of reference and orientations of values render deeper understanding of these people. For instance, if you grow up in a country where it is forbidden to express your own views, you will be confused if asked for your opinion. This is a good example of what people face in education and schooling where they are often asked for their opinion. Obviously, it has become a focal point in education.

When talking about migrants, I do not mean migrants that move to some other country for business, who are starting a company or branch there, the top executives from other countries, but I mean people from the lowest social classes of society, many of whom are in situations of neglect. This situation reflects the inequality-socio-economic relationship of the minority position compared to the majority position of the indigenous people. Their negative image influences their success on the labour market, the housing market and in education (after all, they are lagging behind in their language skills). Having a job and an income is an important precondition for social participation and integration. Of course, much more could be said about multiple cultures living together in a single country. Just think of the Universal Declaration of Human Rights which forms the basis for living together in equality, respecting one another's identity.

Research and exploration of the various backgrounds people come from will hopefully lead to better mutual understanding and free development.

In the next section I will weave everything together and give shape to professional social work.

Consolidation assignment

Analyse events in your own life that can be compared to migration (moving house; your parents' divorce). Considering what you went through, could you imagine the predicaments migrants go through?

Do this assignment in pairs and write down the findings, exchange them with the entire group and take an hour.

Consolidation assignment

Considering the culture dimension of femininity versus masculinity, find an example to express the influence of this dimension on your own frame of reference.

Do this in groups of four and take an hour.

Professional social work, gender and multi-cultural groups

In this section I want to start with the description of the starting points which more or less make up the general model of social work among mixed cultural groups. After that I will proceed to the description of the starting points as developed by black women (women from the multi-ethnic groups) from the feminist point of view. Finally I will deal again with the culture dimensions, the frame of reference and the orientation of values.

A general model for providing professional social work to people of mixed ethnic backgrounds is the **cross-cultural approach** (Hoffman and Ögünç-Serap: *Allochtone Hulpvragers*, or Non-indigenous social work enquiries). This approach means that professional social work can be provided by someone from one's own ethnic background as well as by someone with another background. Professionalism takes priority. Hoffman and Ögünç-Serap describe the general starting points as follows:

1. The principle of equality, all human beings are equal irrespective of sex, religion, ethnic background and values. This means that any client is first and foremost a client with a request for social work and not a person with a certain background with a request for social work.
2. The principle of recognised inequality, all human beings are different and require an individual approach. Each client is an individual who renders meaning to one's own environment.
3. The principle of inclusive thinking, not to think in terms of *us* or *them*, but *us*, includes the other person. This means that professional social work should be easily accessible to all categories of clients, including members of a so-called ethnic group. For institutions this means that they will have to pay attention to communication with clients, in particular with such group as do not understand or speak the language well. (v.d. Stouw, 1999, p113).

The above-mentioned three starting points have consequences for the social worker:

- Considering the ethnic mix of the target group the social worker pays attention to such variables as sex, social class, age, sexual orientation, religion, values, and ethnicity with each client and from the position of the migrant and to the mutual interrelations.
- The social worker has to think critically about their own performance, attitude and frame of reference. The social worker should be able to bring forward for discussion their own views, judgements and prejudices.
- The social worker should be aware of the social power strata in society, the influence of their own position as a professional person in society, the influence of the position of the institution (where the social worker is employed) within society and the position the client assumes within society.

The social worker working against these starting points and principles pays much attention to communication and language and carefully investigates whether there is mutual understanding.

Even though the principles and starting points described above have not been selected gender-specifically, they do not seem to be contrary to the starting points of gender-specific social work. (Schilder, 1999):

1. Gender is considered a fundamental characteristic of social relations and a primary vehicle for achieving power and giving meaning to power. Gender is not linked to differences between physical men and women. The meaning of gender is considered a cultural mechanism prioritising *male* to *female* in all kinds of aspects of society, dividing men and women as it were into dominant and subordinate categories.
2. Besides, gender-specific social work is aimed at combating observable inequalities between men and women relating to their social positions and socialisation. Gender-specific social work stimulates clients to liberate themselves from the oppressive consequences of the inequalities in their lives.

For some time the women from the **black women's movement** (black women originating from the (former) colonies, from migrant groups and refugee women) have been working on feminist social work in relation to social work and black women. Black women fail to recognise themselves in the ideas developed by indigenous feminist women. The equality principle ('we are all women') reigned supreme, all women had to be treated on an equal basis, and no difference was made between black and white women.

Essed brought forward the subject of **Racism and Feminism**. She declared that black women not only had to deal with suppression on the basis of their sex but also on the basis of their skin colour. Black women have adapted the concepts used in women's social work to the social work among black women. In this form of social work the following issues are important:

- For the female social worker to make sure that in her work, words have the same emotional value for either party, for instance what is the emotional value of having children, what does your mother's help in raising your children mean?

- The right of self-determination: the striving for treatment as equal as possible.
- The meaning of the *we*-culture. This culture regards the individual as part of a larger unit. What is its influence on *I* and *we*?
- The importance of authority in the *we*-culture. What power does authority have in a woman's life?

Women's problems should be related to their social problems in society. When dealing with a black woman and when converting the request for social work into real social work, the social worker needs to relate this premise to the client's socialisation and social position in both the country in which she is living now and to the country in which she used to live, and to the present position of the woman within her own ethnic group.

The complex position of black women requires much attention. The extent to which these women have to face discrimination, e.g. racism and sexism, is being researched; is she facing discrimination in person or in the media, advertising using implicit prejudice, etc. Reference is also made to the question whether women suffer from internalised oppression (this is the embedding and acceptance in the dominant culture of prejudice relating to minorities).

The starting points of gender-specific social work can be found in the approach championed by black women. Both emphasise the guidelines for women's behaviour and experience (the so-called feminine codes) which women acquire during socialisation.

When one considers the **cultural dimensions** and social work with multi-cultural groups, one cannot fail to notice that the dimensions can always be found in the starting points and principles; they determine the social framework within which social work takes place.

The frame of reference of both the female social worker and the person requesting social work are emphatically put forward, including the investigation whether words have the same emotional value. The orientation of values always plays a part, they can be found in all starting points. It is in fact an exploration of how and when the cultural dimensions, the frame of reference and the orientation of values play a role and affect each other.

What is lacking in gender-oriented social work and multi-ethnic groups is social work with men. As far as I know a specific approach for men from mixed ethnic groups has not been described.

Consolidation assignment

In order to link the starting points to everyday practise, try the following assignment:

Analyse a case of social work with someone belonging to an ethnic group and pay attention to how the request for help affects gender, the cultural dimensions, the frame of reference and orientations for values. Allow 45 minutes.

Write down your analysis and exchange your case and analysis with another sub-group. Comment on each other's work and eventually discuss your findings in both sub-groups.

Time: about 1½ hours – groups of four.

The present situation

In this section I will discuss a number of developments taking place in the field of multi-culturalisation and gender.

First I will deal with 'The empowerment view of migrant, refugee and black women', who have developed their own views and analysis of their emancipation and integration processes in society. They take empowerment to mean converting force and qualities into power and influence of multi-cultural groups in general and migrant, refugee and black women in particular. They are aiming at a lasting change within society in all its elements.

As their starting point they take 'diversity', this concept brings better expression of the mutual changes among women in, for instance, the experience of one's own position in society, the legal status, the level of schooling and economic participation. The experience of one's own position in society is very diverse. Having the position of a black woman, i.e. a woman from a (former) colony, constitutes a major difference; they emphatically combat the daily racism they are facing. Migrant women used to come to the Netherlands to re-unite their families with their partners who had been here as migrant workers for some time. In their experience the migrant worker system still determines their positions. Refugee women had to leave everything behind when they had to flee. In their experience admission and shelter greatly determine their positions.

There are great differences among the women's legal status. Women originating from the colonies can enter the country without any problems; after all they are 'simply' citizens of this country. The women from the former colonies and migrant women can enter the country (if the partner meets certain criteria) to re-unite their families, however, they get a partner-dependent status and have to remain married for three years if they ever want to be granted a permanent status. Refugee women are subject to long and complex processes before they are granted permanent residence. Their reasons for fleeing their country are not always understood (for instance a woman who flees because she has resisted religious oppression in the country of origin, or a woman fleeing sexual violence in times of war).

The diversity of the various groups has to do with the differences in culture, socio-economic backgrounds and the reasons and experience of their migration.

Empowerment is to be realised on two levels: within their own societies and within society in general.

Between migrant, refugee and black women on the one hand and indigenous men and women on the other hand, there are great differences in accessibility of schooling, the labour market, etc. This pervasive neglect is based on the fact that both sex and ethnicity are the principles of order in society according to migrant, refugee and black women. However, these principles are recognised neither by the authorities nor society. This is a major point for discussion with the authorities. Further, migrant, refugee and black women are working for an independent legal status (independent of their partners). Migrant, refugee and black women suffer from stereotyping by the media, researchers and policy makers. This

is mainly due to the fact that hardly any women from these groups work in these fields, and as long as this remains the case, the stereotyping will stay. Migrant, refugee and black women do not think the integration concept is the right approach as it leaves existing power structures and orders intact. What they are aiming at is a **transformation** of the society in which empowerment of migrant, refugee and black women has been embedded.

Of course, there are a great number of new initiatives and discussions relating to better or different forms of integrating multi-ethnic groups in this country. One can think of schooling and youth centres.

Consolidation assignment in groups of four

For this assignment you need some of last week's newspapers. Analyse some present themes in the framework of being multi-ethnic, are they correct or are there also other ones.

Exchange your findings and finally analyse what has been written about women's and men's positions.

Time: 45 minutes

Instead of newspapers you can also work with a recent video.

References

Theme: Multiculture and gender

Babel, M. and Hitipouw, D. (1992) *Langzaam Gaan de Deuren open*. Uitg. Stichting de Maan, Amsterdam.

Boedjarath, I. (1997) *Een Blik in de Transculturele Hulpverlening*. Uitg. van Arkel, Utrecht.

Bolhuis, S. (1997) *Leren en Veranderen bij Volwassenen*. Uitg. Continho, Bussum.

Essed, P. (1991) *Inzicht in Alledaags Racisme*. Uitg. Het Spectrum, Utrecht.

Equality, (1997) *Lezingenbundel* Uitg. Den Haag.

Hoffman, E. and Arnts, W. (1995) *Interculturele Gespreksvoering*. Uitg. Bohn, Stafleu en v. Loghum, Houten.

Karimi, F. and Kalka, J. (1996) *Met Kracht naar Empowerment*. Uitg. Project Aisa, Utrecht.

Keesing, R. (1974) Theories of Culture, In: Siegel, B. *Annual Review of Antropology*. Uitg. Palo Alto.

Meijer, E. and Pereira, E. (1991) *Hulpverlening uit de Crisis.* Uitg. Bohn, Stafleu en v. Loghum, Houten.

Meulenbelt, A. (Ed.) (1998) *De Eerste Sekse*. Uitg. van Gennep, Amsterdam.

Oomkes, F. (1986) *Communicatieleer.* Uitg. Boom, Meppel.

Pinto, D. (1993) *Interculturele Communicatie*. Uitg. Bohn, Stafleu en v. Loghum, Houten.

Procee, H. (1991) *Over de Grenzen van Culturen*. Uitg. Boom, Meppel.

Rooijendijk, E.A. (1988) Turken en Marokanen in Hollands Welzijnsland. Uitg. Nelissen, Baarn.

v.d.Stouw (red) (1999) *Verkenning in doelgroepen en werkvelden*. 15–45, 109–44. Uitg. Wolters Noordhoff, Groningen.

v.d.Stouw (red) (1993) *Maatschappelijk werk Doelgroepen.* 100–28. Uitg. Wolters Noordhoff, Groningen.

Tastenhoye, G. (1993) *Naar een Multiculturele Samenleving*. Uitg. Davidsfonds, Leuven.

Tennekes, J. (1993) *Culturele Identiteit in het Strategisch Gebruik van Cultuur*. Intern paper N.S.A.V. studiedag Dynamiek en cultuur, Amsterdam.

Vermeulen, H. (1992) *De Cultura, Migrantenstudies* 8. Uitg. Bohn, Stafleu en v. Loghum, Houten.

Vroegindewey, M. E. A. (1989) *Nieuwe Ontwikkelingen in het Maatschappelijk Werk*. Uitg. Nelissen, Baarn.

9. Substance Dependence

Irmgard Vogt

The images of women and men in theories of addiction

Historically it was initially men who were seen to be addicts. In the 19th century it was alcohol addicted men for whom the first institutions were established, and in the 20th century therapeutic communities and other institutions were set up for drug dependent men. Masculinity and addiction are therefore associated with each other, or more precisely: deviance from masculinity and addiction. The image of man underlying theories of addiction is based on masculinity and male stereotypes and on deviance thereof considered typical of addicts. Under this aspect gender was originally of no relevance. Since the mid 20th century, however, the percentage of women with addiction problems or more precisely, with problems related to substance abuse, has been slowly but steadily on the increase. These changes have not been sufficiently accounted for in theories on addiction. The deviance of addicted women is still measured with reference to the deviance of addicted men with regard to standards of masculinity. This becomes especially obvious with reference to moral judgement of substance use and substance dependence. Addicted women are considered to have moved much farther down the morality scale than addicted men (see: Hoppe, 1904). In today's jargon we don't find references to 'immoral' any more but, for example, 'sick' or 'emotionally stressed' or 'disturbed'. Addicted women are seen as 'sicker' than addicted men and therefore their treatment is considered to be particularly difficult and they are often characterised as 'resistant to therapy' (Feuerlein, 1984). Modern diagnostics confirm these interpretations by coming up with more and more new findings (e.g. Vertheim et al., 1998), without taking the underlying gender bias into account. As a result addicted women on the whole are described in more negative terms in addiction theories than addicted men (Vogt, 1990, 1994). The misogyny thus expressed in this context serves as an additional negative factor in the course of this illness in women.

Women-specific and men-specific forms of addiction development

Recent studies on the gateway to substance use and abuse, excessive use, the gradual or sudden development of addiction, as well as the course taken by the disease are characterised by typical gender-specific differences. In (late) childhood and during adolescence, in the case of some drugs, for instance alcohol, certain adaptation processes can be observed over a certain period of time between genders, in particular when we talk about consuming such drugs in peer groups. After a relatively short period of time, however, gender-specific differentiation processes set in. If we generalise we can speak of a 'hard' male drug consumption style and of a 'soft' female one. The adaptation of drug consumption styles of the genders is thus paralleled by gender-specific differences which modify the development of addiction (Helfferich, 1994; Kolip, 1997).

Gender-specific differences in behaviour

Epidemiological studies on the use of, the abuse of, and the dependence on psychotropic substances provide detailed proof of gender-specific differences. Since there are differences between the risks related to drug use, drug careers vary not only by gender but also by the substances used. **Careers** take a different course depending on whether the substances are licit or illicit. As a rule careers are more rapid, steeper, and linked to more self-inflicted damage if the substances used are illicit. Careers extend over a longer period of time and offer more opportunities for getting away from the drug, if the addictive substances are licit. The **life spheres** of addicted women and men clearly differ from each other. The lives of addicted women are dominated by the experience of violence, which while also playing a role in the lives of addicted men, is not dominant there. On the whole self-inflicted damage in the case of addicted women is greater than with addicted men (Vogt, 1998a). In spite of this, addicted women have a higher potential for recovery from addiction than men. This is probably related to the fact that, all in all, women have better social networks than men, or that, compared to men; they can reactivate and make use of these networks more rapidly (Weber and Schneider, 1992).

Problems with (non-gender-specific) assessment

Although there is highly differentiated evidence of gender variations in patterns of use, abuse, and dependence, medical and psychological assessment are highly indifferent to gender when it comes to describing disturbances (compare ICD-10 and DSM-IV, for details see Wetterling and Verltrup, 1997). Dealing with well-established forms of assessment therefore requires creativity.

In order to fairly assess the severity of emotional disturbances in addicted men in particular it will be necessary to take their potential for aggression more into account than it has been done so far. Conventional assessment barely takes into account or assesses the violence of addicted men. It is, however, a gender-specific indicator of emotional disturbances in addicted men, and should therefore be assessed accordingly and integrated into treatment plans.

Counselling and therapy for women and men with addiction problems

The Federal Republic of Germany provides an extensive **support system** for women and men who have problems with the use, the abuse of, and the dependence on psychotropic substances or who are family members of dependent persons. The support system consists of three sectors: residential,

non-residential, and self-help. The support system still has historical features and therefore addresses primarily men. Women can also use this support system but must, with a few exceptions, adapt to the structures which are geared to the needs of men. These are also the roots of residential treatment institutions for alcoholics which to date accept either only men or only women, whereby services for alcohol dependent men outnumber those for alcohol dependent women by far. In addition there is a small network of women-specific facilities for women who are dependent on illicit drugs. These facilities are the result of the women's movement or approaches in feminist therapy (Vogt, 1997; Vogt and Krah, 1998; Vogt et.al., 1998). It is therefore possible to define differences between the various services with regard to orientation and working methods. There are no studies, however, evaluating these services.

Counselling, casework, group works have proven successful in working with persons with substance dependencies and their family members. What has not been successful in working with women is confrontation, an intervention strategy which is based on conflict resolution among men and was used extensively in the seventies and eighties in casework as well as in group work. Today intervention strategies are most widely used, such as motivational interviews (Miller and Rollnick, 1999) working with the motivation of clients as well as with strengthening their trust in the effectiveness of self-help and self-efficacy, which must however be activated in each individual case.

The special problem situations of pregnant women and mothers with children are taken into account in out-patient as well as in in-patient services. These approaches are however comparatively young (Bucher, 2000; Steinhausen, 2000; Vogt, 1996). Further differentiation may be expected in the future (Leopold and Steffan, 1997; Mattejat and Lisofsky, 1998).

On the other hand, what is missing to date is **counselling specifically geared to fathers**. Men are not perceived as fathers who have obligations, needs, wishes, and (ambivalent) feelings towards their children. Substance dependent men who have children have no one to turn to (Schmid et al., 1999).

Relapse prevention has meanwhile become an integral part of residential and outpatient treatment programmes. This has put an end to the dogma that any breach of abstinence must result in a catastrophe. Relapse prevention builds up the abilities of persons for self-control. It is an important element in 'helping people help themselves'.

The problems of helpers

Gender is a major determining factor regarding the prestige which women and men enjoy in society. This is reflected in the positions of male and female helpers in the support system. Men are almost exclusively found in leading positions only, whereas women are assisting and subordinate staff. With the status of women in institutions being lower than that of their male colleagues, women have a different access to the clients than men. There is less distance between female counsellors and their clients than between male counsellors and their clients. Making contact and building trust is to a certain extent made easier through this greater closeness. Furthermore, men in particular turn to women when they are looking for help with their emotional problems. Women counsellors are therefore in high demand. The situation becomes more difficult, however, when their expert status is important or when they set demands on the clients and insist on their implementation. Compared to female counsellors male counsellors have greater problems winning the clients' trust, but it is easier for them to make clients meet their demands (Vogt, 1998b).

The training of counselling staff must reflect these differences and work with them. It must also raise sensitivity levels with regard to the gaps between counsellors and their clients, for the effects of bridging these gaps, or violating them, with the inherent dangers of possible sexual exploitation (Moggi, 1997).

Gender-specific prevention

'Gender-related prevention of addiction has its roots on the one hand in the prevention of

addiction and on the other hand in the work with girls and boys' (Franzkowiak et al., 1998, 24). The very limited extent to which gender is a consideration in addiction prevention is problematic. This need not be the case, since the work in fact focuses on the life spheres of clients. The gender aspect obviously gets lost in the implementing process; clearly, something has do be done about this (Schmidt and Hurrelmann, 2000). On the other hand work with young girls and boys has tended to focus on work with young girls. Belatedly, and only slowly, working with young boys is becoming an established field, into which the aspect of the prevention of drug abuse must be integrated.

No evidence exists for any approaches to gender-specific prevention activities which go beyond adolescence. With a view to the increasing risk of addiction in older age groups (from 60 years of age onward) through psychotropic prescription drugs and alcohol, the existing approaches are not far-reaching enough and require further development.

Didactic assignments

The importance of self-awareness training

Participants of courses or seminars on the subject of addiction are asked to take a closer look at their own use of psychotropic substances (coffee, tea, cigarettes, alcohol, etc.). A number of topics can be covered using cigarettes as an example: initial consumption of the substance, circumstances of starting, developing a habit, status quo, development of dependence or addiction, problems quitting, relapses, possible renewed attempts to quit.

Suitable teaching aids: Ad-hoc-interviews, self-observation questionnaires, weekly schedules. The students are asked to retrace their own development as smokers or non-smokers, to mark the most important stages of this development, to define seductive situations, and to record potentials for resisting temptation.

Instructional goal: Addiction is everybody's business. Addiction is part of everyday life as demonstrated by examples of cigarette smoking. The onset of addiction can be trivial, unspectacular. As a rule this applies to licit psychotropic substances. And: not every addiction stigmatises the addict. But there are forms of addict behaviour which signal deviance. Differentiation is thus just as important as generalisation.

Perception and assessment through others

Students are asked to use pictures and rating scales to document their impression of intoxicated women and men.

Suitable teaching aids: Video recordings of intoxicated women and men taken from films. Scales to rate each individual scene. Evaluation of the results in small groups (using stencils). Discussion of the results with the whole group.

Guiding questions: How are intoxicated women and men judged? Are there differences between the assessments of female and male students? Which factors result in more critical assessments and which tend to mitigate?

Instructional goal: We share our prejudices regarding addicts with the theorists. These prejudices also have gender-specific aspects. Addicted women are usually condemned more severely than addicted men. These activities show the mechanisms and effects of prejudices, and how they control our perceptions and impact our emotions.

Working with statistics and life histories

The object of this activity is the transfer of knowledge. The students should learn how to read and interpret statistics. Before they can do so they must have sufficient knowledge about the compilation of questionnaires, the collection of data, the aggregation of data, and their evaluation as well as – the last and decisive step – the interpretation of the results. These are contrasted to life histories, investigated by qualitative methods, which detail the development of individuals.

Suitable teaching aids: Consumption, abuse and dependence statistics; statistics based on statements by the persons concerned and statistics which are based on so called objective measurements (blood-alcohol values etc.); results of qualitative studies; case histories from counselling practice.

Instructional goal: Introduction to methods of empirical social research; introduction to the interpretation of quantitative and qualitative data; the transfer of knowledge.

Role play: counselling

Two (or more) persons enact a scene at a counselling agency (fish-bowl-setting). Person A has a drug problem and therefore comes to a counselling centre where they meet counsellors. Person B does the counselling. During the interview it becomes clear that person A has been consuming cocaine for some time. Until three months ago they had been able to control consumption quite well. More recently, however, there have been problems. Two weeks ago they started to smoke crack. Since then the problems have been increasing. They don't know what to do and have therefore come to the counselling centre. The counselling interview begins. Duration of the role play: 15 minutes. The audience agree not to interrupt the play and to listen carefully. If there are no interruptions the play is stopped after 15 minutes. Follow-up: Questions to person B: how did they feel as a counsellor, etc.; questions to person A: How did they feel as someone seeking advice. Discussion of the observations of the group.

Prerequisites: table and chairs; volunteers who are willing to engage in the role play.

Instructional goal: Gaining experience with a counselling situation. Discussing the counselling process.

References

Brunner, E. and Franke, A. (1997) *Ess-Störungen*. Hamm.

BMFSFJ (Bundesministerium für Familie, Senioren, Frauen und Jugend) (Ed.). *Verbundprojekt zur gesundheitlichen Situation von Frauen in Deutschland*. Berlin (Publication in Preparation).

Bucher, H. U. (2000) Neugeborene drogenabhängiger Mütter. In: Uchtenhagen, A. and Zieglgängsberger, W. (Eds.) *Suchtmedizin*. Munich, 473–7.

Feuerlein, W. (1984) *Alkoholismus*. Stuttgart.

Franzkowiak, P., Helfferich, C. and Weise, E. (1998) *Geschlechtsbezogene Suchtprävention*. Cologne.

Helfferich, C. (1994) *Jugend, Körper und Geschlecht – Die Suche nach sexueller Identität*. Opladen.

Helmert, U. and Maschewsky-Schneider, U. (1998) Zur Prävalenz des Tabakrauchens bei Arbeitslosen und Armen. In: Henkel, D. (Ed.) *Sucht und Armut*. Opladen, 153–66.

Hoppe, H. (1904) *Die Tatsachen über den Alkohol*. Berlin.

Kolip, P. (1997) *Geschlecht und Gesundheit im Jugendalter*. Opladen.

Kolip, P. (1999) Geschlecht und Gesundheit im Jugendalter: Theoretische Konzeptionen und Gesundheitswissenschaftliche Konsequenzen. In: Röhrle, B. and Sommer, G. (Ed.) *Prävention und Gesundheitsförderung*. Tübingen (DGVT), 221–32.

Krah, K. (1999) *Gebrauch, Missbrauch und Abhängigkeit von psychotropen Medikamenten bei Frauen*. Frankfurt (unpublished).

Kraus, L. and Bauernfeind, R. (1998) Repräsentativerhebung zum Gebrauch psychoaktiver Substanzen bei Erwachsenen in Deutschland 1997. *Sucht. 44*, Special Issue 1.

Leopold, B. (1998) Konsumgewohnheiten und Abhängigkeitsgefahren von Ecstasy bei jungen Frauen. In: Akzept e.V. (Ed.) *The times, they are a-changin'*. Berlin (VWB), 257–72.

Leopold, B. and Steffan, E. *Special needs of children of drug misusers*. Council of Europe, Strassburg.

Maschewsky-Schneider, U. (1997) *Frauen sind anders krank*. Weinheim.

Mattejat, F. and Lisofsky, B. (Eds.) (1998) *Nicht von schlechten Eltern*. Bonn.

Meulenbelt, A., Wevers, A. and van der Ven, C. (1998) *Frauen und Alkohol*. Reinbek.

Miller, W. R. and Rollnick, S. (1999) *Motivierende Gesprächsführung*. Freiburg.

Moggi, F. (1997) Sexuelle Übergriffe in Beratung und Psychotherapie: Grundlagen über einen professionellen Kunstfehler. In: Amann, G. and Wipplinger, R. (Eds.) *Sexueller Missbrauch*. Tübingen (DGVT), 697–712.

Schmid, M., Simmerdinger, R. and Vogt, I. (1999) *Ambulante Suchthilfe in Hamburg*. Statusbericht 1998. Frankfurt (ISS).

Schmidt, B. and Hurrelmann, K. (Eds.) (2000) *Präventive Sucht- und Drogenpolitik*. Opladen.

Steinhausen, H.-C. (2000) Kinder suchtmittelabhängiger Eltern. In: Uchtenhagen, A. and Zieglgängsberger, W. (Eds.) *Suchtmedizin*. Munich, 478–81.

Vertheim, U., Degkwitz, P., Kühne, A. and Krausz, M. (1998) Komorbidität von Opiatabhängigen und psychische Störungen – Ergebnisse einer Verlaufsuntersuchung. *Sucht. 44*, 232–46.

Vogt, I. (1985) *Für alle Leiden gibt es eine Pille*. Opladen.

Vogt, I. (1994) *Alkoholikerinnen*. Freiburg.

Vogt, I. (1996) Drogenabhängige Frauen, Schwangerschaft und Mutterschaft. In: Vogt, I. and Winkler, K. (Eds.) *Beratung süchtiger Frauen*. Freiburg, 92–117.

Vogt, I. (1997) '*Bella Donna*'. Die *Frauendrogenberatungsstelle im Ruhrgebiet*. Berlin.

Vogt, I. (1998a) Frauen, illegale Drogen und Armut: Wiederholungszwänge im Elend. In: Henkel, D. (Ed.) *Sucht und Armut*. Opladen, 191–208.

Vogt, I. (1998b) Geschlechtsspezifische Aspekte von Beratung am Beispiel der Sucht- und Drogenhilfe. *Päd*. Forum 11, 446–550.

Vogt, I., Krah, K. (1998) Klientinnen beurteilen Fraueneinrichtungen. In: Akzept e.V. (Ed.) *The times, they are a-changin'*. Berlin, 97–110.

Vogt, I., Leopold, B., Tödte, M. and Breuker-Gerbig, U. (1998) *Frauen und Sucht*. Düsseldorf.

Wetterling, T. and Veltrup, C. (1997) *Diagnostik und Therapie von Alkoholproblemen*. Berlin.

Weber, W. and Schneider, W. (1992) *Herauswachsen aus der Sucht illegaler Drogen*. Düsseldorf.

Wilde, H. and Spreyermann, C. (1997) *Action, Stoff und Innenleben*. Freiburg.

Winkler, K. (1997) *Zur Behandlung alkoholabhängiger Frauen in Fachkliniken*. Regensburg.

10. The Social Work Profession

Elfriede Fröschl

Introduction

As a profession mainly concerned with the disadvantaged, social work ought to have particularly high standards to safeguard against discrimination within its own ranks. However, this is hardly the case, particularly as regards reflection on gender relations. The following pages undertake to describe the development of the 'social work profession' as a profession which, while consisting mainly of women, has nevertheless always been a profession in which women had very little say.

Currently the trend is to move social services from the control of public authorities; on the one hand by seceding social tasks hitherto undertaken by public services to private societies and on the other hand by expecting citizens to take over certain functions, implicitly expecting women to do them. Social work may increasingly divide into a professionalised and a voluntary sector. The increasing focus on economic aspects further harbours the danger of social work splitting into an 'administrative and managing' branch and one that actually carries out the work. The current structures of gender relationships in social work give us a hint as to who will be found where.

Parallel to these developments there is also the effect of the women's movement which has not only had its impact on the development of the social work profession, but has also exerted a decisive influence on the issues and methods of social work since the 1970s. This influence is one of the main reasons that there is an awareness of gender-hierarchical structures, of the necessity to see social work fields from a gender-specific perspective in order to prevent practical work being performed mainly on the basis of male dominated theories while failing to take the specific life situations of female clients into account. The direction social work will take in its development is as yet undecided.

The following reflections on gender relationships in specific areas of the 'social work profession' are designed to come closer to bringing about gender democracy in social work.

Insights into the history

The origin of social work as a profession is linked to various societal and social change processes which resulted from the gradual dissolution of feudalistic forms of production in the 18th and 19th centuries. This led to two antagonistic opposing tendencies: the release, expulsion and uprooting of workers on the one hand and their inclusion, integration, and control on the other (Schmidbauer, 1994). Release and uprooting led to great poverty, in particular in the cities to which the landless rushed in their search for work.

Correction houses, work houses, and poor houses were established for those who did not have the strength to integrate into the new work processes or who for other reasons had lost their social networks. The poor houses combined elements of welfare, health care, penal procedure, and economic development (Schmidbauer, 1994). The times prior to social work were characterised by aspects of social control and the administration of poverty. Sexuality, violence, disease, mental illness, and death were spheres which were subject to public control. Due to strict role concepts and the rigid moral rules linked to them, women were particularly subject to control. There were a large number of unmarried mothers and former prostitutes in the poor houses. Up to the beginning of the 20th century this form of 'care' on the part of cities and communities was provided and administrated on a volunteer basis by citizens who had the right to vote (Zeller, 1994, p22). These volunteer 'poor bailiffs' were supported by paid male assistants.

Industrialisation, which started in the first half of the 19th century gave rise to the division of labour by sex and location, on the basis of the model of the bourgeois nuclear family according to which the man provides for the family through his work outside the house, whereas the woman takes care of the house and the children and 'makes the house a home'. The ideological underpinning for this model was the biological difference of the sexes. It was said that a woman was destined 'by nature' to have children and care for them, whereas it was the task of a man to work in the outside world. This model corresponded, however, primarily to the situation in the rich upper classes. Working class women nearly always had to work outside the home, which, however, provided them at least with a minimum income of their own, in contrast to women of the bourgeoisie. The poverty of the lower classes provided the ladies of the higher classes with an opportunity to do good deeds. 'Slumming' for instance meant that aristocratic or bourgeois women tried to mitigate the misery in the poor quarters of English (but not only English) cities through charity (Fox-Wallner, 1994, p14). Such activities provided the only acceptable opportunity for upper class women to engage in a meaningful occupation outside the home.

The main concern of the bourgeois women's movement which developed in the second half of the 19th century was, in addition to women's suffrage and the access of women to higher education, fighting for spheres of activity in society for women. The key concept used in this context was 'spiritual motherhood', which was an ingenious way of taking up the bourgeois biological concept of motherhood and using it to expand in an acceptable way the female sphere of activity which permitted them to undertake activities outside the home. The term 'Geistige Mütterlichkeit' ('spiritual motherhood') was coined by Henriette Schrader-Breymann and means in principle that men and women are different, but that 'female' and 'male' qualities complement each other and are therefore both equally necessary for a well functioning society. 'In total conformity with idealistic gender philosophy the ideal of spiritual motherhood permits even women who strive to cast off the shackles of bourgeois marriage, to live a woman's life and enjoy recognition. It prepares the ground for the public and at the same time 'respectable' appearance and activity permitted to women.' (Simmel-Joachim,

1990, p44). The concept of 'spiritual motherhood' may therefore, particularly in retrospect, be interpreted as a strategy which combines adaptation to ascribed roles with the simultaneous resistance against them. The concept of 'resistance', however, may be questioned: the patriarchal division into 'good' and 'bad' mothers is retained, by having the 'good' caring for the 'bad'. And, after all, this is a concept devised by women of 'pure soul and kind spirit' (Simmel-Joachim, 1990, p45). In view of current tendencies towards returning social work to the family (i.e. to women) this foundation of the profession is becoming an unwanted heritage.

In spite of all this the expansion of female activities outside the domestic world resulted in a leap forward in terms of emancipation and proved to be a great attraction to women who strove for a less conventional life. Many women who felt a part of the women's movement had an impact on social work. In 1892 Jeanette Schwerin founded the 'Deutsche Gesellschaft für ethische Kultur' (German Society for Ethical Culture) in Germany which advocated a reform of the care for the poor (Zeller, 1994, p33). In 1893 she was on the founding committee of the Berlin 'Mädchen und Frauengruppen für soziale Hilfsarbeit' (Girls' and Women's Group for Charitable Works) whose public appeal to 'upper class' daughters to do volunteer charitable work was followed by many young women, among them by Alice Salomon. In 1899 Jeanette Schwerin initiated a 'Jahreskurs zur beruflichen Ausbildung in der Wohlfahrtspflege' (a one year course for professional training in welfare work) and after her death the same year Alice Salomon took over the coordination of this course which eventually developed into the first two-year 'Soziale Frauenschule' (Social School for Women) in Germany, founded in 1908. The objectivating of these schools was to systematise the competencies and skills required for welfare work and make them 'learnable', i.e. professionalised. 'The social schools for women were targeted at socially interested women and developed their own definition of a profession, which was different from the concept of bureaucratic social administration in a system of law and order'

(German original: Puch 1994, 31). The teaching contents were designed to be practice-oriented (in contrast to universities) and the training was focused on personal values, attitudes, and ideology, since Alice Salomon, in particular, was convinced that social work was a vocation requiring specific personal qualities (see Zeller, 1994). A main point of criticism regarding this type of training, which was meant to be a combination of professional and social character education, was the fact that it was oriented towards an image of women based on ideology (see, for instance, Berndt, 1999, p27). 'This ideological value orientation, however, was balanced and rectified in the curriculum by the objectivity influence of scientific findings, derived from traditional university disciplines (national economy, medicine, and sociology)' (German original: Puch, 1994, p31).

In parallel to these developments the above mentioned 'welfare bureaucracy' developed further at the beginning of the 20th century – with men in the leading positions whereas the grassroots work was done by the graduates of the social schools for women, who had virtually no decision-making powers with regard to the allocation of financial resources.

The fields of practice were mainly 'respectability' and the supervision of women: target groups of the 'services' were in particular: unmarried mothers, women in need, and prostitutes. Many authors point to the contradictory attitudes in a society, which could not be counterbalanced by idealistic, active women who met the moral requirements of society: 'the 'idealistic representation of the role of women' was coupled to the 'legal and social discrimination' of women, especially unmarried mothers.' (German original: Berndt, 1999. p27).

After the First World War, in the course of general social reforms social welfare became more and more the concern of government. Voluntary charitable work for the poor lost its importance.

At the same time some demands of the women's movement were met in many countries, women's suffrage for example, and access to the universities and to most professions. Women, however, continued to work mainly in the social sector. A minimal pay was introduced for this type of work, as

opposed to the former voluntary work, as it was becoming obvious that the growing demand and the legal provisions for a reformed modern welfare system, in particular child and youth welfare, could no longer be met with volunteers alone. In Vienna, for instance, up to the year 1913 welfare services for infants and toddlers were only provided by volunteer workers with hardly any training. It was repeatedly pointed out that there was no guarantee for continuity in this work since ... volunteer workers in conflict between the needs of their families and the needs of their clients had to decide in favour of their families, whereas professionals had to decide in favour of their clients. Even the most committed volunteer worker will, and must, care for her own child in the case of a mass epidemic ... the professional civil servant will have to fulfil her duty first.' (Arlt, quoted in the German original: Mittermeier, 1994. p108). Even so the division between men in the administration and in government offices with little professional knowledge of social problems and women working in the field with poor working conditions, low pay and little or no decision-making power still prevailed. This separation resulted in the division of professional procedures which essentially belonged together. 'They [the female welfare workers *Ed. note*] had no power to decide on the type, the volume of services, and the amount of the welfare benefits applied for. The welfare workers remained investigators and recorders of mass poverty' (German original: Zeller, 1994, p114).

Whereas professional social work in Austria and in Germany developed mainly from charitable 'casework' the so-called 'Settlement Movement' which began in England around 1880 was decisive for the approach to social work taken in the Anglo-Saxon countries. It developed from the attempt to promote contacts between rich and poor, with the rich going to the slums and doing charitable work in the community. 'The activities were manifold: caring for infants and toddlers, working with children and adolescents, working with women and families, working with offenders, providing recreational services for children and adults, providing educational and club facilities; there was hardly any field of social work practice which was not represented there.' (German original: Sachße, 1994, p123). This movement spread quickly to the United States, where it involved mainly working with poor immigrants. In 1889 the famous Hull-House was opened in Chicago by Jane Addams and Ellen Star. The main difference between England and the United States was that the Settlement Movement in England was primarily the work of young Protestant men, whereas in the United States the work was predominantly done by young women with a college education, which meant that in the US the religious element was less dominant than in England.

It appears that female social workers in the US had, independently of the Settlement Movement, tried at a very early stage (1930) to go a 'more political' way than their European colleagues. 'In Chicago ... there was the strongest and most explicit tendency to consider social work primarily as the organisation of social reform. However from the very beginning, supporters of individual casework had also paid serious attention to the problems involved. Richmond claimed that the knowledge and expertise of caseworkers should be the basis of any social legislation.' (Waaldijk [no year given], p336). These were early attempts to overcome the separation of administration and legislation, which were in male hands, and the practice fields given to women, as was the situation in Germany and Austria described above.

The Settlement Movement as well as the scientific writings of Mary Richmond who had systematised and further developed the methods of 'casework' exerted a great influence on Germany and in particular on Alice Salomon through her international contacts. Alice Salomon was particularly concerned with the further development of the social work profession and towards this goal wrote text books for training purposes and in 1925 founded a 'Deutsche Akademie für soziale und pädagogische Frauenarbeit' (German Academy for Social and Pedagogical Work for Women) to provide additional education for female welfare workers.

In Germany and in Austria this development was interrupted by the rise of National Socialism. Political and racial persecution forced many of the most creative women working in the social field, among them Alice Salomon, to leave Germany.

'National Socialism reduced *ad absurdum* the principle of motherhood, according to which women are *a priori* responsible for humaneness. Women took an active part in the extermination machinery of the Third Reich, often in their capacity as welfare workers. On the other hand motherhood in its biological sense serving the "preservation and reproduction of Arian genetic heritage" is recognised by the awarding of the "Mutterverdienstkreuz" (Order of Motherhood).' (German original: Fox-Wallner, 1994, p20). The most important basis for Nazi 'Welfare' was the concept of 'Rassenhygiene' (racial hygiene). Desirable persons were to be supported, undesirable ones annihilated, a process in which female welfare workers also participated, mainly through investigations in homes. The theory according to which certain character traits are inborn and inherited makes any form of resocialisation unnecessary. A clear distinction is made between desirable 'families rich in children' and undesirable 'asocial large families'. Female welfare workers were mainly employed as investigators of an inhuman regime. Karin Windaus-Walser writes about social work under National Socialism: 'Womanhood was by no means the stronghold of humaneness ... the gender as such had proven to be without any quality, as an invariable of human existence without any influence on the resistance against barbarity.' (German original: Windaus-Walser, 1991, quoted in Meinhold, 1993, p73). The behaviour of the greatest part of female welfare workers under National Socialism shows that the concept of 'spiritual motherhood' which was the basis of the profession did not provide a source for resistance under extreme conditions. On the contrary, the research available to date on the behaviour of the 'Volkspflegerinnen' (People's Carers) shows that their adjustment was fast and smooth despite (or because of) the 'high moral standards' provided during training. (see German original Berndt, 1999).

After the Second World War welfare work training became accessible to men in most European countries. This, however, had no impact on the fact that there were virtually only women in social work, that this work was poorly paid, and had little societal impact.

The political phase

A change in this situation occurred during the socio-political discussions of the sixties and the seventies, when sociological theories were increasingly used to explain the causes of social problems. Societal frameworks and the resulting social inequalities were seen as the main factors in the origin of social problems. A logical consequence was that the methods had to change; community work or political work aiming at changing society became the focus of the predominantly theoretical discussion (but not so much in social work practice).

'In the seventies approaches to solutions for social problems were oriented towards social criticism. ... Social work was supposed to be political work and was to develop into a strategy which should make it possible for marginalised groups to gain a place in society and thus undermine the foundations of the system which rest on extreme inequality' (German original, Brückner, 1992, p7). In those years criticism of traditional (social work) institutions gave rise to many new projects, such as women's refuges, living units for adolescents, non-residential projects for psychiatric patients etc. Changes also occurred in existing organisational structures and in social work methods. Training for the social work profession was extended to include new fields of practice. (For Austria see Simon, 1995). Status and pay levels increased, which resulted in a higher percentage of men in the field (see also Brückner, 1992), with these men striving for a further increase in status. In those years men, step by step, took over the posts of directors of Akademien für Sozialarbeit (Schools of Social Work) which up until then had been held almost exclusively by women. In 1976 five of eight directors were women, three were men. In 1993 there were eight male directors and only one woman, and this one remaining woman was only a 'programme director' which meant that she was in fact only the deputy of a male director. In 1998 the ratio was seven men to two women (including the above-mentioned 'programme director')

(Schauer 1994). 'From the 1970s on more and more men became social workers which gave rise to the so-called debate on professionalisation. Men 'naturally' wanted an upwards evaluation of their work, which should become visible in the form of better pay and a higher status for the profession.' (German original, Glaser, 1998, p252).

At the same time the new women's movement gave rise to a discussion on the position of female clients in social work. Women-specific approaches were developed for many fields, some problems were virtually 'discovered' by feminists and brought to the awareness of society through persistent campaigning, in particular the subjects 'violence against women in families' and 'sexual abuse'. Women were mainly seen as 'victims' of a patriarchal system and as morally virtuous. This view of women was originally important in order to raise awareness of their disadvantaged position in society but eventually it caused women to be tied to their traditional roles and added support to the continued polarisation of gender relationships (see the concept of 'spiritual motherhood'). This perspective in some cases had the (then unintended) side effect that moral expectations were higher with regard to women than with regard to men.

The therapeutic phase of the 1980s

The social work context of the eighties saw a shift from sociological explanations of social problems towards psychotherapeutic concepts.

'Now a new start, for one self and for the clients, appeared to depend to a great extent on working up one's own biography, as well as personal difficulties and the suffered grievances.' (German original, Brückner, 1992, p8). It became difficult to find employment as a social worker without additional qualifications as a therapist. This shift in focus is assumed to stem from the decrease in material resources. It is true that during the eighties significant budget cuts were made in many countries affecting in particular the social sector. Social work therefore had virtually no choice but to make this shift from material support to other services.

As in many other contexts this development of social work is ambivalent: on the one hand training as therapists has always been important for professionalisation and to strengthen the reflective skills of social workers, with regard to interaction with clients as well as with colleagues, and is equally important to address the clients' self-responsibility. On the other hand, however, focussing on biographies may lead to individualising social problems.

The decade of the 1980s also saw the further development of feminist institutions as well as the origin of theories on feminist counselling, group work with women, political work, etc. Women's 'own share' in their disadvantaged situation became an issue. In this phase, very few projects for men developed, which for the first time addressed the (social) problems men have because of their gender role. Less attention was devoted however to men who cause problems because of their traditional gender role (e.g. violent men). On the contrary: male clients are allowed a much higher amount of resistance, refusal, and aggression than female clients (see Burden and Gotlieb, 1987).

The management phase of the 1990s

The so-called management phase of the nineties is characterised by 'the recognition that every institution must provide for its own support or survival and in doing so must prove its efficiency' (German original, Brückner, 1992, p9). The dominant concerns are the integration of economic issues into social work, the planning of processes, the professionalisation of the representation of social organisations in public, and the documentation of supportive auxiliary processes. All these measures are to serve quality assurance. Documentation serves not only for the reflection of the helping process but also as proof for those providing the funding that the financial resources have been used as efficiently and economically as possible. Quality in this context is not only seen as the product of professionalism but also as the result of an interactive process of adjustment between the social organisation, the clients, and the public and private providers.

In addition to political and societal conditions this process depends on the organisational skills of the organisation in question, developing and improving these skills is the objective of social management training.

Badelt (1991) in a paper presented at a meeting on social management listed commonalities between economic and social organisations. In his opinion the main differences lie in the difficulty of measuring the 'successes of social work and in the low societal status of the clients and of social work itself. As social work is mainly a woman's profession, the link to housework and housewives seems logical: this work too, is hard to measure and of low esteem. Although professionalised sectors of housework, e.g. chefs de cuisine, or pedagogical experts, enjoy high esteem, this does not improve the status of housewives and mothers. Social management could therefore be seen as an attempt to revalue the often obscure relationship-oriented work carried out by social workers by applying market-oriented concepts, which could also benefit the women working in this profession. At the same time, however, social work could increasingly develop an even stronger tendency to be split into an administrative and a practical sector.

It appears important to ask for a definition of the 'success criteria'. Will the presence of women at all hierarchical levels, the development of women-specific approaches in social work practice, be defined as 'quality' and 'success'? The question whether women in social work will gain the power of definition through social management or lose it (even more) has not been answered. There are hardly any publications which make the gender aspect an issue or take a self-reflective view of it (according to the experience of the author during research and classroom work). There are however many pessimistic outlooks: although women in their traditional sphere (household and child care) fulfil several management functions, management and leadership are concepts rather associated with 'male' qualities. In social work too, men usually very soon aspire to management positions. (see Glaser, 1998; Cree, 1996, see also Chapter: Gender Hierarchy in Social Work). Training should therefore specifically teach women aspects of management and leadership, since there might be a danger of 'social work developing into a male profession in which women perhaps will not even have a chance in the lower ranks.' (German original, Rabe-Kleeberg, 1992, quoted in Glaser, 1998, p163). Relationship work could more and more be shifted to the volunteer sector, according to the slogan 'unpaid work is priceless' (German original: Notz 1990). There are therefore critical voices which call for the increased (re)integration of ethical and political issues into social work. 'It is for these reasons that it appears to be vitally significant to complement this concept of 'trainability' (i.e. within the framework of social management; note by the author) through retaining political analysis and the appreciation of a self-reflective psycho-social competence.' (German original, Brückner, 1992, p14). Brigitte Sellach in a paper on quality assurance in women's refuges points out similar issues: 'Quality of social work in women's refuges is not neutral, but must meet the demand of individually and collectively enforcing women's rights to their physical integrity as a human right.' (German original, Sellach, 1995, p1). The neutral concept 'quality' is therefore clearly determined by value concepts which are related to the power of definition. The question will therefore be: which values will persevere, which 'quality' will be recognised.

Social work as a human rights profession

There has been a continuous increase in the professional, ethical and political perspective of social work as a human rights profession, perhaps as a counter-movement to the rather pragmatic market orientation of social management (Staub-Bernasconi, 1993). This could be interpreted such that 'the profession has moved on from dealing with the morals of the clients in the late 19th century to the current issues of ethical dilemma, ethical decision-making, and ethical risk management' (German original, Reamer, 1999, p137). Social workers are seen as advocates of their clients, whom they support in enforcing their human rights. Issues of discrimination through social work itself and the ensuing ethical questions are also gaining increased attention.

Although these human rights have been criticised as being Eurocentric, individualistic, and androcentric, they are still an important source of argumentation aids for women when it comes to fighting politically to achieve their causes. The women's movement used the Charter at a relatively early point in time to draw attention to the violation of the human rights of women (e.g., the slogan 'Women's Rights are Human Rights'). Feminist social workers often refer to human rights when they deal with 'typically' female discrimination or violence against their female clients. Sylvia Staub-Bernasconi considers human and social rights issues to be very closely linked to the theoretical traditions of social work of the early 20th century. She sees a refusal to open social work to socio-political aspects in the German speaking countries only as a later aspect (Staub-Bernasconi, 1993; Waaldijk, [no year given]). The human rights orientation gives the social work profession the opportunity to orient itself more to the needs of people and to work politically for the enforcement of their rights. This corresponds to the expectations social workers have of their profession; they wish primarily to support persons who are deprived of their rights (see also Müller, 1999, p18). Staub-Bernasconi sees the orientation towards human rights as an opportunity to arrive at a professionalisation of social work through 'the capability of assigning oneself self-determined tasks' (German original, Staub-Bernasconi, 1993, p322). She sees the mandate of professional social work as follows:

- *To draw attention on the basis of scientific research to the conditions and consequences of unfulfilled needs.*
- *To turn privatised needs wherever possible together with the addressees into public issues.*
- *To trigger off individual and collective assessment processes in connection with unanswered needs, which are oriented along the concept of universal needs and corresponding universal values.*
  (German original, Staub-Bernasconi, 1993, p323)

The method used for the enforcement of human rights for clients is the method of empowerment, which basically aims to expand the scope of thinking and acting and builds on the clients' strengths rather than on their deficits. This approach has proven particularly helpful in working with women since expanding the scope of thinking and acting means to work actively against the restrictions imposed by traditional gender roles and against every other form of discrimination.

The United Nations and also some social workers' organisations in the United States suggest in a manual, which was published in 1992, making human rights issues a larger part of social work training (Wronka, 1999, p197; United Nations, 1992). On the subject of gender discrimination the Manual provides the following suggestions with regard to implementation: 'Possibilities for action by social workers in promoting gender-equitable legislation and in raising awareness of gender-related issues could be described and studied. Other avenues could be work with self-help groups, women's groups and others.' (United Nations, 1992, p54). The United Nations list a number of social problems which women and girls have because of their gender and explain why the majority of social work clients are women:

- Inequality in the eyes of the law or established custom.
- Inequality in education, work, property inheritance.
- Women as heads of families, poverty.
- Discrimination and sexism.

One further point should be added here:

- Women affected by violence.

One of the tasks of social work is its fight against the discrimination of women: 'As a predominantly female profession, social workers have great potential for women's consciousness and development. They are especially well placed to impact knowledge of rights to women, though they are aware that this may lead to an increase of their women client's conflicts with their men. Research is an important tool for the advancement of women, and one which social work profession is well equipped to undertake. For positive and concerted action, social workers should link up with women' s non-governmental organisations at the local, national and international levels, not least to keep women's issues before governments at every level.' (United Nations, 1992, p65).

Applying human rights principles to the social work profession as such would make numerous forms of discrimination visible. The number of members of ethnic minorities, for instance, qualifying for the profession fails by far to correspond to the percentage of these minorities in the number of clients in the individual fields of social work practice. The same is true for social workers who are physically challenged. After all, this imbalance constitutes an obstacle to empowerment work with the client groups in question; but it is a separate subject the discussion of which would go far beyond the framework of this chapter.

The outline of the history of social work shows clearly that, from a gender perspective, social work is a female profession under male control and that men have had decisive influence either through their positions in administration, science, and politics or, since the 1970s, in social work itself. In many social work programmes (with the exception of special agencies for women) and training institutions they hold far more leading positions than would correspond to their actual numbers in social work (for Austria see: Gruber and Schmidbauer, 1991). They have therefore been the ones who have primarily shaped theory development and the analysis of social problems, and thus have the power of defining social problems and training contents. Nevertheless women who work in self-determined settings have succeeded in acquiring theories and methods, in redefining or developing them, and in fighting for their cause through lobbying and public relations and thus have contributed significantly to the professionalisation of social work, though often not in the limelight.

Professional motivations of women and men

The image of a profession is shaped by the professional motivations of those who choose this profession – on the other hand assumptions and expectations with regard to a profession also shape professional motivation. The following section describes two studies on gender-specific differences.

According to a survey in Scotland the following motives are of paramount importance for choosing social work as a profession: 'Caring for others came much higher up the agenda for these largely middle-class women than other concerns such as financial remuneration or career advancement' (Cree, 1996, p66). Carol Gilligan in her model of the moral development of women also found that women were more drawn to other human beings than men (Gilligan, 1982). In order to verify these theories and results Vivienne Cree carried out research with the purpose of finding out more about the link between 'caring' and the professional motives of women and men. The central question was: 'Assuming that women choose to become social workers because caring is somehow central to their sense of self, why do men choose to become social workers?' (Cree, 1996, p67). The study was carried out in 1993/94. At that time of all students in Scotland who started social work training 29 per cent were men (137) and 71 per cent were women (334). 17 of these men and 18 women were interviewed; in addition questionnaires were evaluated.

Most respondents chose the profession as adults; hardly anyone had heard anything about social work before that time. Many therefore had working experience in other fields, however with clear differences between men and women. While women had mainly worked in jobs which permitted a reconciliation of family and employment or had done only traditional reproductive work, men had worked in many different fields. Their reason for a change of occupation was their wish for more autonomy or for career development. Women often chose the social work profession after a phase during which they had been taking care of their children and the household. A clear motive was independence through a profession combined with the knowledge that social work mainly dealt with issues which women already had experience in – namely relationship work. Men and women alike chose the profession more for professional factors (responsibility, variety etc.) than for salary and career opportunities.

Other studies which investigated family background and its influence on the choice of profession to a greater extent concluded that men who choose professional settings dominated by women often come from non-traditional families (lone parents), whereas women who choose male dominated professions more often came from traditional families with close ties to father and mother (Lemkau, 1984; Chusmir, 1983, quoted in Cree, 1996).

Hardly any gender-specific differences were noted with regard to the main contents of social work, but there were differences with regard to the personal career opportunity expectations of the respondents. All men assumed that they would be promoted faster than their female colleagues, but they also described additional advantages of their gender in social work 'Because social work is not considered a male profession, it's as if there's not a protocol which is expected of you ... you are open, freer as a man ... there are not so many expectations of you.' (Cree, 1996, p80). Another study reinforces these findings '... qualities associated with men are more highly regarded than those associated with women, even in predominantly female jobs ... This fact reflects a widespread cultural prejudice that men are simply better than women.' (Williams, 1993 quoted in Cree, 1996, p80). Cree comes to the conclusion that most respondents do not see social work as a female profession. 'This means that men in social work, while enjoying the advantages of being male in a non-traditional environment (better promotion and more autonomy), experience fewer difficulties than men in other women's settings such as nursing' (Cree, 1996, p81).

The author concludes that in spite of similar family backgrounds of men and women there are great differences with regard to the motives for choosing social work as a profession. Men who want to become social workers consider themselves different and are convinced that they have qualities which are not seen as typically male. They thus see themselves as something special. They enter the profession in the conviction that they will climb the career ladder. Women by contrast enter a profession which expects qualities which are seen as typically female. They do not consider themselves exceptional or unconventional. They are aware that their career opportunities are not as good as those of men.

The author's conclusion is therefore: one should avoid praising men for their social skills while taking the same skills in women for granted. 'Another area which demands urgent attention is the reappraisal of the 'feminine' side of social work. Social work practice is rapidly becoming more technical, more bureaucratic, more 'masculine' in style, whether carried out by men or by women, and my research has shown that it is the personal, caring, 'feminine' aspects of social work which both women and men social work students see as most worthwhile.' (Cree, 1996, p84).

In a study which was mainly geared to the professional motivation of female social workers Birgit Rommelspacher (1992) came to the conclusion that women stay close to their familiar immediate social environment when they choose the profession: 'Frauen kommen nicht weit weg von zu Hause' (women don't get far from home) (Rommelspacher, 1992, p138, see also Cree, 1996). The closeness between social work and reproductive work is pointed out in many publications, just as the 'need' of women to care for others, which is based on gender-specific socialisation. Thus one of the most important sources of power for women is their power of relationship (Rommelspacher, 1999). It is striking that none of the respondents aspired to professional success and career. Their main aspirations were the wish for horizontal development and diverse facets of this field of work. This is probably linked to a lack of role-models. There are not many women in social work who have had great careers.

Despite the parallels between private and professional helping there are important differences which constitute sources of power for women: 'Professional relationship work offers an opportunity to make publicly known how much time, knowledge and skill is required and that relationship work cannot be done on the side, automatically, or even instinctively.' (German original, Rommelspacher, 1986, quoted in Glaser, 1998, p253). Another difference lies in the power of controlling and sanctioning (Rommelspacher, 1992, p191) which comes with the professional position and not 'only' the precarious relationship power derived from private relationships. Female social workers are also far more insecure than male social workers – 'if relationship work at home isn't worth anything at home why should it be in

a job?' (German original: Rommelspacher, 1992, p192). This could be one of the reasons why female social workers strive less for higher salaries or more prestige for the profession than their male colleagues. Unlike men, women sometimes choose a traditionally female profession because they do not feel confident enough to do 'more', i.e. enter a 'male' profession. 'The interviews have shown how highly suspicious women are of the criteria of professionalisation and how bad they feel in positions which separate them from the real lives of their clients' (German original, Rommelspacher, 1992, p193). Many women are aware of the ambiguous character of professionalisation, since relationships with people can never be equated to other services and social work is most successful in relationship work. There is a danger however that this work is being pushed further and further down the hierarchical ladder. There, however, we are faced with the central contradiction of 'wishing to help others but being powerless ourselves' (German original, Rommelspacher, 1992, p195). On the other hand it is important to cope with desires for power which develop particularly easily when working with dependent and underprivileged persons and harbour the danger of the abuse of power.

Many women however choose the social work professions for reasons of self-actualisation and to give meaning to their lives. 'Since social work is a world full of diverse professional landscapes, glossy expectations of competence and manifold chances of identification, it appears to be the ideal projection field for multiple expectations. The attraction of social work to today's women is not that it is a traditional female profession but that it permits the projection of all sorts of hopes. This carries risks and promises alike.' (German original, Heinemeier, 1994, p214). The choice of social work as a profession remains an ambivalent decision for women: on the one hand it is a 'typical' female profession and on the other hand it is a diverse, meaningful profession. Both motives were already present in the earliest social workers: helping others as the only opportunity for a woman to work outside the home and at the same time self-actualisation and emancipation.

The gender-hierarchical structure of social work

At first sight one cannot help noticing that very few publications are devoted to gender relationships in social work. One of the first was a survey by Hans Drake (1980) who found that 'It appears as if women in social work do not feel discriminated against professionally because of their gender. Investigations however have shown that they are at a disadvantage compared to their male colleagues: with regard to pay, career opportunities, and actual exclusion from certain professional functions'. (German original, Drake, 1980, p46).

On the labour market women are, as a matter of principle, seen as taking on a professional as well as a gender role and very often presumptions become the reason for women missing out on a career 'Since they prefer working with people they remain on the lowest hierarchical level, in contact with customers, patients, clients, and children; since they prefer getting along well with their colleagues they shy away from competition for higher or leading positions; since they anticipate the interruption of their career they do not seek to improve their qualifications; since they tend to personalise their relationship with their supervisors they choose individual career strategies or choose to do without them in the interest of keeping up a good relationship.' (German original, Rabe-Kleberg, quoted in Bader et al., 1990, p30).

These factors, which are certainly true for some women, are however projected on all women, no matter whether this is their orientation, and whether they plan to have children or not. They are considered to be only partially available in the labour market and the same appears to be true in social work. An Austrian study in 1991 (Gruber and Schmidbauer) investigated fields of social work in which men and women worked examining factors such as remuneration and access to managerial positions on the basis of social work graduates between the years 1976 and 1986. According to this study women work predominantly (43%) in the field 'Children, Youth and Family' (only 17% of the men work in this field). The predominantly male field is 'Probation and Offenders', in which 32% of the male but only 4% of the female graduates were found. Women earn significantly less than men, which stems partly from shorter weekly hours of work. Statistics however show that 'remuneration is gender-related, whereas weekly working hours are not gender-specifically different, and that there is a link between workload and pay.' (German original, Gruber, 1995, p120). Women are found less often in leading positions than men (eight per cent of women and 19 per cent of men). If the category 'partly in a leading position' is included, the share of women increases to one fifth and that of men to one third. (Gruber, 1995, p121). Further results of this study were: women cannot delegate clerical work as often as men and acquiring higher qualifications does not result in expanded responsibilities. A German study in 1991 analysed all youth welfare offices in the German federal state, the Rhineland: in Germany 69 per cent of social workers are women. At the lowest level of the youth welfare offices 69 per cent of the workers are women and 31 per cent men. In middle management (group leaders) 50% are women and 50% men, while at the next higher level 66% of the positions are held by men and only 34% by women. These results are not only the result of the often quoted female 'fear of success', or women's fear of loss of affection (e.g. from a team). In the investigation carried out by Marianne Meinhold (1993) 56 per cent of the female social workers she interviewed said that they would apply for a higher position. Two thirds of them believed that they would meet with greater recognition after promotion and that their relationships with their colleagues would not deteriorate. The greatest obstacles for women with regard to applying for leading positions, in addition to the well-known sexist barriers, are definitely also the high expectations placed on a woman to do everything 'better' in such a position, as described by Brückner (1992) and also mentioned by Meinhold (1993). 'As a greater number of women rise to leading positions there will be an increased awareness of the multitude of different competencies and deficits among individual female managers, as has always been the case with male managers

(German original, Meinhold, 1993, p77). The author takes a critical view towards 'female' orientation: 'All investigations which place particular emphasis on the skills of women as therapists should be looked at with some reservation, if they indifferently refer to 'women' and if they neglect interactive aspects: for instance the expectations of clients. What appears to be true is that most women are more experienced and successful at establishing and maintaining interpersonal contacts, than men are said to be.' (German original, Meinhold, 1993, p58).

Interpersonal relations, in particular those with men, very often constitute an obstacle to the careers of women, and this is also true for social work: 'A study carried out in the United States is of interest in this respect. It shows that in 'dual-career families' (in the field of social work; *author's remark*) it takes usually only a few years until women, having identical starting positions, lose in status and that for female social workers living together with a partner is a greater obstacle to their careers than caring for their children.' (Stacey, 1986, quoted in the German original, Rommelspacher, 1992, p185).

The effects of the gender-hierarchical structure are manifold. There are remarkable deficits with regard to gender-specific services in particular in larger social agencies. According to investigations by students in Vienna in 1998 there were no women specific programmes in the field of 'illicit drugs' and many other women specific programmes are not sufficiently funded. The situation is different in some Western European countries but social work publications, show that gender-specific issues are only dealt with in a rather marginalised manner. The relatively new book *Soziale Arbeit in Europa* (Puhl, Ria and Maas, 1997), for example, contains no gender-specific aspects. On the whole only female authors of social work literature mention the 'gender factor', if it is mentioned at all. 'There are hardly any institutionalised women specific programmes. Social work agencies are all somehow gender neutral. Male decision-makers don't care about the fact that being a woman results in specific problems in all aspects of society.' (Homm, 1994, quoted in German, Gruber, 1995, p123). Among the gender neutral services we very often find programmes which are tailored to the male biography without however explicitly referring to the 'male' factor. In the 'Children/Family' sector, where many 'general' services implicitly address only women (the fact that the counselling centres for mothers at youth and family welfare offices in Austria were renamed 'Counselling Centres for Parents' a few years ago does not make much difference) it is exactly the other way round, which obscures who does the work involved in caring for children.

There are only a very small number of social work programmes which assist and support women on the labour market, compared to the range of services addressing women in their function as mothers. Many social work services must therefore be seen as rather traditional in their gender role orientation.

The gender hierarchy also has an effect on the image of women held by clients: 'This gender hierarchy prevents any emancipatory features of social work. Female clients see female social workers in subordinate roles. This conveys, to female as well as to male clients, the notion that women are simply subordinate,' (Homm, 1994, quoted in German, Gruber, 1995, p123). Since many social problems stem from traditional role concepts, this situation certainly is not conducive to prevention.

Conclusions

Women's professions in the social field depend specifically on socio-political definitions. They define which aspects of reproductive work are to be done by women in an employed capacity and which is to be done in the private sphere. Furthermore, female professions are much affected – much more than most male professions – by cyclical and ideological changes.

(German original, Schmidbauer, 1994, p30)

The crucial question is, whether female social workers will be able to overcome their heritage of 'spiritual motherhood', since otherwise the proximity to (unpaid) reproductive work will repeatedly trigger the debate on whether social work is a profession or voluntary charitable work. The tendency towards social management is certainly a further step towards greater professionalisation. Whether women will be able to participate in this development or whether they will be pushed to the (then even more) controlled sidelines of relationship work is unclear. Social work should, also where it is taught and where it is the subject of research, be made a truly female profession (see also Schmidbauer, 1994). Specific plans for the advancement of women or an increased reflection on social management from a gender-specific point of view are still lacking. The concept of 'advancement of women' is highly controversial, since it could be understood in the way that women require special assistance to establish them in the employment market. As part of an overall policy of gender equality this concept, however, means much more: 'The instruments for the advancement of women – institutions for gender equality, advancement programmes, legal provisions, should serve to reduce the structural disadvantages women face. In this respect the advancement of women is a political issue.' (German original, Meinhold, 1993, p78) It can contribute to gender democracy in social work. Experts agree that the advancement of women should include the following criteria:

- Job advertisements: women should feel directly addressed.
- Hiring procedures: women should be given preference until they are proportionally represented at all levels of the profession (performance-related quotas).
- Training and continued education should be organised in a women-friendly way – near their place of residence or with child care facilities; women's or gender-specific topics should be offered. Gender-specific aspects should be integrated into all subjects taught.
- Reconciliation of family and employment: this includes special leave arrangements and part-time work, also for higher positions (see Meinhold, 1993).

One disadvantage of measures for the advancement of women is the lack of sanctions in case of non-compliance with a given measure. In social work there would, however, be enough opportunities, in particular on the part of the funding bodies to exert their influence. Programmes for the advancement of women should, if possible, be developed by the agencies and training institutions themselves. 'The polemic arguments against performance-related quotas hide the fact that there have always been 'quotas' in force (mainly to the detriment of women) either quotas for political parties, or some other non-transparent rules.' (German original, Meinhold, 1993, p82)

On the whole it appears to be important for the future of the profession to put greater emphasis on 'gender' as a central structuring category, not only with regard to interaction with clients but also with regard to the segregation of professional fields and career opportunities of female social workers.

Audrey Mullender lists five central spheres in which 'gender' should be integrated into social work:

- *Gender must be on the agenda in all matters relating to the organisation and practice of social work.*
- *Women have traditionally been discriminated against in society and its institutions, including social work.*
- *Women's needs and experiences of life are different from men's.*
- *Groups and organisations established by women for women and run to women's agendas are the best means of empowering women.*
- *Men, too, both as professionals and as service users, need to be challenged to rethink their traditional roles and assumptions.*

(Mullender, 1997, p43)

Although women have laid the foundations of the professionalisation of social work and have always played a decisive role in its development, this has not brought them leading positions and the power of definition. The women's movement has succeeded in 'occupying' important approaches and issues in social work, which have now become widely recognised. 'Nevertheless it would be desirable for female social workers to develop greater ''income consciousness''. This would mean, among others, to bring ''hidden'' qualifications in the professional profile into the limelight and to free themselves from the heritage of spiritual motherhood.' (German original, Schmidbauer, 1994, p31). A crucial question will be the extent to which social work will succeed in overcoming the often gender-specific dichotomies described above, between theory and practice, between emphatic helping and the rational analysing of the causes of social problems and to achieve gender democracy in the social work profession.

Didactic assignment: Sexism in social work agencies. (This exercise was developed in cooperation with Rosa Logar.)

Method

Group work, discussion, theoretical input.

Duration

30 minutes.

Assignment

Recall a situation during your practicum or during training in which you experienced or observed discrimination based on gender.

Questions

What was the nature of the discrimination?
How did you feel?
What did you do?
What would you have liked to change? What would be needed to bring about this change?
Report to the whole group, discussion, theoretical input on strategies against sexism

Exercise: Discrimination in social work

This exercise was developed in cooperation with Rosa Logar.

Objective

Raising awareness of specific discriminations experienced by certain client groups.

Equipment

Flipchart, pens.

Methods

Group work/brainstorming/discussion.

Duration

total time: 1 hour, group work: half hour.

Assignment

Consider which specific prejudice/discrimination people may experience in social work agencies because of:

- nationality
- religion
- class/stratum
- disability
- sexual orientation

Write down the results and present them to the whole group.

Variant

Consider if and how such discrimination affects men and women differently.

Fundamental References

Brückner, M. (1992) Sozialmanagment-Der neue Blick auf soziale Arbeit. In Brückner, M. (Ed.) *Frauen und Sozialmanagment*. Freiburg im Breisgau, 7–19.

Glaser, M. (1998) Der dornige Weg. Vom Muttertier zur mütterlichen Sozialarbeit. In Perko, G. *Mutterwitz*. Vienna, 248–74.

References

Andersson, B.S. and Zinsser, J.P. (1995) *Eine eigene Geschichte – Frauen in Europa. Vol. 2: Vom Absolutismus zur Gegenwart*, Frankfurt/Main.

Badelt, C. (1991) Unterschiede und Gemeinsamkeiten von wirtschaftlichen und sozialen Organisationen. In: ÖKSA (Ed.) *Sozialmanagment, planen-leiten-handeln im sozialen Bereich*. Vienna, 11–32.

Bader, C., Cremer, C. and Dudeck, A. (1990) (Eds.) *Frauen in sozialer Arbeit*. Weinheim and Munich.

Berndt, H. (1999) Pathos und Appell – Zum moralischen Rüstzeug der frühen Sozialarbeit, dargestellt an Alice Salomon. In: Pantucek, P. and Vyslouzil, M. (Eds.) *Die moralische Profession, Menschenrechte und Ethik in der Sozialarbeit*. St. Pölten, 25–48.

Brückner, M. (1992) (Ed.) *Frauen und Sozialmanagment*. Freiburg im Breisgau.

Brückner, M. (1996) *Frauen und Mädchenprojekte. Von Feministischen Gewißheiten zu Neuen Suchbewegungen*. Opladen.

Burden, D. and Gottlieb, N. (1987) *The Woman Client*. New York and London.

Cree, V. E. (1996) Why do men care? In: Cavanagh, K. and Cree. V.E. *Working with Men, Feminism and Social Work.* Routledge, 65–86.

Dominelli, L. and McLeod, E. (1989) *Feminist Social Work*. London.

Drake, H. (1980) *Frauen in der Sozialarbeit*. Neuwied.

Feiler, L. (1991) Ist Sozialarbeit managbar? In: ÖKSA (Ed.): *Sozialmanagement, planen–leiten-handeln im sozialen Bereich*. Vienna, 33–42.

Fox-Wallner, W. (1994) Frauenbewegung und Entwicklung der Sozialarbeit – Ein verflochtenes Thema, In: Verein für Bewährungshilfe und Soziale Arbeit (Ed.) *Frauen und soziale Arbeit*. Vienna, 13–23.

Gilligan, C. (1982) *Die andere Stimme. Lebenskonflikte und Moral der Frau*, Munich and Zurich.

Glaser, M. (1998) Der dornige Weg. Vom Muttertier zur mütterlichen Sozialarbeit. In: Perko, G. *Mutterwitz.* Vienna, 248–74.

Gruber, C. and Schmidbauer, I. (1991) Wodurch unterscheiden sich drei Viertel von einem Viertel? Geschlechtsspezifische Unterschiede zwischen Frauen und Männern in der Sozialarbeit. In: ISOSO. *Sozialberufe. Untersuchung über Veränderungen der Anforderungen an Sozialarbeit.* Unpublished Project Report. Vienna, 85–102.

Gruber, C. (1995) Sozialarbeit – ein Frauenberuf? Geschlechtsspezifische Unterschiede in der Sozialarbeit. In: Wilfing, H. *Konturen der Sozialarbei.* WUV Univ.-Verlag, Vienna, 116–24.

Heinemeier, S. (1994) Sozialarbeit: Notnagel oder Sinnquelle? In: Schatteburg, U. (Ed.) *Aushandeln, Entscheiden, Gestalten – Soziale Arbeit, die Wissen schafft.* Hannover, 173–218.

Meinhold, M. (1993) *Sozialarbeiterinnen – Frauenkarrieren*, Münster.

Mittermeier, S. B. (1994) Die Jugendfürsorgerin. *L'Homme, Zeitschrift für Feministische Geschichtswissenschaft*. Fifth Year, Issue 2, 102–20.

Mullender, A. (1997) Gender. In: Davis, M. (Ed.) *The Blackwell Companion to Social Work*. Oxford, 42–9.

Müller, W. C. (1999) Selbsterziehung-Umerziehung-Lebenshilfe, Kreuzwege Sozialer Arbeit in Deutschland. In: Pantucek, P. and Vyslouzil. M. (Eds.) *Die moralische Profession, Menschenrechte and Ethik in der Sozialarbeit.* St. Pölten, 17–24.

Notz, G. (1990) Ist unbezahlte Arbeit unbezahlbar? In: Cremer, C., Bader, C. and Dudeck, C. *Frauen in sozialer Arbeit, Zur Theorie und Praxis feministischer Bildungs und Sozialarbeit.* Weinheim and Munich, 95–106.

Puch, H-J. (1994) *Organisation im Sozialbereich, Eine Einführung für soziale Berufe.* Freiburg im Breisgau.

Puhl, Ria and Maas, U. (1997) *Soziale Arbeit in Europa*, Weinheim and Munich.

Riedl, G. (1991) Begrüßungsrede. In: ÖKSA (Ed.) *Sozialmanagment, planen-leiten-handeln im sozialen Bereich.* Vienna, 9–10.

Rommelspacher, B. (1992).*Mitmenschlichkeit und Unterwerfung, Zur Ambivalenz der weiblichen Moral*. Frankfurt/New York.

Rommelspacher, B. (1999) Weibliche Ambivalenz und gesellschaftliche Rahmenbedingungen. In: Verein Wiener Frauenhäuser: *Fortschritte. Wege aus der Ambivalenz*. Vienna.

Sachße, C. (1994) *Mütterlichkeit als Beruf, Sozialarbeit, Sozialreform und Frauenbewegung 1871-1929*. Opladen.

Schauer, U. (1994) Zusammenhang zwischen Frauengeschichte, Frauensozialisation und der Berufswahl zur Sozialarbeiterin. In: Verein für Bewährungshilfe und soziale Arbeit (Ed.): *Frauen und soziale Arbeit*. Vienna, 33–42.

Schmidbauer, I. (1994) *Sozialarbeit als Frauenberuf*. Linz.

Sellach, B. (1995) *Qualitätssicherung: Was kommt auf die Frauenhäuser zu?*. Lecture, Vienna.

Simmel-Joachim, M. (1990) Frauen in der Geschichte der sozialen Arbeit – zwischen Anpassung und Widerstand. In: Cremer, C., Bader, C. and Dudeck, A. *Frauen in sozialer Arbeit, Zur Theorie und Praxis feministischer Bildungs-und Sozialarbeit.* Weinheim and Munich, 42–59.

Staub-Bernasconi, S. (1989) *Ermächtigung von Frauen als Prozeß*. unpublished manuscript, Boldern.

Tillmann, J. (1994) Sozialarbeitswissenschaft im Werden. In: Schatteburg, U. (Ed.) *Aushandeln, Entscheiden, Gestalten – Soziale Arbeit, die Wissen schafft*. Hannover, 17–50.

United Nations (1992) *Teaching and Learning about Human Rights – A Manual for Schools of Social Work and the Social Work Profession*. New York.

Waaldijk, B. (no year given) *A New World for Women – Gender and History of Social Work in the Netherlands and the United States.*

Wilfing, H. (1995) *Konturen der Sozialarbeit*. Vienna.

Wronka, J. (1999) Teaching Human Rights to Social Work Students. In: Pantucek, P. and Vyslouzil, M. (Eds.) *Die moralische Profession, Menschenrechte und Ethik in der Sozialarbeit*. St. Pölten, 197–210.

Zeller, S. (1994) *Geschichte der Sozialarbeit als Beruf, Bilder und Dokumente 1893–1939*. Pfaffenweiler

11. Men, Masculinity and Social Work

John Bates and Neil Thompson

Introduction

In this chapter we explore the role of men as clients, carers, social workers and managers as well as men as part of the solution to the problem of gender-based discrimination and oppression. For many years now the importance of gender as a factor in social work has been recognised within the UK literature. However, the main focus has understandably been on women and femininity. Here we seek to balance matters out to a certain extent by focusing primarily on men and masculinity. This is not intended to undermine the attention given to issues of women and femininity, but rather to broaden the debate so that we can begin to work towards a fully holistic picture of the issues that affect both men and women in the social work world.

Our aim is not to provide a definitive statement relating to men in social work, but rather to present a number of points and arguments which, it is to be hoped, will encourage further debate, study and analysis.

Men as clients

It has long been recognised that the vast majority of users of social services are women. However, we should not forget that a significant proportion of social work's clients are men. This leads us to pose the question as to whether we need a different approach in working with men. For example, Mullender (1996) asked whether one of the main reasons why men feature so little in social work is that their needs are not met by an approach that is geared primarily towards the needs of women. Feminism quite correctly placed women at the heart of the social work agenda, and it has been remarkably successful in developing services for women over the last few decades. Rape Crisis, Women's Aid plus numerous smaller but influential pressure groups and service providers have changed the landscape for women service users and indeed the thinking and teaching of social work academics. Although it has been a momentous struggle, feminist social workers and their supporters have had their work recognised as 'woman-centred' practice which has been incorporated into mainstream social work and social work education (Hanmer and Statham, 1999). However, one outcome of this development may be the:

> ... uncomfortable implications ... that men's behaviour may have gone unchecked and that we may have played a part in reinforcing stereotypes about women's caring role within the family and within the social welfare net.
>
> (Cavanagh and Cree, 1996, p5)

Another implication is that the focus on feminist social work has meant a paucity of serious discourse about men as recipients of services. This has its dangers, as the vacuum may well be filled by either anti-feminist literature and practices ultimately so damaging to men and women alike or by an analysis which sees the problem as the responsibility of one gender or another. The questions for both men and women practitioners are: How do we work with men? How do we construct an intervention that acknowledges the damage that patriarchal social relations inflict on both men and women? Although men's experience of gender oppression can never be equated with that of women, men too are casualties of patriarchal myths and stereotypes (Thompson, 1995).

Masculinity is an overlapping and complex knot of socially constructed expectations that shape how men are expected to behave (norms) and how they should think (attitudes). One example of this is the reluctance of men to ask for, and accept help. A factor that is well documented in the literature (Bowl, 2001). We may theorise that this relates to patterns of upbringing in which, amongst other things, men are socialised into roles of protector and breadwinner. Such roles are not easily compatible with the notion of asking for help or accepting it when it is offered. This can lead to a number of problems for men for example, in not asking for help in the early stages of the problem. Intervention at a later stage may be much less likely to be effective because matters have developed to such an extent that helping becomes far more difficult. This is a parallel with health care matters where reluctance on the part of men to ask for help with their health problems may lead to many men reaching a position where their illness is no longer treatable because medical intervention has begun at too late a stage in the development of the disease process (Luck et al., 2000). Male pride, as a feature of socialisation into masculine patterns of behaviour, can therefore be seen as something that can lead to critical, life or death situations, with many men suffering as a result of their socially defined attitudes towards help and assistance.

It is also important to note that the range of problems men face is likely to be different from those that women encounter in their day-to-day lives. While many of the underlying causes will often be similar (for example, poverty and deprivation), there are also likely to be significant differences because of the ways in which men and women operate differently within the social structure. For example, men's roles, not only in the world of work, but also in the domestic sphere of the family, show significant differences in terms of socially constructed expectations of the respective genders.

The reluctance of men to explore and articulate their feelings or acknowledge their vulnerability is well established (Seidler, 1994; Thompson, 1997). For many women the lack of emotional closeness with their partner can be seen as the prime cause of difficulties within their relationship (Hite, 1987). One of the basic, socially constructed qualities of 'masculinity' is being in control of not only oneself, but also of other people and things, thus exposing vulnerability becomes a challenge to the very nature of what it is to be a man (Bates, 1997). Emotional tenderness therefore exposes a man's vulnerability to ridicule or exploitation, thereby creating obstructions to the development of meaningful relationships with other men and women. In other words, men cultivate the carapace of 'hardness', often with disastrous consequences for them and those around them. Masculinity provides a sense of wholeness or, as Giddens (1993) describes it, 'ontological security'. If, during times of acute stress, this sense of who we are becomes challenged or confronted, then the obvious option is to retire behind masculine excesses. If the oft-stated message to young boys in pain is not to cry, as big boys don't do that, the options are to stop feeling or to find other ways of expressing pain and distress (Riches, 2002). When that command comes from the same person who earlier 'kissed it all better', it is little wonder the confusing messages to little boys and young men comes back to haunt us all.

Many writers have pointed out the cost of maintaining this masculine persona and have emphasised the heavy burden of being able to express only a restricted range of feelings, of living in a world of distorted relationships, emotional illiteracy and distant communicating (Bowl, 1985; Harris and Sullivan, 1988; Thompson, 1997, 2001). One outcome of this is an inability to see when things are beginning to go wrong, perhaps exacerbated by the illusion of a trouble-free, compensatory home life. As Tolson argues:

More often, deeply troubled masculine feelings are swept away by feminine tension management and the cost of harmony in the home can be a masculine superficiality towards feelings in general, in relationships within the family, and in a man's relationship with himself.

(Tolson, 1977, p70)

This, of course, can then spill over into a reluctance to seek help when overcome with stress. In this regard, Busfield (1998) shows that the experiences of mental health problems are very different between men and women. Women are far more likely to experience depression than men, but men are likely to encounter other disorders at a higher rate than women. Men are also, on average, likely to have less social support than women. Of course, this is not to say that men are more deserving of help than women, but simply that their needs are likely to be different, and therefore need to be addressed in a different way if we are not to make the mistake of oversimplifying the complex realities of men's lives and the problems that they face. For example, by returning to one of our earlier themes (that of emotional hardness and the high cost of this in terms of men's inability to make and sustain close relationships), we can recognise that holding out unrealistic expectations of men's abilities to assume greater responsibility for acts of caring is simply setting them up to fail. That failure may then rebound on them, and their families. We need to acknowledge that there is a much bigger project waiting, in the retraining of men to ensure that they can fulfil the roles required to challenge gender oppression. Otherwise, as Chesler (1990) points out: 'The disconnected men who have been socialised to reproduce sexism are the very men whom feminists have been calling upon to participate equally in child care' (cited in Richard-Allerdyce, 1994, p3). Change will be slow, but at least by recognising that there is a problem within traditional masculinity, we might be able to start redressing it. This is a theme to which we shall return below.

In addition, we need to consider the fact that, in many social work situations, men are considered to be problems in their own right, rather than people who have problems. That is, in many situations the problems that women and children encounter are as a result of the behaviour of some men. For example, although it is now established that many women do indulge in child abuse (Blues et al., 1999; Cawson et al., 2000), it remains the case that the vast majority of child abuse perpetrators are men. Similarly, while women may at times become violent towards their male partners, the issue of domestic violence remains primarily that of men being violent towards their female partners (Mullender, 1996). A clear danger to avoid here is that of demonising men, that is, seeing them primarily as sources of problems, rather than looking at the wider context with its many levels. For example, we need to enrich our understanding of the impact of socialisation and the stereotyping of men by engaging in the complex discourses around male identity as just one illustration. It has been argued that male identity is inherently unstable, being built around elements of masculinity that are themselves oppressive (Jackson, 1982; Bowl, 1985; Thompson, 1995):

The centrality of competitiveness, competence, aggression and objectification creates a masculinity characterised by anxiety and instability. Failure to impress, compete or acknowledge competence particularly in areas of sexuality may well lead to inadequacies and fears which, not surprisingly, can then be projected onto women and children.

(Bates, 1997, p220)

We have to avoid the extremes of oversimplification. At one extreme, it would be naïve indeed not to recognise that the behaviour of some men is at times extremely problematic. However, we should not go to the opposite extreme of automatically seeing men as problems. This question of reductionism is one that has haunted work relating to anti-discriminatory practice in general and anti-sexist practice in particular. It is therefore a mistake that we are very keen to avoid here.

Men as carers

Although there is little doubt that the world of caring is predominately a female world brought about by the socialisation of children into the traditional patterns of thought, behaviour and language which include the expectation of the woman as the 'natural' carer (Hanmer and Statham, 1999), we should not allow this to lead us into neglecting those men who do act as carers. Although in a minority, men are none the less a significant body of carers (Bowl, 2001). While research has shown that men as carers will often receive additional support compared with the levels of support offered to women, this remains a complex situation (Fisher, 1994). While not wishing to support an unequal distribution of support services between men and women we would wish to draw attention to the more complex problems related to the allocation of services and support to informal carers.

First, we would wish to return to the point made earlier relating to men's reluctance to accept help. It can be argued that women in general have many years' experience of supporting and being supported which is something that is not always the same pattern for men. Men will often find it difficult to swallow their male pride and accept help. We therefore have a complex situation in which men as carers are more likely to be offered help, but also ironically are more likely to decline it, or are less likely to seek out such help in the first place. We should also recognise that the type of support that men need is likely to be different. For example, research undertaken by Lund and Caserta (2001) shows that men and women who had been bereaved as the result of the death of their partner experienced different problems because of their different lack of skills, that is, women found it difficult to cope without their husbands because there were skills and tasks which were performed by their husbands which they did not know how to complete themselves. On the other side of the coin, the men who had lost their wives also found it difficult to cope because of the absence of the practical skills that their wives had practised prior to their death. Concrete examples of this would be men finding it difficult to deal with day-to-day matters such as cooking, operating the washing machine and so on, while women in many cases had no idea about their financial position, insurance arrangements and so on, because these had, over the years, been dealt with by their husbands. The argument we would therefore wish to put forward is not that men or women should be regarded as more or less skilled, but rather that the allocation of skills and knowledge relating to practical matters within the household tend to be distributed according to gender. This means that, where people are in need of support, it is likely to be along gender lines. In view of this, those people offering support and services to carers should be careful to ensure that they do not:

(a) Offer more support to men simply because they feel that men are less competent than women in household tasks and more in need of support.

(b) Should not assume that both men and women will require the same type of support. What is clearly called for is an accurate assessment of specific needs, rather than generalised assumptions based on gender stereotypes.

Men as social workers

Given that the vast majority of social workers are women and that social work, along with the other caring professions, is generally seen as 'women's work' (Davis, 1997), it is not surprising that men in social work are often viewed with suspicion.

Such suspicion tends to fall into three main categories. First, men may be seen as ambitious and only spending time in practice as a short stepping stone to the level of management and policy making. Second, men in social work may be seen as 'failures as men', that is, they may be seen as people who are not capable of getting work deemed more suitable for men. They are seen as not being real men, too weak and incompetent to do 'proper' men's work. This fear is well exemplified by Savage writing of the male nurse who:

> ... is emasculated by taking on 'women's work' in which he is expected to demonstrate 'feminine qualities' such as caring and gentleness and in which, at least to begin with, he will be subordinate to women. And if his masculinity is in question, so too is his sexuality.
>
> (Savage, 1987, p76)

Third, men may be mistrusted because they are seen as people who wish to exploit their position, for example, in relation to children. This may be linked to stereotypes and discriminatory assumptions about gay men; the assumption is that gay men are a threat to children (Ruxton, 1992). Alternatively, there is the fact that child care is seen as a gendered occupation and, as such, largely the preserve of women which presents immediate tensions for men who enter it. Murray (1996) suggests that, in analysing the experiences of men in child care, we are 'more likely to reveal constructions of gender that may otherwise be obscured' (p1).

In view of the above, we need to ask the main question, namely: Can men be trusted as social workers? Hicks gives an example of this from his own practice:

> Many of the women, mothers of the children with whom I worked, told me that they were not used to men who did child care, or

actively listened to them. Instead, often the women themselves were the survivors of men's sexual, physical or emotional violence. They had every reason to distrust me as a man, and to distrust me with their children. However, I believe that my statements of 'outrage' and their violent treatment by other men, by declared opposition to such violence, and my re-framing of the abuse as being a consequence of men's violence, helped us to build a working and trusting social work relationship.

(Hicks, 2001, p50–1)

This passage shows that men as social workers can overcome such mistrust and suspicions. However, as Hicks makes clear, it is necessary to do a lot of groundwork to be able to get past such problems. In many aspects of social work at least, men start from a disadvantage, in so far as they have to prove themselves as genuine carers in order to overcome the stereotypical assumptions about their role in social work. Another danger is to see men in children's services social work as the strong, masculine father figure. NCH research noted that some male workers felt that, on occasions, they had been pushed into acting as project 'policeman': 'They didn't want me because they wanted a caring man; they wanted me primarily as a strong disciplinarian father figure' (unnamed source quoted in Ruxton, 1993, p21). This 'disciplinarian father' is the very figure that causes so many problems and so much distress for women and children, and so it is vital that it is not recreated in a different guise.

Another issue relating to the potential or actual role of men as social workers relates to the matter of women's predominance within the social work world: i.e., given that the majority of social work clients are women, are men in a position to understand their perspective and their view of the world? This is a complex question, and so it is important to avoid simplistic responses. Sibeon (1991) introduces the concept of 'insiderist epistemology'. What he means by this rather strange-sounding term is the view that one has to have a particular experience in order to be able to understand that experience e.g. only women can understand women's problems; only black

people can understand black people's problems, and so on. While this argument has some degree of validity, there is also a danger of taking it too far. The naive assumption that being a woman *per se* gives insight into the intricacies of gender oppression has the risky potential of shifting the responsibility onto the victim. If we extend its argument to its logical extremes, no one would be able to work with another person, unless matched with that person in terms of their experience across a number of dimensions. Clearly this would be immensely complex and unworkable. It also misses the point of practising within an anti-discriminatory framework. The issue of fighting, and ultimately banishing, sexism has to be a joint project between men and women. What is required is the skill and flexibility to be able to make the effort to understand another person's perspective, to empathise with that person and to take on board what they are saying about their situation, their experiences and their feelings. While it can be argued that women are generally much better at such tasks than men, we should not allow ourselves to be led into making the mistake of assuming that men are therefore not capable of being empathic listeners and thus not able to be competent social workers.

Men as managers

In recent years, authors such as Adams (1998) have been very critical of what they term 'managerialism'. This term refers to the process by which managers have amassed more and more power in organisations, giving less voice to their employees. In some respects this is a paradoxical development, as it has occurred in tandem with an emphasis on the notion that an organisation's most important asset is its people – its human resource. One distinct characteristic of managerialism is that it has emphasised what can be regarded as masculine qualities. For example, in recent years there has been a development of a strong emphasis on numerical indict – that is, a focus on counting and measuring and being able to justify decisions and the use of resources in statistical terms. This has paralleled the emphasis on evidence-based practice, a notion which has become more and more influential as a result of its predominance in medicine and related occupations (Sheldon and Chilvers, 2000). The idea behind evidence-based practice is that whatever actions are taken, the person taking that action should be in a position to justify his or her practice on the basis of evidence or research to demonstrate the effectiveness of such steps. In management terms this has led to a very strong emphasis on such matters as performance indicators, targets and the importance of quantitative measures (Adams, 1998; Coulshed and Mullender, 2001).

The rise of managerialism as an approach to local government has led to a number of criticisms across public services generally and in social work in particular. These criticisms hinge on the argument that an overemphasis on statistical data and hard evidence fails to take account of the more human side of caring and supporting people through difficulties (Jordan, 2000). It has, therefore, been argued that the heart has gone out of social work as a result of this masculine tendency towards being able to account for everything in statistical terms. Some have argued that one of the main reasons for the development of managerialism has been the predominance of men in management positions. That is, while, as mentioned earlier, the majority of social work clients and indeed of social work personnel are female, the majority of managers are male. The argument, therefore, is that an over representation of men at the management level leads to typically masculine concerns being given considerable attention, while the more typically feminine concerns have to take a back seat. It is again ironic that such developments should take place in contexts of growing recognition in the management literature that women have an important part to play in management because of their generally less confrontational and more co-operative approach (Newman, 1995; Coulshed and Mullender, 2001). That is, women's recognised greater level of skill at an interpersonal level, greater ability to be able to listen and communicate effectively at various levels can be recognised as key management skills. However, traditionally these skills have been devalued in management with greater focus given to more executive concerns which are typically seen as being within the male domain.

An important conclusion to draw here, therefore, is that men in management positions need to look very carefully at the role they are adopting to ensure that they are not slotting into masculine stereotypes, that is, that they are not falling into the rut of assuming a managerialist statistical position without taking account of the more human side of the organisation in which they work, and the people that the organisation is intended to serve. Clearly what is called for here is a balance in which the need for evidence-based practice is not fulfilled at the expense of recognising the other more complex needs within the human services in general and social work in particular.

Men as part of the solution

Bryson (1999) distinguishes between two main perspectives on the role of men in challenging sexism. First she quotes Hester (1984, p33): 'Whatever activities an anti-sexist man becomes involved in, and whatever opinions he chooses to hold as an anti-sexist man it appears that the motivation is egotistical and for his own enhancement' (p198–9).

However, she then goes on to counterbalance this by stating that other feminists argue that:

> ... the analysis of men's patriarchal power cannot be so simple. Rather, it involves complex issues of structure and agency through which it may be possible to distinguish between male power and male persons, and to understand that the former is socially constructed rather than embodied in all biological men. Such an approach makes it possible to oppose patriarchy without assuming that all men are necessarily immune to the considerations of justice, denying the very possibility of non-exploitative relationships with men, or treating all forms of male support as automatically suspect. As such it can appear to provide a comfortable solution for the majority of feminists, who continue to have personal, working and political relationships with men.
>
> (Bryson, 1999, p199).

We have argued elsewhere that the challenging and ultimate elimination of sexism as an ideology has to be a joint project (Thompson and Bates, 1997). Our starting point is well exemplified by Mason and Mason (1990): 'We believe that patriarchy damages men's quality of life as well as women's, that it constrains men rather than enabling them to develop' (p210).

For social work education, the training of future social workers allows one opportunity to begin the process of engaging men in the struggle. Current social work training programmes can provide an opportunity for exploring the nature of masculinity in particular and the gendered approach to social work in general. As men teachers of social work we have for many years attempted to produce a curriculum that places anti-discriminatory practice at the very core of everything we do, with anti-sexist teaching central to every element of the programme. As Mullender (1996) points out, the big danger of patriarchal thinking is that it not only pervades all of society's thinking but extends to 'professional thinking in numerous direct and indirect ways' (p37). For example, there exists a wealth of teaching and learning opportunities for social workers to begin to understand and make sense of this complex discourse. The Cleveland Report (1988) could be read as a straightforward account of a child care disaster but a closer analysis reveals a language that supports Mullender's earlier contention: 'The mythical "traditional" family, and by implication the role of the father within this – the father as patriarch – is defended' (Nava, 1992, p150).

Using social work reports can also enhance the sensitivity of men social workers to their use of language and the potential for collusion with male clients. This approach can encourage male social workers to challenge language in reports and case studies that minimises the oppression and violence of women by, for example, exploring phrases like 'marital dispute' or 'relationship problems'. Farmer and Owen (1998) report on the gendered nature of professional responses and how, for example, language can obscure the real story behind a situation. They observed a particular process when a male worker became strongly identified with the father's view of the situation under investigation, siding with his perspective that the children were disobedient and failed to take action when the children were beaten: 'The father's abuse was reconstructed as discipline, albeit occasionally excessive' (p555).

The establishment of men's groups on training programmes can also allow opportunities for men social workers to engage in debates and discourses about the very nature of masculinity. Men's groups can allow the free exploration of such issues as 'emotional hardness' and how emotions in men have become a 'no go area' where feelings like tenderness, compassion and humanity become 'off limits'. By giving permission to put them back 'on limits' negative characteristics like competence, competitiveness, dominance and aggression can be replaced by nurturing, patience, sensitivity and kindness as *acceptable* attributes for men to aspire to. Themes for discussion like Segal's powerful quotation can also provide opportunities for men to explore normally forbidden territory:

> ... there has always been a close link between misogyny and homophobia in our culture ... although the persecution of homosexuals is most commonly the act of men against a minority of other men, it is also the forced repression of the 'feminine' in all men. It is a way of keeping men separated off from women, and keeping women subordinate to men.
>
> (1994, p16).

We have also used techniques whereby identical case studies were given to men's and women's groups, with the result that the very different conclusions and recommendations allowed a much more profound debate as to how responses to problems are constructed. For example, using child protection case studies in this way allows trainee workers to challenge many current child protection practices which seek to make women responsible for the offending behaviour of men.

There is little hope for the future if we fail to engage men in the struggle, or simply see men social workers, clients, managers and students as people to blame. Changing men is a joint venture that, by its very nature, will be slow and problematic but, by engaging with them and attempting to demonstrate that traditional masculinity is as damaging for them as it is for women, progress can be made. For men in social work it is vital that they address their own sexism and deal with it as not only a prerequisite to successful practice as a social worker, but also as a creative ally in the struggle against discrimination and oppression. What is needed is a desire by both men and women to see the world anew by engaging together in a fresh, invigorating debate which constructs a social work that embraces the changes already established and pushes back even further the limiting experiences of gender stereotyping.

To be responsible inventors and discoverers, though, we need the courage to let go of the old world, to relinquish most of what we have cherished, to abandon our interpretations about what works and what doesn't work. As Einstein is often quoted as saying: 'No problem can be solved from the same consciousness that created it. We must learn to see the world anew'.

(Wheatley, 1994, p5)

Conclusion

The issue of men, masculinity and social work is clearly a complex one. Much has been written about the role of women in social work, with relatively little attention given to men and the role they can play for good or ill. It is to be hoped that, in this chapter, we have enabled the reader to see the broader picture, to be able to recognise that simplistic assumptions about men and women have no place in a sophisticated analysis of the underpinnings of effective social work practice.

It is unfortunate that much of the literature relating to gender and social work has tended to oversimplify matters. Our aim here is not to present a full analysis of the issues, for that would leave us open to the charge of oversimplifying. Instead what we have more realistically attempted to achieve in this chapter is an outline of the broad range of issues that need to be considered in more depth. It is to be hoped that this chapter can pave the way for further research, further debate and a greater awareness of the complexities of the issues involved.

References

Adams, R. (1998) *Quality Social Work,* London, Macmillan – now Palgrave.

Bates, J. (1997) 'Men, Masculinity and Childcare', in Bates *et al.* (1997).

Bates, J., Pug, R. and Thompson, N. (Eds.) (1997) *Protecting Children: Challenges and Change*, Aldershot, Arena.

Blues, A., Moffatt, C. and Telford, P. (1999) 'Work with Adolescent Females who Sexually Abuse: Similarities and Differences', in Erooga and Masson (1999).

Bowl, R. (1985) *Changing the Nature of Masculinity: A Task for Social Work?* Norwich, University of East Anglia Monographs.

Bowl, R. (2001) 'Men and Community Care', in Christie (2001).

Bryson, V. (1999) *Feminist Debates: Issues of Theory and Political Practice*, London, Macmillan – now Palgrave.

Busfield, J. (1998) *Men, Women and Madness: Understanding Gender and Mental Disorder*, London, Macmillan – now Palgrave.

Chesler, P. (1994) *Sacred Bond*, London, Virago.

Cavanagh, K. and Cree, V, (1996) *Working With Men: Feminsim and Social Work*, London, Routledge.

Cawson, P., Wattam, C., Brooker, S. and Kelly, G. (2000) *Child Maltreatment in the United Kingdom: A Study of the Prevalence of Child Abuse and Neglect*, London, NSPCC.

Christie, A. (Ed.) (2001) *Men and Social Work: Theories and Practices*, Basingstoke, Palgrave.

Cleveland County Council (1988) *Report of the Inquiry into Child Abuse in Cleveland 1987*, DHSS Cmnd. 412, London, HMSO.

Coulshed, V. and Mullender, A. (2001) *Management in Social Work*, 2nd edn, Basingstoke, Palgrave.

Davies, M. (Ed.) (1991) *The Sociology of Social Work*, London, Routledge.

Davis, A. (1996) 'Women and the Personal Social Services', in Hallett (1996).

Erooga, M, and Masson, H. (Eds.) (1999) *Children and Young People who Sexually Abuse Others: Challenges and Responses*, London, Routledge.

Farmer, E. and Owen, M. (1998) 'Gender and

the Child Protection Process', *British Journal of Social Work*, 28(4).

Fawcett, B., Galloway, M. and Perrins, J. (Eds.) (1997) *Feminism and Social Work in the Year 2000: Conflicts and Controversies*, University of Bradford.

Field, D., Hockey, J. and Small, N. (Eds.) (1997) *Death, Gender and Ethnicity,* London, Routledge.

Fisher, M. (1994) 'Man-made Care: Community Care and the Older Male', *British Journal of Social Work,* 24(5).

French, M. (1993) *The War Against Women*, London, Hamish Hamilton.

Giddens, A. (1993) *New Rules of Sociological Method*, 2nd edn, Cambridge, Polity.

Hallett, C. (Ed.) (1996) *Women and Social Policy: An Introduction*, Hemel Hempstead, Harvester Wheatsheaf.

Hanmer, J. and Statham, D. (1999) *Women and Social Work*, 2nd edn, London, Macmillan – now Palgrave.

Harris, J. and Sullivan, J. (1988) 'Addressing Men's Roles', *Social Work Today*, 8 September.

Hester, M. (1984) 'Anti-Sexist Men: A Case of Cloak-and-Dagger Chauvinism', *Women's Studies International Forum* 7(1).

Hicks, S. (2001) 'Men Social Workers in Children's Services: "Will the *Real Man Please Stand Up*?"', in Christie (2001).

Hite, S. (1987) *Women and Love*, Harmondsworth, Penguin.

Itzin, C. and Newman, J. (Eds.) (1995) *Gender, Culture and Organizational Change: Putting Theory into Practice*, London, Routledge.

Jackson, S. (1982) *Childhood and Sexuality*, Oxford, Basil Blackwell

Jordan, B., with Jordan, C. (2000) *Social Work and the Third Way: Tough Love as Social Policy*, London, Sage.

Luck, M., Bamford, M. and Williamson P. (2000) *Men's Health: Perspectives, Diversity and Paradox*, Oxford, Blackwell.

Lund, D.A. (Ed.) (2001) *Men Coping with Grief*, Amityville, NY, Baywood.

Lund, D.A. and Caserta, M.S. (2001) 'When the Unexpected Happens: Husbands Coping with the Deaths of Their Wives', in Lund (2001).

Mason. B, and Mason. E, (1990) 'Masculinity and Family Work' in Perelberg and Miller (1990).

Mullender, A. (1996) *Rethinking Domestic Violence*, London, Routledge.

Murray, S.B. (1996) ' "We All Love Charles" Men in Child Care and the Social Construction of Gender', *Gender and Society*, August.

Nava, M. (1992) *Changing Cultures, Feminism, Youth and Consumerism*, London, Sage.

Newman, J. (1995) 'Gender and Cultural Change', in Itzin and Newman (1995).

Perelberg, R.J. and Miller, A.C. (Eds.) (1990) *Gender and Power in Families*, London, Routledge.

Richard-Allerdyce, D. (1994) 'Hearing the Other', *Feminist Issues*, Spring.

Riches, G. (2002) 'Gender and Sexism', in Thompson (2002).

Ruxton, S. (1992) *'What's He Doing at the Family Centre?'*, London, NCH Research Report.

Savage, J. (1987) *Nurses, Gender and Sexuality*, London, Heinemann.

Seidler, V.J. (1994) *Unreasonable Men*: *Masculinity and Social Theory*, London, Routledge.

Segal, L. (1994) *Slow Motion: Changing Masculinities, Changing Men*, London, Virago.

Sheldon, B. and Chilvers, R. (2000) *Evidence-based Social Care: A Study of Prospects and Problems,* Lyme Regis, Russell House Publishing.

Sibeon, R. (1991) 'The Construction of a Contemporary Sociology of Social Work', in Davies (1991).

Thompson, N. (1995) 'Men and Anti-Sexism', *British Journal of Social Work* 25(4).

Thompson, N. (1997) 'Masculinity and Loss', in Field *et al.* (1997).

Thompson, N. (2001) 'The Ontology of Masculinity', in Lund (2001).

Thompson, N. (Ed.) (2002) *Loss and Grief: A Guide for Human Services Practitioners*, Basingstoke, Palgrave.

Thompson, N. and Bates, J. (1997) 'Men Promoting Anti-Sexism: Progress and Pitfalls', in Fawcett *et al.* (1997).

Tolson, A. (1977) *The Limits of Masculinity*, London, Tavistock.

Wheatley, M.J. (1994) *Leadership and the New Science*, San Francisco, Berret-Ko.

12. Gender and Social Work: Research on Gender Differences in the Treatment of Clients in Welfare Institutions

Christian Kullberg

Introduction

In the 1960s and 1970s, in the area of social work, there was considerable interest among both theoretical and practical social workers in the questions of how non-repressive methods can be developed in the daily work with 'social problems' (e.g. Becker, 1967; Bailey and Brake, 1980; Corrigan and Leonard, 1981). The class society and the treatment of marginalised groups by society were two issues that attracted a relatively large amount of attention during these two decades. Since the 1980s, more attention has been paid instead to inequality between women and men, based on a gender-hierarchical and segregated society. Scientists have been studying conditions in the labour market (Hartmann, 1976; Cockburn, 1983) and in the family (Haavind, 1882; Björnberg, 1994; Holter and Aarseth, 1994; Björnberg and Sass, 1997). It is only in the last 10 years that studies of conditions in other areas such as health care and social services have attracted more attention. Questions concerning, for example, what treatment women and men receive in social welfare or other institutions of the welfare state have until recently been paid relatively little attention in Swedish as well as Scandinavian research.

In research performed in the 1990s (Kullberg, 1994, 1996, 1997) and in an on-going research project (Kullberg, 2000), I address the question of social welfare officers' perception and handling of male and female clients. The overall aim of this research is to obtain systematic knowledge of the content and meaning of such genderising processes that form a part of the daily activities of the practice of social work. The theoretical point of departure for the research is

the understanding of the patriarchal structure, namely men's domination over women within such specific institutional arrangements, the kind of specific discourses and the practices that form the field of activity called social work.

In this chapter, I will report on some of the findings from research on gender differences in the treatment of male and female clients in welfare institutions. However, I will start by giving a short account of a theoretical perspective of the gender system.

Genderising processes: The dynamic aspects of the gender system

The order between the sexes, the 'gender system' (Hirdman, 1988, 1990) can be understood as a more or less routinised (taken for granted and constantly recurrent) 'production of meaning'. This ongoing process is accomplished by both men and women, with reference to those differences between the sexes that are perceived and understood as 'natural' (West and Zimmerman, 1987; Goffman, 1977). The active mechanism in the production of the gender system is a hierarchicalisation and segregation between the sexes and in society as a whole (Connell, 1995).

Culture-specific notions of the gender differences in all cultures have always been related to the biological differences between the sexes, but are primarily socially produced (Douglas, 1987; Kulick, 1991; Connell, 1995). The gender of the individual is culture-specific and given for the specific context that is studied. At the same time, the gender system and the arrangements between the sexes are open for negotiation (Haavind, 1985; West and

Zimmerman, 1987; Björnberg and Bäck-Wiklund, 1990). What is understood as being 'male' and 'female' is in a constant (but slow) state of change. In our daily actions, we constantly contribute to displaying and maintaining an image for ourselves and for others of the gender category we belong to, we are inevitably involved in the genderising processes. The meaning of 'male' and 'female' is intertwined in intricate patterns, which are specific to each social activity. A theory of the formation of the socially produced meaning of gender must therefore include the two sexes' relative 'positions' (cf. Davies and Harré, 1989) in relation to each other in the specific field of activity to be investigated.

The gender system is maintained in different ways and with different logic in different areas of society. These rationales involve intricate processes, which are contextually shaped (Connell, 1995; Kullberg, 1994, 1996, 1997; Kullberg and Cedersund, 1996) and should be studied on the basis of these premises. Each society develops a number of specific institutions where practices are based on specific conceptions of the meaning of 'male' and 'female'. It can be argued that institutions in all different areas of society (the labour market, family and other institutions) are 'genderised', and that a systematic theory concerning processes that produce these conditions is required. The gender order in institutions such as the welfare system can be described as being made up of five parallel processes (Acker, 1991).

1. First, it is manifested through the division between men and women, and male and female. This separation is most evident in the segregation, differentiation and hierarchicalisation of jobs at certain workplaces. It is also manifested by the segregation, differentiation and hierarchicalisation of different areas within the labour market or in the labour market as a whole. Here this process is evident in the division between low-income and high-income jobs, between skilled and unskilled labour and between technical and 'caring' professions.

This first process is very evident in social work (Pringle, 1995). In the case of professionals, men are often found in positions giving higher status and better pay, e.g. managerial positions, while women are more likely to work in 'street-level' positions, doing the actual client work. It is also men who are responsible for most of the theoretical development in the field, since the majority of the textbooks on social work are written by men.

2. Secondly, the gender system in institutions is maintained through the existence of symbols and notions that justify, explain, and express (but in some cases also contradict) the gender order. The symbolic meaning of gender-specific female and male 'social problems' can be traced in both theoretical and practical social work. Such notions are very important for the maintenance of the gender system and are, among other things, manifested in such routines that contribute to the attribution of specific problem labels to female and male clients. (The problem of the gender-specific attributions of social problems is discussed in greater depth in the section: Gender-specific typifications of social welfare and welfare workers perceptions of clients, below).

3. The third type of genderising process that contributes to the gender order is the interaction between men and women in the different institutions of society. In the case of social welfare, this involves both the interaction between male and female professionals as well as the interaction between male and female professionals and clients. (How the interaction between female welfare officers and female and male clients contributes to the maintenance of the gender system is discussed more thoroughly in the section: Gender differences in the treatment of clients in welfare institutions).

4. The fourth type of process which contributes to the production of the gender order is manifested through the male and female actors' way of representing their own identity and their way of representing the genderised order to which they belong in the institution in question. In the case of social welfare, this process involves the actors 'display' and enactment of themselves in the interaction between female and male welfare professionals and welfare clients.

5. The fifth type of process, through which the gender order is maintained, is the existence of a specific kind of reasoning, or logic or rationality that forms the prerequisites of the institution and the different kinds of practices that the institution develops.

Gender differences in the treatment of clients in welfare institutions

The position of women in the welfare state has been debated in the field of gender studies and has resulted in a large body of literature (see e.g. Bryson, 1992; Sainsbury, 1999). The transformation of the social political reforms into the everyday actions of the employees of the welfare institutions has, however, not received the attention of social scientists until recently. This question concerns if and how the daily activities carried out by the employees contribute to the maintenance of the gender system. The interaction between individuals is of great interest in the study of these 'genderising processes' since it can be claimed that it is in these encounters that our social identity is formed (Goffman, 1959). The daily interaction between men and women can be seen as the basis of how our understanding of male and female is created and maintained and how our gender-specific acts are formed (Holmberg, 1993; Hydén, 1992, 1994).

On a general level, research on the encounter between professional and citizen in an institutional context reveals that these encounters show elements of considerable professional dominance. Particularly in the case of conversations between doctors and patients, there are a large number of studies that confirm this (Mishler, 1984; Sätterlund Larsson, 1989).

There are a growing number of studies addressing the problem of how female and male clients are treated when they meet representatives of the welfare institutions (applying for assistance or asking for other services).

Doctor–patient interaction

Some researchers have been able to demonstrate how doctors, in the interaction with their patients, display a professional dominance, which contributes to maintaining the gender system. In a study of conversations performed in the United States between male gynaecologists and female patients, Alexandra Todd (1983) has, for instance, illustrated how male doctors prevent consultations from leading to the social reality faced by their female patients. Instead, the doctors use different communicative strategies to keep the conversation focused on, or bring it back to, the clinical and medical aspects of the problems the women bring up (Todd, 1983). The study also shows how the manner in which the male doctors treat their female patients contributes to traditional and stereotype values about the woman's role (such as when and how a woman should be sexually active and when to reproduce) being maintained in society.

Another American researcher, Howard Waitzkin (1991) has used studies of conversations to show how doctors in the United States, in interaction with female and male patients, contribute to the reproduction of patterns that exist on a structural level in society. The working routine of the doctors is described as ideology-preserving as regards the conditions of production in society and relations within the gender system, as well as the role of medical science in our capitalist society.

Waitzkin (1991) observes that doctors in their interaction with married male patients, who are having difficulties in their work situation, encourage and make it easier for these patients to be able to return to work quickly. This is done in two ways, partly by transforming the difficulties of these men in their work situation into solely physical or mental problems. This means that social or contextual aspects of the problems are not attended to, and also partly by encouraging the patients to adapt or accept the problems facing them at work. The men are given medicine to be able to go back to work quickly. A patient with muscle pains in his back and neck, which began and worsened at work, is nevertheless encouraged to return to work as soon as possible. Instead of rest at home, the man is prescribed a special neck collar, which can be used at work. The collar is supposed to relieve the injured muscles.

Other parts of the male patients' lives are thus given considerably less attention. One such important question is their relations with their family. According to Waitzkin (1991), discussions concerning this part of the lives of the patients are very limited. When the patients nevertheless bring up problems that are related to this area, they get no actual attention from the doctors. In the interaction, the male patients' in most cases marginal role in the home instead appears to be taken for granted (and unchangeable).

Also in the interaction with the female patients, the different parts of life, work and family life are given very different attention. However, in the case of women, the conditions are reversed. Most attention is paid to the home and the role of housewife. In the doctor-patient interaction, the position of the married female, as patient and housewife and responsible for the household is reproduced, even though it emerges in the conversations that they are dissatisfied with this role. No attention is paid to the anxiety and frustration of the women and the dialogues are concentrated on the medical aspects of the problems. As a result, the doctors prescribe various medicines. In this way, the focus of the discussions leads to an adjustment of the women to their role as housewives.

The study by Waitzkin (1991) is interesting in several ways. Firstly, it illustrates in a concrete and detailed way how the gender system is perpetuated. According to Waitzkin, this takes place as a part of a general conservative discourse, which includes the reinforcement of the capitalist conditions of production. Secondly, the study contributes to the understanding of the way in which the interaction in the welfare institutions of society plays a central role in this self perpetuating system. Thirdly, it shows how the strongest principle of the gender system (Hirdman, 1988), the principle of segregation, is reproduced in an important institution of society. In the interaction between doctors and patients, the male gender role is shown mainly as being related to the sphere of paid work in the labour market, while the female role is represented as belonging to the area of unpaid work within home.

Interaction in social insurance offices

The results from the studies of doctor-patient interaction referred to above can be compared with Scandinavian research on the treatment of male and female clients in welfare institutions.

A study conducted by Hetzler (1994) shows that in the case of the administration of disability allowance to the handicapped, men and women are treated quite differently. Empirical findings on an aggregated level (statistical data) show that men are in an advantageous position compared to women. Men are granted an allowance more frequently than are women (Hetzler, 1994). Hetzler discusses what the cause of these differences could be, but does not attempt to make any systematic study of the circumstances in the processing of the male and female clients that constitute the differences. Instead, she claims that the differences found are due to constructions that we, as members of a patriarchal society make of handicapped men and women. Another study of Swedish social insurance offices shows that male and female clients on long-term sick leave are treated differently (Bäckström and Eriksson, 1989; Bäckström, 1994). The empirical material consists of information taken from social insurance office files, records from decision-making meetings and interviews with clients and the officials responsible for decisions on rehabilitation measures. All clients were or had been involved in various kinds of rehabilitation measures aimed at getting them back to work. The results show that the institution made greater efforts to get the male clients employed compared with the female clients. They also show that these efforts for the men were initiated at an earlier stage than in the case of the women. Bäckström (1994, p48) notes that despite the fact that all officials in interviews with the researcher made it clear that they made no distinction between male and female clients, there was a significant difference between the treatment of the male and female clients.

Interaction between social workers and clients

The issue of gender differences has also been addressed in Scandinavian research for which authentic data has been used to study the encounter between social workers and clients. Kullberg (1994, 1995, 1997) has conducted a study of the work of case workers in two different areas. One is the case worker's conduct and conversations with respect to the topics of paid work and children (family) in encounters with social welfare clients who are single fathers and mothers. The encounters studied are 'interviews' at the social services' office regarding financial assistance. The second area involves the case worker's way of presenting arguments and making decisions in decision-making meetings concerning cases involving amounts above the norm where the clients are men and women with varying problems. Outcomes from the social worker's interaction with male and female clients show that the conversations proceeded in very different ways depending on the client's gender, which was reflected in both the structure and content of the conversation.

When the topic of paid work was discussed in conversations with men, social workers took the initiative. The social workers controlled the interaction and a large part of the conversation was taken up by the social worker's questions, directives and statements about the men's unemployment. All of these speech acts were aimed in different ways at trying to ascertain whether the men had legitimate reasons for being in need of social welfare. The social workers attempted in this way to determine whether the man had taken adequate measures to avoid requiring assistance. In conversations with female clients, paid employment was a rare topic of conversation. The social workers asked few questions and the conversations had a statement-statement character rather than a question-answer character (as was the case in the interviews with the men). The same thorough examination of the causes of welfare dependency did not occur in these conversations, as was the case with male clients. Instead, the social workers tended to investigate the issue in a more formal way and thus restricted themselves to economic calculations to a greater extent.

The results thus show that when clients visited the social services office, social workers placed more emphasis on men obtaining means to support themselves as soon as possible than they did with women. They also examined what legitimate reasons the men had for being on welfare more thoroughly than was the case in their conversations with women.

When the topic of children was discussed with male clients, the dialogue was in most cases part of the formal investigation conducted by the social worker aimed at determining the amount of the welfare grant. In four cases, however, the interacting parties tried to introduce talk about the topic from another perspective. In two of these cases, the clients initiated a line of reasoning that involved a wish to get closer to their children, but the social workers did not respond to their attempts. Instead, they abruptly steered the conversation back to the institutional procedures and continued to investigate the circumstances that needed to be investigated in order to evaluate the client's application. In the two other cases, the social worker took the initiative to the line of reasoning about the client's children. In both cases, however, the social worker seems to be giving a picture of a father who is somewhat distanced from his children. For instance, in one of the conversations, the social worker seems to be defending the inevitability of a father losing touch with his children when they get older. In the second conversation, the social worker is clearly anxious to encourage the client to contact his children. Despite this, what she actually says is that children usually wonder who their father is and usually want to know about their origin. This could also be seen as the social worker in question painting a picture of a rather absent father. As she puts it, a father appears primarily to be someone whom it could be 'interesting to meet' and not someone who is responsible for his children's well-being in their daily lives.

Results from the part of Kullberg's (1994) study that had to do with decision-making meetings show that the participating social workers talked about the causes of the problems of male clients in such a way that they are described as being responsible for their own problems to a greater extent than the female clients. The economic difficulties of female clients were presented in such a way that they appear to be victims of their problems to a greater extent than the male clients. Moreover, clients described as responsible (in most cases male clients) were granted social welfare at these meetings to a significantly lesser extent than clients described as victims (in most cases female clients).

The fact that, as Kullberg (1994) found, female social workers could control the conversation about both topics with male clients, linguistically and with respect to content, may be compared with a study conducted by Berg Sorensen (1995) in Denmark. In this study, it appeared that social workers were more dominant in their interaction with male clients than they were with female clients. Male clients spoke less and did not dominate the interaction to the same extent as female clients. The men also contributed more to wrapping up the conversation. They both gave and received less feedback. Conversely, female clients overlapped and interrupted the social workers more frequently.

The results from the Danish study are the opposite of what one might expect in the light of similar international studies of interaction within various institutional environments (see e.g. West, 1984; West and Zimmerman, 1985). However, the similarities with the results from Kullberg (1994) are striking. Berg Sorensen (1995) comments on the first of these facts as follows:

These observations are in clear opposition to other studies of the connections between gender, interaction style and linguistic usage, which have shown that men purportedly have the most aggressive and least considerate interaction style, while women purportedly have a more humble, self-effacing role as those who, heedless of personal costs in the form of reduced prestige, sought to ensure harmony and equilibrium; see the previously discussed study by Zimmerman, West (1975) as well as, among the more recent studies, that by Holmes (1993), where it was found

that women were, from every observed angle, both the most pleasant and most competent communication partners.
(Berg Sorensen, 1995, p250)

Berg Sorensen (1995) has also studied whether there are differences between how male and female social workers act in the encounter with clients of both genders. The most important result from this part of the study is that male social workers had a relationship that could be characterised more as a 'relationship of respect', while the women's way of conversing was more in the nature of a 'caretaker relationship' (Berg Sorensen, 1995, p248). Characteristic of the first of these interaction patterns was that the men more frequently adjusted their speech according to the client's manner of speaking and were more removed from what may be termed bureaucratic usage. The way that female case workers conducted conversation was characterised by a style anchored in the bureaucratic organisation, while elements of closeness and involvement in the topics brought up by clients also occurred. According to Berg Sorensen (1995), differences between male and female case workers were, however, not as prominent as they were with respect to clients.

In summary, the studies mentioned above point to the fact that there are differences in how women and men are treated and how their cases are handled in welfare institutions.

On the basis of the findings of two of the authors (Hetzler, 1994; Bäckström, 1994) it can also be concluded that the differences found indicate that the male clients are in an advantageous position compared with the female clients. In these studies, it seems evident that male clients get more adequate and better treatment in terms of their specific situation. However, the results from Kullberg (1994) and, the study by Berg Sorensen (1995) contradict the former authors' somewhat simplified interpretations of the treatment of male and female clients. These studies of social work can instead be said to show that the social work practice encompasses a number of separate, more or less intricate and sophisticated 'methods' (see West and Zimmerman, 1987), which social workers and clients jointly, in interaction, use to maintain the gender system. One way through which these differences are manifested is the linguistic interaction, between professional and client and professionals and professionals.

Somewhat surprisingly, compared to other studies of institutional discourse (Zimmerman and West, 1975; West, 1984; West and Zimmerman, 1985; Holmes, 1993) the analyses in the studies by Kullberg (1994) and Berg Sorensen (1995) show that the male clients do not dominate the interaction with the professionals. Another important result from Kullberg's (1994) study is that the question of which gender is favoured in contacts with the welfare institutions is not easily answered and is instead dependent on the theoretical perspective applied when the analysis is performed. Instead, the most significant result is the segregating and differentiating aspects of the client work. Male and female clients are treated according to traditional conceptions of the sexes, and the professional's attribution of responsibility for social problems seems to have a connection with the client's gender. The results found by Kullberg show that the social welfare officers place more responsibility on male clients than on female clients with respect to how soon they are expected to be able to contribute to supporting themselves. Female clients, on the other hand, are given more responsibility for the well-being of their children and conditions at home.

Gender specific 'typifications' in social welfare and welfare workers' perception of clients

The above-mentioned results of studies of interaction between professionals and clients in welfare institutions can be compared with studies in the field of research on attribution which deal with differences in how men and women are ascribed different types of social problems. A comparison with this type of research reveals that the professionals' understanding of the implications or meanings of men and women's situations varies depending on the types of 'social problems' involved. An examination of other studies in the field of social work and the field of research on

attribution indicates that the gender differences in the treatment referred to above can be interpreted as being 'gender-specific typifications' made by welfare workers in their work with male and female clients.

Clients' parental responsibility

In a Swedish research project, the written language in 20 files concerning cases of the placement in custody of children were analysed (Kåhl, 1995). The researcher's analysis also concerns the role of the two parents, as regards the children. Kåhl finds that there are large differences in how themes or subjects such as motherhood, fatherhood and parenthood are described in relation to the female and male clients. The study shows that the two parents are described in very different ways. According to the author, the files have a mother-child focus (p113), and the fathers are not described as being equally as responsible as the mothers for the well-being of their children. From the files, it can also be seen that the authors concentrate on the relation between mother and child and that the fathers are not described as resources when it comes to the taking care of their children. Kåhl finds that the mothers are attributed the sole responsibility for the children while the fathers are not expected to take an active part in the upbringing of the children. Using Kåhl's own words, the fathers are to a large extent 'excused' for their lack of involvement in their children. Eriksson and Mohlin (1996), who carried out a survey inspired by Kåhl's theoretical and methodological ideas, present similar results. Eriksson and Mohlin's study focused on 10 cases consisting of files concerning placement in custody of children according to so-called 'environmental cases' in social welfare in a small Swedish municipality. This study also shows that social welfare describes the roles of the two parents in gender-traditional ways. The authors observe that the women are attributed care of the children, while the men are given a subordinate role in this respect. Results that seem to support these conclusions have also emerged in a study carried out by the National Swedish Board of Health and Welfare

(Pettersson, 1990). In this study, which was carried out in the county of Gävleborg in Sweden, it was found that out of 64 files examined, concerning placement in custody of children, only in nine cases was there information about the children's fathers. Five of the 55 files, where the fathers were not mentioned, included data explaining why they were not included. In the remaining 50 files, there was no information whatsoever about the fathers.

The relative lack of involvement of fathers in the ongoing investigations or treatment in social work mentioned here has also been identified by other researchers. Similar results have been obtained from Swedish studies (Lennéer-Axelsson, 1989; Berg and Berg, 1992) as well as from studies from the rest of the world (see Day, 1979; Jaffe, 1983; Bryson and Edwards, 1988; Lazar, Sagi and Frazer, 1991; Pringle, 1995).

Results from research imply that the social workers have a tendency to regard and treat men as 'secondary care-takers' (Lazar, Sagi and Frazer, 1991, p297). This means that the social services under certain circumstances only treat men as 'distanced fathers', more or less 'incapable' of taking responsibility for the daily care of their children.

Clients' responsibility for social problems

The results from the studies on attribution of parental responsibility for problems with their children referred to above can be compared with research on attribution of responsibility for other categories of 'social problems'. Studies on attribution of responsibility show that men and women are assigned responsibility for different categories of behaviours. Among other things, research shows that men to a greater extent than women seem to be assigned personal responsibility for psycho-social problems, crimes they commit, but also offences that they are exposed to, for example sexual abuse. Women, on the other hand, are ascribed responsibility for problems within the family and the well-being of the children to a greater extent.

Crime

As regards criminality, it has been found that young men face the greatest probability of standing trial if they have committed a crime for which society, so to say, demands protection from or requires that they be made responsible for. At the same time, young women face the greatest probability of being placed in the custody of the social authorities of society if society feels that they are in need of protection or supervision, e.g. in cases involving their sexuality (Shaklady Smith, 1978). Research from the United States has shown that there is a much greater possibility of young women being held in detention centres for status offences (often for behaviour labelled as 'promiscuity'). In many of these cases, the protection of the girls is the main reason for society's intervention. Young men are more often sentenced for criminal offences such as burglary and car theft (Chesney-Lind, 1977).

Scientists have also discovered that young female perpetrators are less likely than young men to be arrested for crimes they have committed (Armstrong, 1977). The same researchers also found that when women do get arrested, it is also less likely that they get convicted. Others (Abbott and Wallace, 1997) claim that women, if their cases are taken to court, are more often than men given a suspended sentence. According to the same authors, women are more seldom fined than men and given shorter sentences for the same offence.

In another study, an analysis was made of how responsibility is attributed for child abuse (Howe, Herzberg and Tennen, 1988). After questioning professional social workers and psychologists, the researchers discovered that sexual abuse and physical abuse (for instance, assault) were considered more serious if they were committed by the father than by the mother. The authors' note, on the basis of the results, that it is certainly not unreasonable to assume that the differences found in professionals' assessment could correspond to the knowledge of the professionals, concerning the degree of damage that abuse from the mother or father causes the child. However, because so few studies are available, such hypotheses have yet to be verified empirically. According to the researchers, the few empirical studies that now exist (but also a large proportion of the theories in psychology) show tendencies in the opposite direction. Since children in our culture generally have a stronger attachment to the mother, abuse from her side could have more serious consequences than corresponding acts committed by the father.

Mental health

It is a well-known fact that women, to a greater extent than men, are diagnosed and they themselves report having mental problems (Hällström, 1996). Women are also being prescribed medicine for their problems to a greater extent than are men (Hällström, 1996). Whether these circumstances are due to inherent or constitutional differences between the mental health of men and women, respectively, is, however, questioned in research circles. Researchers holding a constructionist perspective of gender differences in association with different kinds of 'deviant behaviour' have argued that women, as a result of the gender order within all sectors of society, more often than men are categorised as having mental problems. This means that differences in diagnoses and prescriptions of medicine can be interpreted as gender stereotypical behaviour and as assumptions from both professionals and clients.

A study by Israel, Raskin, Libow and Pravder (1978), reported on how stereotypes of women's and men's mental health can actually function in the welfare institutions. Israel, Raskin, Libow and Pravder found that social workers in their assessment of four allegedly authentic cases of social problems placed greater responsibility on male clients than on female clients for the situation they were in. The male clients were considered, for instance, to have caused their own problems to a large extent.

Another researcher (Allen, 1997) has also questioned whether differences in professionals' treatment of clients really are due to 'real' differences, or if such differences are reflections of biases in how the welfare institutions work. Allen claims that women who

have committed crimes similar to those committed by men, are described and talked about as having mental problems to a larger extent than men during court hearings. Women are more often than men described as having problems that make them not responsible for the crimes committed. As a result of this women are more often than men sentenced to psychiatric treatment, instead of being convicted.

Conclusions

To sum up, the studies referred to indicate that welfare institutions play a part in the construction or 'moulding' of specific types of individuals or clients. In this construction work, gender-specific processes are constantly present.

On the basis of the research report here, a tentative conclusion that can be reached is that gender stereotypical attributions of responsibility play an important part in professionals' work with social problems. Another conclusion is that the attribution of responsibility for various types of social problems follows certain patterns. The attribution of responsibility seems, for instance, to be based on certain specific conceptions of such opposites, dichotomies or segregating differentiations as those 'spheres' of activities that men and women are 'traditionally' associated with, that is, paid work versus domestic work (Kullberg, 1994). These dichotomies also seem to be based on such specific acts as e.g., violence versus care and such characteristics that perhaps can best be defined as character traits (for instance, the distinctions between strong and weak or active and passive) that, by tradition, are associated with men and women, male and female. This means that the understanding of the segregation and hierarchicalising mechanisms of the gender system are tied to deeply rooted images of the characteristics of men and women, male and female. According to Abbott and Wallace (1997), patriarchal conditions, ideologies concerning how women should behave and the role of women in the family can be used in explanations of why women are treated differently to men when it comes to those actions that are categorised as 'deviant behaviour'.

Another conclusion that can be drawn from studies of attribution of responsibility for social problems is that individuals who differ from expected signs of 'deviation' or social problems that are ascribed to their gender are perceived to have more serious problems than those individuals who meet gender-specific expectations. This, for instance, seems to be the case with men suffering from mental problems (Malchon and Penner, 1981; Robertson and Fitzgerald, 1990). This also seems to be the case with women who do not meet expectations as regards their responsibility for their children's situation (McCollum and Russel, 1991) or, for example, in the case of women who have committed crimes (Lee, 1986).

One further distinctive feature indicated by research is that the attribution of responsibility seems to be connected with how conditions in general are in the specific area of the 'social problem' in question. This is evident in results showing that men who have been exposed to sexual abuse by women are held more personally responsible for what has occurred than are women in the corresponding situation. This circumstance can probably be explained by the fact that the majority of such crimes are usually committed by men, against women or children (Smith, Pine, and Hawley, 1988). In other words, it can be assumed that social workers' attribution of responsibility to clients to some extent reflects the welfare officers' knowledge of the situation that they conceive actually exists in society concerning the specific social problem in question. This means that social workers' own knowledge and their own assessments of conditions in society are probably an important resource in the work of typifying cases of male and female clients.

Another important conclusion is, in my opinion, that the positions men and women are given, and take, in the gender system to a large extent also form the conditions for, but also are conditioned by, the positions that the other gender is ascribed. It seems, in other words, as if the positions that one gender is ascribed in many cases have an imperative influence on the way that we comprehend the positions of the other gender.

Finally, it can be said that the research referred to above indicates a number of dimensions that could be used to acquire knowledge of 'gender-typing processes' in social welfare work. So far, however, there has been no large-scale study of the importance of the welfare client's gender to the professional social worker's conceptions and explanations of such 'social problems', which can be described as 'typical cases'.

References

Abbot, P. and Wallace, C. (1997) *An Introduction to Sociology, Feminist Perspectives*. London: Routledge.

Acker, J. (1991) Hierarchies, Jobs, Bodies: A Theory of Gendered Organisations. In: Lorber, J. and Farell, S.A. (Eds.) *The Social Construction of Gender.* Newbury Park: Sage Publications.

Allen, H. (1997) *Justice Unbalanced*. Milton Keynes: Open University Press (referred to in Abbot, P. and Wallace, C. (1997) *An Introduction to Sociology. Feminist Perspectives*. London: Routledge).

Armstrong, G. (1977) Female Under the Law – 'Protected but Unequal'. *Crime and Delinquency*, 23, 109–20 (referred to In: Sagatun, I. J. (1989) Gender Biases in Probation Officers: Attributions of Juvenile Delinquency. *International Journal of Offender Therapy and Comparative Criminology*, 33, 131–40).

Bäckström, I. (1994) Rehabilitering för män? En undersökning om arbetsrehabilitering av langvarigt sjukskrivna kvinnor och män. Umea Universitet: *Institutionen för socialt arbete, rapport, 37.*

Bäckström, I. and Eriksson, N. (1989) Rehabiliteringsgrupper till vilken nytta? – En studie av fyra lokala rehabiliteringsgrupper och deras klienter. *Umea Universitet: Umea Studies in Sociology, no 97.*

Bailey, R. and Brake, M. (Eds.) (1980) Radical Social Work and Practice. London, Arnold.

Becker, H. (1967) Whose Side are we on? *Social Problems*, 15, 239–47.

Berg Sorensen, T. (1996) *Den Sociale Samtale-mellem Klienter og Sagsbehandlare*. Århus: Forlag Gestus.

Björnberg, U. (1994) Mäns Familjeorientering i Förändring. Björnberg, U., Kollind, A. K. and Nilsson, A. (Eds.) *Janus och Genus. Om kön och Social Identitet i Familj och Samhälle*. Stockholm, Brombergs Bokförlag.

Björnberg, U. and Bäck-Wiklund, M. (1990) *Vardagslivets organisering i familj och närsamhälle* Göteborg: Diadalos.

Björnberg, U. and Sass, J. (1997) *Families with small children in Eastern and Western Europe*. Aldershot: Ashgate.

Bryson, L. (1992) *Welfare and the State. Who Benefits?* Basingstoke: Macmillan.

Bryson, L. and Edwards, A. (1988) Gender, Social Control and Community Services. *Australian and New Zealand Journal of Sociology*, 24: 3, 398–419.

Canaan, J. E. and Griffin, C. (1990) *The New Men's Studies: Part of the Problem or Part of the Solution?* In: Hearn, J. and Morgan, D. (Eds.) *Men, Masculinity and Social Theory*. London: Unwin Hyman.

Chesney-Lind, M. (1977) Judicial Paternalism and the Female Status Offenders. Training Women to Know their Place. *Crime and Delinquency*. 23 (April), 121–30.

Cockburn, C. (1983) *Brothers. Male Dominance and Technological Change*. London: Pluto Press.

Connell, R. W. (1995) *Masculinities*. Cambridge: Polity Press.

Corrigan, P. and Leonard, P. (1981) *Kritisk syn pa socialt arbeid – en marxistisk tilnærming*. Oslo: Universitsforlaget.

Davies, B. and Harré, R. (1989) Positioning: The Discursive Production of Selves. *Journal for the Theory of Social Behaviour*. 20: 1, 43–63.

Day, P. (1979) Sex-role Stereotypes and Public Assistance. *Social Service Review*. 53: 1, 106–15.

Douglas, M. (1987) *How Institutions Think*. London: Routledge and Kegan Paul.

Eriksson, N. and Mohlin, A-M. (1996) *Dikotomiseringar av moders- och fadersrollen i LVU-utredningar* Hogskolan i Örebro: Institutionen för socialt arbete. C-uppsats i socialt arbete.

Goffman, E. (1959) *The Presentation of Self in Everyday Life*. New York: Doubleday.

Goffman, E. (1977) The Arrangement Between the Sexes. *Theory and Society*, 4, 301–31.

Haavind, H. (1982) Makt och kjærlighet i ektenskapet. Hakaa, R., Hoel, Marit, Haavind and Hanne (Eds.) *Kvinneforskning: bidrag till samfunnsteori*. Oslo: Universitetsforlaget.

Hällström, T. (1996) Psykisk ohälsa – könsskillnader. Förekomsten av psykiska sjukdomar hos män och kvinnor. Östlin,P., Danielsson, M., Didrichsen, F., Härenstam, A. and Lindberg, G. (Eds.) Kön och ohälsa. *En antologi om könsskillnader ur ett folkhälsoperspektiv*. Lund: Studentlitteratur.

Hartmann, H. (1976) Capitalism, Patriarchy, and Job Segregation by Sex. In: Blaxall, M. and Reagan, B. *Women and the Workplace*. Chicago: University of Chicago Press.

Hetzler, A. (1994) *Socialpolitik i verkligheten. Den handikappade och försäkringskassan*. Lund: Bokbox Förlag.

Hirdman, Y. (1988) Genussystemet – reflektioner kring kvinnors sociala underordning. *Kvinnovetenskaplig tidskrift*. 3, 49–63.

Hirdman, Y. (1990) Genussystemet. In Statens offentliga utredningar, 1990: 44. *Maktutredningens huvudrapport*. Stockholm.

Holmberg, C. (1993) *Det kallas kärlek. En socialpsykologisk studie om kvinnors sociala underordning och mäns överordning bland unga jämställda par*. Göteborg: Anamma Förlag. (Dissertation).

Holmes, J. (1993) New Zealand Women are Good to Talk to: An Analysis of Politeness Strategies in Interaction. *Journal of Pragmatics*, 20, 91–116. (Referred to in Berg Sorensen, T. 1995. Den sociale samtale – mellem klienter og sagsbehandlere Århus: Forlaget Gestus).

Holter, Ø. G. and Aarseth, H. (1993) *Mäns livssammanhang*. Stockholm: Bonnier Utbildning.

Howe, A. C., Herzberger, S. and Tennen, H. (1988) The Influence of Personal History of Abuse and Gender on Clinicians Judgements of Child Abuse. *Journal of Family Violence*, 3:2, 105–19.

Hydén, M. (1992) *Woman Battering as Marital Act. The Construction of a Violent Marriage*. Stockholm University. Stockholm Studies in Social Work 7. (Dissertation).

Hydén, M. (1994) Det upprepade valdet mot kvinnor i äktenskapet och fragan om manlig ansvarsbefrielse. *Socialvetenskaplig tidskrift*, 2–3, 193–205.

Israel, A., Raskin, P., Libow, J. and Pravder, M. (1978) Gender and Sex-role Appropriateness: Bias in the Judgement of Disturbed Behaviour. *Sex Roles*, 3, 399–413.

Jaffe, E. D. (1983). Fathers and Child Welfare Services: The Forgotten Client? In: Lamb, M. E. and Sagi, A. (Eds.) *Fatherhood and Family Policy*. Hillsdale, NJ: Lawrence Erlbaum Association.

Kagle, J. D. and Cowger, C. D. (1984) Blaming the Client: Implicit Agendas in Practice Research? *Social Work*. 29: 4, 347–51.

Kahl, I. (1995) *Socialarbetarkaren – den lindansande professionen*. Lund: Bokbox Förlag. (Dissertation).

Kulick, D. (1991) Hur man blir en riktig kvinna eller man. Kulick, D. (Ed.) *Fran kön till genus. Kvinnligt och manligt i ett kulturellt perspektiv*. Stockholm: Carlsson Bokförlag.

Kullberg, C. (1994) Socialt arbete som kommunikativ praktik. Samtal med och om klienter Linköping Universitet: Linköping. *Studies in Arts and Scien*ce, 115. (Dissertation).

Kullberg, C. (1996) Swedish Fathers and the Welfare State Institutions. In: Björnberg, U. and Kollind, A-K. (Eds.) *Men's Family Relations*. Stockholm: Almqvist and Wiksell International.

Kullberg, C. (1997) Arbete eller socialbidrag? Socialsekreterares samtal med och om kvinnliga och manliga klienter. Bladh, C., Cedersund, E. and Hagberg, J-E. (Eds.) Kvinnor och man som aktörer och klienter. *En antologi som skildrar tidigt 1800-tal och framat Stockholm*: Nerenius and Santérus Förlag.

Kullberg, C. (1999) Men's Lack of Family Orientation. Some Reflections on Scandinavian Research on Families. Ervø, S. and Johansson, T. *Images of Masculinities: Moulding Masculinities.* vol. 1. London: Ashgate.

Kullberg, C. (2000) *Gender and Social Work. Genderising Processes in Social Work Practice. Research Plan.* (stencil). University of Örebro. Department of Social Sciences.

Kullberg, C. and Cedersund, E. (1996). Forskning om värdering av kvinnors och mäns arbeten. Cedersund, E. and Kullberg, C. *Arbetsvärdering. Teori, praktik, kritik*. Stockholm: Arbetslivsinstitutet.

Lazar, A., Sagi, A. and Frazer, M. W. (1991) Involving Fathers in Social Service. *Children and Youth Service,* 13: 4, 287–300.

Lee, S. (1986) Losing Out: Sexuality and Adolescent Girls. Harmondsworth: Penguin. (referred to in Abbot, P. and Wallace, C. (1997) *An Introduction to Sociology. Feminist Perspectives*. London: Routledge).

Lennéer-Axelsson, B. (1989) *Männens röster i kris och förändring*. Stockholm: Sesam.

Malchon, M. J. and Penner, L. A. (1981) The Effect of Sex And Sex-role Identity on the Attribution of Maladjustment. *Sex Roles*, 7: 4, 363–78.

McCollum, E. and Russel, C. (1991) Mother Blaming in Family Therapy: An Empirical Investigation. *American Journal of Family Therapy*, 1, 71–6. 1992.

Mishler, E. (1984) The Discourse of Medicine. *Dialectics of Medical Interviews*. Norwood, NJ: Ablex.

Öberg, B. and Öberg, G. (1992) *Pappa se mig. Om förnekade barn och maktlösa fäder*. Stockholm: Förlagshuset Gothia.

Östlin, P., Danielsson, M., Didrichsen, F., Härenstam, A. and Lindberg, G. (Eds.) (1996) Kön och ohälsa. *En antologi om könsskillnader ur ett folkhälsoperspektiv*. Lund: Studentlitteratur.

Pettersson, G-M. (1990) *Utredningar om barn och ungdomar*. Socialstyrelsen: Individ och familjeenheten. Remissupplaga.

Pringle, K. (1995) *Men, Masculinities and Social Welfare*. London: University College London Press.

Robertsson, J. and Fitzgerald, L. F. (1990) The (Mis)treatment of Men: Effects of Client Gender Role and Life-Style on Diagnosis and Attribution of Pathology. *Journal of Counselling Psycholog*y, 37: 1, 3–9.

Sainsbury, D. (Ed.) (1999) *Gender and Welfare State Regimens*. Oxford: Oxford University Press.

Sätterlund Larsson, U. (1989) Being Involved. Patients Participation in Health Care. Linköping University. Linköping. *Studies in Arts and Science*, 36. (Dissertation).

Shaklady Smith, L. 1(978) Sexist Assumptions and Female Delinquency. In: Smart, C. and

Smart, B. (Eds.) *Women, Sexuality and Social Control*. London: Routledge and Kegan Paul.

Smith, R. E., Pine, C. J. and Hawley, M. E. (1988) Social Cognition About Adult Male Victims of Female Sexual Assault. *Journal of Sex Research*, 24, 101–12.

Sudnow, D. (1965) Normal Crimes. *Social problems*. 12, 255–76.

Todd, A. (1983) The Prescription of Contraception: Negotiations Between Doctors and Patients. *Discourse Processes*. 171–201.

Waitzkin, H. (1991) *The Politics of Medical Encounter. How Patients and Doctors Deal with Social Problems*. New Haven: Yale University Press.

Van Dijk, T. (1989) Structures of Discourse and Structures of Power. *Communication Yearbook*, 12, 18–59.

West, C. (1984) When the Doctor is a 'Lady': Power, Status and Gender in Physician-Patient Encounters. *Symbolic Interaction*. 7: 1, 87–106.

West, C. and Zimmerman, D. (1985) Gender, Language and Discourse. *Handbook of Discourse*, vol. 4. London: Academic Press.

West, C. and Zimmerman, D. (1987) Doing Gender. *Gender and Society*, 1:2, 125–51.

Zimmerman, D. H. and West, C. (1975) Sex Roles, Interruptions and Silence In Conversation. In: Thorne, B. and Henley, N. (Eds.) (1975) *Language and Sex. Difference and Dominance*. Rowley, Mass. Newbury House Publishing. (Referred to in Berg Sørensen, T. (1995) Den sociale samtale – mellem klienter og sagsbehandlere. Århus: Forlaget Gestus.)

13. Are Boys and Girls Treated in the Same Way by the Social Services?

Elinor Brunnberg

Introduction

Boys and girls can, in identical situations be treated differently by social workers from the same social welfare department. An associative gender approach seems to influence the execution of their duties. Boys get more help and protection than girls. For girls, the information about their situation is more often queried and checked by the social services than is the case for boys.

According to the United Nations Children's Convention (UD informerar, 1996:2), children should not be discriminated against on the grounds of their or their parents' race, gender, ethnic origin, handicap, birth etc. Boys and girls are to be treated equally. Responsibility for raising children is to be shared between men and women. According to the United Nations Human Rights Convention (UD informerar, 1996:3), men and women shall have equal rights and responsibilities as parents in all matters concerning children. Prejudices, customs and traditions which are based on the notion that one gender is inferior, or on set roles for men and women will no longer be acceptable.

Now, most of the countries in the world have agreed to follow the regulations in the United Nations Children's Convention. Sweden was one of the first countries to sign the convention, but the impact of the convention has, in practice, been limited. In 1998, the Child Ombudsman mapped out how the principles of the Children's Convention had influenced the child perspective of the Swedish authorities, and came to the conclusion that the Children's Convention views on children had not in any systematic way changed or developed most authorities' perspectives on children (Barnombudsmannen, 1998). On the 1 January 1998, the key paragraph of the Swedish law on

social services was changed in accordance with the UN Children's Convention, and the child's perspective was emphasised by giving priority to what was best for the child in all measures concerning the child.

Authorities and institutions should, just like the parents, act on the basis of what is 'best for the child' (UD informerar, 1996:2 p23), The children should be given the opportunity to express their opinion in all matters concerning them. In carrying out their duties, the authorities may not discriminate by making distinctions, exceptions or limitations based on gender or age. Children, particularly girls, and also their mothers are instead to be protected from every form of discriminatory action. Also, authorities working with families in chaotic situations must work to change petrified gender roles, and see to it that children, regardless of whether they are boys or girls, are treated in the same way.

The official statistics (Socialstyrelsen, 1999) concerning children and youths affected by social services actions show that boys slightly more often than girls are the subject of social welfare actions in Sweden. In 1998, of the children who were in placements other than with their families, about 53% were boys and 47% girls. There were bigger gender differences for youth. Of the young people aged 18 or over, almost 70% of those who were immediately taken into care, or who received treatment in accordance with LVU (law about the care of young people) in 1998 were male. Statistics from earlier years also demonstrate a preponderance of boys in social services activities.

In this chapter I shall investigate whether boys and girls are pre-treated equally by social workers when dealing with children at risk. I will do this from a child and gender perspective. In order to make this comparison, the social workers in an average-sized Swedish municipality were asked to respond to a vignette, a fictitious case description. The vignette was arranged in stages, so that the child's situation grew steadily worse. Half of the social workers received a case about Eva; the other half had a case about Erik. The case descriptions about which the social workers were asked to make a judgement were thus identical and about a 4-year old child. The only difference was whether there was a boy's or a girl's name. The questions which I wished to explore were whether social workers have different attitudes to boys and girls, and if a boy or girl receives the same help or protection in the same situation. Do the social services employ the same measures for a boy as for a girl when the child is in the same situation? When working with children, what perspective is taken by the social worker – is it that of the child, the family, or the parents or is it some other perspective?

Traditional conceptions of gender are reproduced

Those adults whom most children in almost all cultures have a lot of daily contact with, apart from their parents, are their teachers. School research shows that there are similarities between the behaviour of teachers and pupils in different nations (Granström and Einarsson, 1995). The teachers pay more attention to the boys than to the girls, at the same time that the boys themselves take up more of the interactive space in the classroom than the girls do. School research also shows that boys can be perceived as more disturbing in the classroom than girls. Girls are also regarded as more well-adjusted than boys and are overlooked more often than boys. Boys, on the other hand, are allowed to misbehave more than girls.

It is only in recent years that studies have been made from a gender perspective of how boys and girls are treated by the social services. An associative approach can lead to the reproduction of traditional conceptions of gender, through the transference of normal associations between social phenomena without counter factorial questioning of the status of the relationship between these phenomena (Sayer, 1999). An associative

approach can thus lead to the fact that social services, just like schools, pay more attention to boys than girls. The boys receive attention because it is assumed that they have problems and need protection. Girls in the same situation may be overlooked or there may be doubts about how to interpret the situation. Traditional conceptions about gender are reinforced when boys get more attention and protection than girls in equivalent situations.

A Swedish study shows that social work seems to strongly conserve gender roles. Social problems are made invisible and are reinterpreted as individual problems, according to Ingela Kåhl (1995). She analysed 20 treatment case-books from three different municipalities where most of the children and young people had been placed in foster homes. The case-book descriptions of women and men and boys and girls were to a great extent from a traditional gender perspective. Assaults on women were redefined as family quarrels and made invisible. The social workers adopted the male perspective by not using words like 'assault', and instead used 'conflict', 'quarrel' and so on. The boys were more noticeable in the case-books analysed, and were described as active subjects to a greater extent than the girls. The girls, on the other hand, were described in a more diffuse way, and their opinions were not made clear in the same manner. A study from a youth clinic – Maria Norra Ungdomsklinik – (Andersson, 1991a) also indicates that the authority documents boys' and girls' cases very differently. There were boy case-files and girl case-files. In the girl case-files there was a clearer negative reaction to the girls' behaviour than in the boy case-files. In the latter, the boys' recreational pursuits were described instead. Traditional motherhood and fatherhood permeated the investigations studied by Ingela Kåhl (1995). The mother was regarded as having the main responsibility for raising the child; the father was not included in this, and escaped responsibility for care of the child. The 'good mother' myth had central symbolic value, while at the same time there was no 'good father' myth. Alleged 'bad mothers' or 'fallen women' were roundly condemned by the social workers. Assaults on women were redefined as family quarrels and made invisible. The social workers adopted the men's perspective by not using words like 'assault', and instead used 'conflict', 'quarrel', etc. The type of family which emerged from the empirical material was 'a chaotic family with neither the energy nor the capacity to set limits', where the traditional gender perspective, with women in an inferior role, was reinforced.

That the social workers reproduce traditional conceptions of gender in their meetings with parents has been shown in a number of studies. In applications for economic assistance (Kullberg, 1994), the social workers put greater emphasis on the men managing to support themselves than they did on the women doing the same. The women were regarded more as being the victims of their economic problems. They were given attention primarily as mothers, and their ability to provide good social care to their children was central. The men's role as fathers did not receive as much attention. The social workers saw it as central that the man upheld the traditional bread-winner's role, and the woman the care-giver's role.

Violence against women is the ultimate expression of lack of gender equality.

In the legislation on social services, it is emphasised that the social services committee should act so that women who are or who have been exposed to violence or other abuse in the home get support and help to change their situation (SFS 2001:453). Statistics for Sweden show that in half of the cases where there has been violence between the parents, the children have also been assaulted (Weinehall, 1997). Children and mothers can often be both witnesses and victims of family violence. An English study showed that children in families where the mothers were assaulted by the father figures often witnessed the violence, but the professionals did not pay much attention to the children's situation (Farmer and Owen, 1995). A Swedish study (Weinehall, 1997), in which 15 young people who had grown up with violence in the home were interviewed in-depth on several occasions during four years, showed that most of them had been both witnesses (15) and victims (13) of their fathers' violence. In none of the families had the mother alone used violence. The children were threatened into silence. There were family rules, and they were

dictated by the father. In school, the children were seen as different and were often bullied by their peers and received no support from the adults. When these young people broke their silence and sought help, they were ignored by the social services.

Interview with a child in an exposed situation

According to the UN Children's Convention, (UD informerar, 1996:2), the views of the child should, with due allowance made for maturity, always be taken into account. In the general guidelines for the social services committee's activities, in the Swedish legislation on social welfare, it is emphasised that when a measure involves a child, then that child's point of view should as far as possible be ascertained. (SFS 2001:453). If the child is living in an exposed situation where there is physical and psychological abuse, it is possible that the child cannot or does not dare to tell an unknown adult outsider what has happened. Lack of confidence, feelings of loyalty, or feelings of guilt about what has happened, or a 'rule of silence' in the family can make it impossible for the child to say anything. The child can, in this exposed position, just like women in abuse cases (Hyden, 1994), hesitate about describing the violence, or personally interpret it so that the perpetrator of the assault is freed from responsibility.

A study of police interviews with children who were suspected of having been sexually abused (Cederborg, 1998) showed that some of the children could relate the entire episode, while others completely denied its occurrence. There were also children who could only talk about what had happened in a fragmentary way. The child's reaction to the abuse situation may be to conceal the episode to protect the parent who is the abuser. Silence may also be one of the family rules dictated by the threatening parent (Weinehall, 1997). The rules are often unexpressed and can be arbitrarily changed. The home environment is unpredictable. The young people in Weinehall's study described how there was a constant state of alert in the family before an act of violence, and an almost total silence afterwards. The members of the family abided by the man's rules in order to avoid further violence.

Establishing the child's viewpoint in a situation where there may be violence in the family not only assumes that the child is mature enough to talk about it, but also that the child is aware of the nature of the family relationships, and that the interviews take place in such a way that the child has confidence in the adult and dares to talk about what has happened.

The vignette as a method

The vignette is a description in words of a social situation. The situation described can be interpreted in many ways, since the description is rather brief. This gives each of the social workers an opportunity to create their own picture of the case. The vignette in this study can be termed a vertical vignette (Jergeby, 1999), since it has various factors which are gradually changed over time. With their own impression of the case based on the brief information given, the social workers have answered open and closed questions. The vignette method is one that has many possibilities for variation, which is useful in comparative studies (Soydan and Stål, 1994) since those interviewed receive the same information. In the vignette in question, only the gender of the child has varied. The case descriptions are fictitious constructions based on a mix of real cases. The vignettes have been constructed from real cases at several social welfare offices. Many of the social workers have felt that the examples were realistic and true to life. They have put a lot of effort into answering the questions posed in the vignettes.

The social workers may, in their answers, have given a rather rosy picture, even though they were asked to answer as realistically as possible. They may have described how they would like to act. The answers can in any case be said to reflect what attitudes and values the social workers have. The advantage of the method is that all of the social workers have had the same situation to react to, regardless of whether it has been a boy or a girl. Comparability is present in the vignette method in a much more absolute sense than it is in reality. In order that it should say something about a real situation, the case description in

the vignette must have 'face validity', that is, be perceived by the social workers as realistic. The social workers seem to have understood the case description in question as a situation they could meet in reality.

Analysis

My overall perspective in the analysis is one of gender. The central question is whether boys and girls are treated equally by the social services. Therefore I do not only wish to know if the social services engage in the same situations for boys and girls, and take the same measures in the same situations, but also what perspective the social workers use in their work, that is, whose situation they mainly focus on, and with whom they have contact.

A child perspective in social work means that the child is regarded as a separate subject with opportunity to express themselves on matters of central importance to the child. In all authority activities, both a child and a woman's perspective is required. Gender discrimination of any age-group is to be combated. A child perspective can emanate from different assessments of the child's relationship to its parents. In the UN Children's Convention, something which can in part be interpreted in part as an *ecological child perspective* (Brunnberg, 2001), and in part as a *child protection perspective* is described. An ecological child perspective (Hessle, 1996; Garbarino and Eckenrode, 1997) can be described as a whole perspective where everything fits into everything else like a Russian doll (Bronfenbrenner, 1979). Regarding the child's welfare, the family is the child's central environment. The family must have the support of the surrounding community and society in order to work for what is best for the child. At the same time that society safeguards the family as the natural setting for the growth of a child, the child should be protected from all forms of physical or psychological violence, injury or acts of cruelty, as well as negligence or neglectful care, abuse or exploitation by the child's guardian. The child may need protection from one or more of the family members. Social workers are a professional category who are likely to meet the child in a situation where assessments based on a child protection perspective are central. Social work can also be carried out from a *family perspective*, where the family's situation is central. The child may then not be visible as a person, and be mainly regarded as an object of care for the parents' attentions. Even when the social worker's point of departure is a family perspective, the child may, in relation to the other individuals in the family collective, be regarded as a visible subject at the same time that they are an object for parental attention.

Selection and instruments

The empirical material was collected in Örebro at the turn of the year 1998/99. Örebro is a municipality where the figure for new placements of children aged 0–12 years was just under the national average for Swedish municipalities. It is thus a medium-sized municipality, with normal placement figures for children of the age mentioned in the vignette. More women social workers than men answered the vignette in 1998. The men accounted for 23% of replies, the women for 77%.

The vignette has been gender-varied. Half of the social workers had a version of the vignette in which the child was called Erik, and the other half had a version in which the child was called Eva. 79 social workers from Örebro answered the vignette. 41 had a case in which the child was called Erik, and 38 received instead a case description in which the child was called Eva. Thus, the gender of the child was varied by changing the name. In all other respects the accounts were identical. In the first stage of the vignette, diffuse second-hand information about lack of care is described. In the second stage, the information is addressed directly to the social services. The information comes from a person who has seen how Erik/Eva has been struck by the father. In the third stage, the child has visible signs of physical abuse, and also other symptoms of not developing in a normal way.

Stage 1

The district nurse has heard from a patient that there is a small child in the district, about four years old, whose parents do not seem to be looking after them properly. Erik/Eva is allowed to be out until late in the evenings. Sometimes it seems that the parents leave them alone at home while they go shopping.

Stage 2

(Your office receives a phone-call some months later about the same family).

A neighbour of the family has phoned the counsellor at the social services office and said that she often hears a little boy or girl screaming in the house. A few days ago she saw the father hit the child hard. The child had broken a window when they were playing football with some older children. The father was very angry and shouted and hit the child. This was not the first time she had seen the father being hard with the child.

When the social workers had progressed this far with the case, they got new information about the state of things about six months later.

Stage 3

During a visit to the child health care centre, a nurse discovers several bruises on Erik's/Eva's back and several round burns on their cheek and one arm. The parents say that Erik/Eva often falls over and gets hurt, because they are such an active child. They have got the burns by walking into people with cigarettes. The visit to the care centre also revealed that Erik/Eva had lost weight in the last six months. The mother had said that the child had had a bad appetite lately, and often had infections.

The social workers have answered open questions, describing their immediate reactions, what they would do if they began to work with the case, what further information they would want, what ideas the information prompted, what they saw as the biggest problem and who they thought was the main client. The social workers were also asked to state what measures they thought they would take -whether the child, with support from the social and medical services could remain at home, whether a contact person or a contact family should be appointed, whether the parents should be encouraged to voluntarily place the child in care outside the home, or whether an application for compulsory placement in care should be made.

Results

Client, non-client or half-client

Working with clients at a social services office is dealt with in different phases which overlap and merge with each other – reception, investigation, measures/treatment and conclusion (Billquist, 1999). A sorting process takes place which decides if the client is to be regarded as a client or not, and who is to be regarded as the main client. In child care, different people can be regarded as the main client. A person is not a client in the formal sense until they have been registered at the social services office. There are also 'half-clients', that is, clients who are not registered and in relation to whom no investigations are conducted or formal decisions made. They are not visible in the organisation. There are also non-clients – those people who are turned away.

In Stage 1 of the vignette, the 4-year-old child's situation was described in a diffuse way and all the information was second-hand. In spite of the diffuse account of possible deficiencies in the care of the child, the social workers were of the opinion that the social services would probably take on the case. Erik's and Eva's social workers reacted differently to a certain extent. Of the social workers assessing Erik's case, over one third (39%) were certain that the case would be something for them to work with, while only one quarter of the social workers assessing Eva's case (24%) were equally certain. This can be interpreted as meaning that Eva and her family were not as often regarded as clients as Erik and his family were, and instead were more often regarded as half-clients.

In Stage 2 of the vignette, when the father was seen to hit the child, most of the social workers were convinced that the child would be subject to social services activities. Only every fifth social worker had any doubts at all. At this stage there was no difference between the social workers assessing the boy's or the girl's situation. In Stage 3 of the vignette, when

Table 1 Percentage of social workers who were sure that the case would be taken up by their social service offices

	Eva	Erik
Stage 1 – first report	24%	39%
Stage 2 – investigative phase	79%	81%
Stage 3 – investigative phase reactive social work	82%	93%

symptoms of suspected abuse were observed by nursing staff, more of the social workers were completely convinced that the child's situation would be taken up by the social services. Somewhat more of those judging Eva's case than those judging Erik's case still expressed a certain hesitation.

It seems that in situations where the report is diffuse, or where the child has probably already been abused, the social services give boys somewhat more unreserved attention than they give girls. However, regardless of whether the case involved a boy or a girl, the social workers were equally certain that it was a matter for the social services when the father was seen to hit the child, that is, they were sure that the social services would have to carry out an investigation to establish whether the situation described was unique or not, and if the family needed help, or the child protection.

Child perspective or family perspective

The social workers' perceptions about who was the main client varied. They thought that it was the child, the child and the family, or just the family that was the main client. A few social workers thought it was one of the parents, or some other family constellation which could be regarded as the main client. In my opinion, those social workers who indicated that it was the child, or the child and the family that were the main clients expressed a child perspective since they indicated that the child was the main client. I judged that those social workers who only indicated the family as the main client had a family perspective. The social workers' assessments varied according to whether they had received a case description about a boy or a girl.

Table 2 Perspectives that social workers had in their work if they met Eva or Erik

| | Child persp | | Family persp | | Other answer | |
	Eva	Erik	Eva	Erik	Eva	Erik
Stage 1	74%	54%	24%	42%	0%	5%
Stage 2	68%	95%	32%	0%	0%	5%
Stage 3	84%	98%	16%	2%	0%	0%

In Stage 1 of the vignette, that is, in the initial process of sorting and establishing the clients, most of the girl's social workers expressed a child perspective. Three-quarters of Eva's social workers and over half of Erik's social workers reacted to the diffusely described situation by taking a child perspective. Almost half of Erik's social workers had a family or parent perspective.

In Stage 2 of the vignette, when the father is seen to hit the child, several of the social workers changed their minds about who should be the main client. The social workers reacted differently depending on whether they had the boy's or the girl's case. When the problems described became worse, all of Erik's social workers abandoned the family perspective. One third of Eva's social workers, on the other hand, had a family perspective, which was an increase in number compared with Stage 1. In Stage 3, when symptoms of suspected abuse were observed, a greater number of Eva's social workers also expressed a child perspective.

This can be interpreted as meaning that the social worker sees the child as the main client, when the child may need protection from someone in the family who uses violence on the child, and that a girl can be exposed to more direct violence than a boy before the social services judge that they must protect the child. The gravity of a violent situation can be judged differently.

Different reception of boys and girls by the social services

Most of the social workers who received a case description of a girl chose the child perspective at Stage 1. The choices were *general child perspective, child protection perspective,* or an *ecological child perspective.* Those social

workers who had a general child perspective emphasised that the point of departure for social work should be the child, but did not describe in more detail how that affected their work:

The interests of the child come first.

(Social worker)

Those social workers, whom in the analysis I deemed to have adapted a child protection perspective, explained why they considered that the child was the main client by saying that the child might be in need of protection:

The girl may need protection. The child should come first.

(Social worker)

There were social workers who throughout all three stages of the vignette adopted a child protection perspective, since the primary aim was to ascertain if the child needed protection. Two-thirds of the social workers were prepared to change their minds about who the main client was when the situation grew worse. When the problem situation grew worse, more and more social workers took the child protection perspective. The social workers who at Stage 1 reasoned from what can be interpreted as an ecological child perspective focused on both the child's and the family's situation. They could explain their perspective in this way:

The child may be being abused. The child is in focus ... What are the family's living conditions? Are they receiving childcare? Have they had any previous contact with the social services?

(Social worker)

The largest group of Erik's social workers chose a family perspective in Stage 1. They considered that the family was the main client. Several of the social workers with a family perspective focussed primarily on the parents' shortcomings or characteristics:

The parents are lacking in their ability to look after the boy.

(Social worker)

Among the social workers who had a family perspective, there were varying views of the child. Those social workers who above all focused on the parents' shortcomings saw the child primarily as an object for the parents' attentions There were also social workers with a family perspective who focussed both on the child and the parents' care of the child. This can be interpreted as the child being perceived both as subject and object:

> *It's about the boy being in some way maltreated. But it is the whole family that needs help. The parents, working with me and/or their network will see to it that the boy's situation improves. The focus is on the child.*

> (Social worker)

A family perspective where the child is seen as both subject and object can be said to be close to an ecological child perspective, in which the family is, of course, a central enveloping setting for the child. Even in social work with a family perspective the child can be made visible as an individual, but if the social worker has to prioritise, they may act differently depending on whether the child or the family is given first priority. Check the information, help the family or protect the child. The social workers were asked to describe their immediate reactions upon reading the case description. They were asked about what ideas the information prompted. Whether they thought that there was not a problem in the situation described, or if there was a problem but that the reliability of the information needed checking. Some also reacted with the feeling that there was a problem, and that the parents needed support and help to be better able to take care of their child, or that the problem meant that something needed to be done to protect the child.

Statutory child care is regulated by the Swedish legislation on social services (SFS, 2001:620), and in the law concerning special regulations for the care of young people (SFS, 1990:52). In social services' activities there is a tension between voluntariness and coercion, and between support and control. There is also a tension between helping the family and protecting the child. The everyday statutory childcare work done by social workers at the social services office can be described as the arrangement of help and support, control and the exercise of authority, treatment-oriented work and work which is solely of an investigatory nature (Andersson, 1991b). It can also be defined as the carrying out of preventive work by social workers to further the favourable physical and social development of the child and its personality (SFS 2001:453), and help the family to look after the child in the best way possible; or the carrying out of reactive social work as a consequence of the possibility that the child has already been exposed to destructive circumstances such as abuse, improper exploitation, care deficiencies or some other circumstance in the home where there is a palpable risk that the child's health or development is damaged (SFS 1990:52). In the circumstance the child may need protection from someone in the family. Regardless of how the everyday work in statutory childcare is described, the content seems to consist to a great extent of sorting into categories, that is, one has to 'decide if a report is to lead to an investigation, if an investigation should lead to an action, and if so, what', (Lundström, 1996, p51).

At Stage 1, when the situation described was based on second-hand information, both Eva's (97%) and Erik's (93%) social workers thought that the reliability of the information should be checked. A few social workers' reaction was that there was a problem that the parents needed help with so that they could take better care of their child.

Check the information, help the family or protect the child

When the problem was made more concrete, and the information was from a neighbour who described certain observations, a majority of Erik's social workers reacted by thinking that the family had problems and needed help (71%). Somewhat fewer of Eva's social workers reacted in the same way, thinking that the family had problems and needed help (55%). More of Eva's social workers (37%) still wanted to check the reliability of the information first. Only a few (7%) of Erik's social workers still wanted to first check the information. On the other hand, more of Erik's social workers (20%) than Eva's (8%) reacted with the immediate feeling that something should be done to protect the child. So the boy's social workers react more unequivocally in their perception that there is a social problem than the girl's social workers do. The girl's social workers are more inclined to question the reliability of the information.

When symptoms of suspected abuse in Stage 3 of the vignette are observed by a nurse at the child health care centre, it becomes central for most of both Erik's (90%) and Eva's (84%) social workers to protect the child. Slightly more of Erik's social workers than Eva's reacted by wanting to protect the child. Among Erik's social workers there were still a few who believed that the family had a problem and needed help. Some of Eva's social workers, even in this situation, wanted to check the reliability of the information. When the child had probably already suffered physical abuse, the great majority of both Erik's and Eva's social workers saw their task to be the protection of the child.

Interviews with the child

Being a client means entering into an administrative and an emotional relationship with the social worker The relationship with the child in this context can be regarded in the light of it 'being about a client' that is, a client with whom the social worker has very limited direct contact. (Brunnberg, 2001), regardless of whether the child, the family or one of the parents is seen as the main client. In the initial categorisation process, even most of the social workers who stated that they worked with a child perspective; saw the relationship as 'being about a client'. Few of them said that they would interview the child if they were dealing with the case.

In Stage 2 of the vignette, which the social workers regarded as an investigative situation, roughly one third of them said that they would

Table 3 Number of social workers who said that they would see or interview the child if they began working on the case

	Erik	Eva
Stage 1	2%	8%
Stage 2	27%	34%
Stage 3	2%	5%

interview or see the child. In Stage 3, when symptoms of suspected abuse were found on the child, there were once again only a few social workers who stated that they would interview the child when they were asked what they would do with this case, and if there were any routines they would be expected to follow in a case like this. There were rather more of the social workers who had the girl's case (40%) than of those with the boy's case (32%) who said that they would interview or see the child.

It is above all in a situation where a neighbour has said that she often hears a small child screaming in the house, and that she has also seen the child receive a heavy blow from the father after breaking a window, that it was recognised as important to interview the child as well. This is a situation in which approximately three-quarters of Erik's social workers and about half of Eva's think that the family has problems and needs help. Talking to the child is not so central for the social workers when the nurse at the child health care centre discovers the symptoms of suspected abuse in the form of bruises and burns, and that the child has also lost weight. Most of the social workers judged that the child needed protecting. Neither was it as important to meet or interview the child about the situation when it was described as based on second-hand information about possible shortcomings in the care of the child. In that situation, the most important thing for almost all of both Erik's and Eva's social workers was to check the reliability of the information that had come to their notice. The checking of information was done by contacting the adults, for instance the informant or the parents. The social worker also gave information to the adults, i.e. the parents. Only a few social workers met the child as well at this stage. It seems to be when the situation has worsened that the social workers first try to see the child. At that stage an investigation may also have been initiated:

Start an investigation, talk to the parents, the child, and other people, for instance at the child health care centre and the nursery school.

(Social worker)

When the problem situation has become even worse, and the child has probably already suffered physical abuse, so that there are visible injuries, the social workers judge that the child needs protecting, and contact with other adults once again becomes the central issue for them. Then for instance parents, police, doctors, the nursery school, referees, colleagues and others are contacted.

The child's relationship with its mother and father

When the social workers write about the mother and father they almost exclusively use the term 'the parents', apart from in Stage 2, when they are describing what they judge to be the biggest problem in the case. Several of both Erik's (42%) and Eva's (26%) social workers believe that the biggest problem in the situation described is that 'the father hits' the child. Somewhat more of Eva's social workers (42%) and as many of Erik's (42%) describe the biggest problem as 'physical abuse', or 'violence', but these terms are not then directly related to the father. When the terms for assault are used, there is an anonymisation of the perpetrator. Seen morally, the term 'assault' can be interpreted as a more condemning expression for an unacceptable violent action than the term 'hit'. The more morally loaded the social worker's description of a problem situation is, the more invisible the person responsible for the action becomes.

When the social workers in the following questions have described what further information they think would be important to have before making their judgement, and what the social worker would do if they were to begin working with the case, the parents are most often regarded as one unit. Only a few of both Erik's (15%) and Eva's (8%) social workers reflected on the parents being two people with different relationships to and ways of acting with the child. The fact that the parents are regarded as one unit seems to contribute to making the father's responsibility for his actions invisible, even though the social workers classify what has happened as assault. The mother is made directly or indirectly an accessory to the assault through the fact that the individual responsibility for the action is made invisible, at the same time that the parents have a joint responsibility for

their child. The social worker's assessment may be that the child should be protected from both its parents because of the father's actions:

Report to the police – Child abuse. Take the girl into care; she needs protection from her parents.
(Social worker)

Making the individual responsibility for a parent's violence towards his/her child invisible can even mean that the social worker directly rephrases who has done it:

That the boy is in a family which instead of giving him security beats him. Perhaps he should be taken into care immediately.
(Social worker)

None of the social workers wonder about whether the mother is also being abused, and, just like the child, in need of protection. An English study showed that when children are physically abused by men, professional attention moves quickly from the man to the mother (Farmer et al. 1995), in spite of the fact that in most of the families where the children were at greatest risk, the woman suffered continual physical abuse from the man.

The parents in this study are most often described as one unit, and not as two individuals. They have joint responsibility to protect their child. If the social worker judges that the child is abused in the family, it seems that a depersonalising of the responsibility for the violence takes place.

Measures

In Stage 2 of the vignette, when a neighbour sees the father hit the child, the social workers envisage several different measures to improve the child's situation. Almost all of them (96%) think that they can offer the family help:

If the parents accept help there are many possibilities – discussions, advice and support.
(Social worker)

Support and motivate the parents and the child too before making a decision about taking into care.
(Social worker)

Most of both Erik's (95%) and Eva's (90%) social workers think that the child can remain at

Table 4 The measures the social workers regarded as options in the situation described

| | At home with support | | Contact family | | Voluntary placement | | Compulsory placement | |
	Eva	Erik	Eva	Erik	Eva	Erik	Eva	Erik
Stage 2	90%	95%	82%	73%	58%	51%	11%	17%
Stage 3	21%	39%	11%	46%	76%	90%	84%	93%

home if the family receives support from the social or medical authorities. However, most of the social workers did have some doubts about this. Only a few of Eva's (8%) and Erik's (17%) social workers were completely confident about the child remaining in the home. About three-quarters (77%) of the social workers thought that having a contact family/person for the child might be a solution. Encouraging the parents to voluntarily place their child in care away from home was also a possible alternative for 54% of the social workers – slightly more for Eva's (58%) than for Erik's (51%). In the situation described, most of the social workers were not yet prepared to recommend a compulsory placement (77%). However, slightly more of Erik's (17%) than Eva's (11%) social workers thought that it actually was the right time to apply for a compulsory placement.

In Stage 3 of the vignette, when symptoms of suspected abuse were observed, the social workers reacted by wanting to place the child in care away from the family. Almost all of the social workers dealing with Erik's case now wanted to apply for a compulsory placement (93%). They would also have considered a voluntary placement (90%). Most of Eva's social workers also wanted a compulsory (84%) or voluntary (76%) placement of the child. Eva's social workers were not as focused as Erik's on a placement outside the home. In a reactive situation, then, it seems that the social workers felt that a boy somewhat more frequently than a girl needed protection by placement away from their family.

Summary and discussion

The social workers seem to react somewhat differently depending on whether the child is a boy or a girl, even when the child is only four years old. It can also mean that they will take different measures in the same situations. The social workers were relatively certain that, in all of the situations described, the case was

something for the social services to work with, regardless of whether it was a boy or a girl. More social workers were, however, convinced that the social services should always get involved regarding a boy. The boy's social workers also judged at an earlier stage than the girl's that there were serious social problems and that the child must be taken into care. The boy's social workers were also slightly more prepared to use compulsory placement than those working on the girl's case. This can be interpreted as meaning that social workers can judge the gravity of a violent situation differently, depending on whether it involves a boy or a girl. They can take measures to protect the child in situations that are less well-documented for a boy than for a girl.

Not only teachers pay more attention to boys than girls. Boys also seem to get more attention than girls in matters concerning the social services. Social workers can feel that a boy's situation is more problematical than that of a girl in an identical situation, even when the child is no more than four years old. The social workers' reaction is that they question and want to check the information about the girl's social problems a little more than for a boy. There seems therefore to be more doubt about the accuracy of the information concerning a girl's situation than there is about the same information on a boy's identical situation. Protecting the child from the family comes into the picture earlier for a boy than for a girl. A girl in the same situation isn't seen as being without problems, however, but does not need protecting from the family. Instead, it is judged that the parents need help to take care of the girl. It can be concluded from the reaction of the social workers that girls are not protected to the same extent as boys. It can also be interpreted that there is a more critical analysis of the information about an unsatisfactory situation brought to the notice of the social services if the case concerns a girl rather than a boy.

From the gender equality perspective, boys and girls should be treated alike. This is not so in the fictitious world of the vignette. There is also statistical information which can be interpreted as indicating that it is not the case in reality either. There is, neither in the fictitious world of the vignette nor in reality, a radical difference between the way small children of either gender are treated, but the social workers seem to choose to protect a boy from violence in the family at an earlier stage than a girl. The signals about something being wrong do not need to be as strong in a boy's case as in a girl's. For small children, this can mean that girls are exposed to more violence than boys before the social services take measures to protect the child. What is deemed to be an unsatisfactory state of affairs can vary from one culture to another, and also vary in one culture depending on time and place. Gender differences, however, seem to be culturally all-embracing.

According to the UN Children's Convention, a child should be given the opportunity to express their thoughts, feelings and opinions in all matters concerning themselves 'where the child is able to form their own opinions' (UD informerar, 1996:2). According to Swedish social services legislation, the child's opinions should as far as possible be ascertained. Neither boys nor girls were given the opportunity, from the standpoint of the family situation and a 4-year-old's terms, to express themselves. Only a few social workers stated that they would interview the child in the situation where it was probable that the child had suffered abuse, and where the majority of social workers intended to apply for a compulsory placement. This is a situation in which the child would probably be removed from the family without the social worker having spoken to the child. Occasional conversations with the social worker in an investigative situation do not give a child that has suffered family violence an opportunity to express themselves properly, since a central feature of the abuse situation is keeping silent about what has happened. The social workers' conversations with the children can be more in the nature of a bureaucratic alibi for a legal requirement than really giving the children an opportunity to express themselves.

The authorities may not in any way discriminate against women, neither girls nor mothers. Mothers and fathers are to have equal rights and responsibilities as parents, and they too must also be visible subjects. The parents were most often regarded by the social workers as one unit, and not as two individuals with different relationships, behaviour and separate responsibility for their actions. Men seem, to a certain extent, to be freed of responsibility for their actions concerning their children, even when this is regarded as abuse, because, amongst other things, parenthood is seen from the authorities' perspective as a dualistic – not an individualistic – relationship to the child.

References

Andersson, C. (1991) 'Flickors väg in i missbruket av alkohol och andra droger' i Järvinen, M. and Rosenquist, P. *Kön, rus och disciplin* ISBN 951-47-5326-7.

Andersson, G. (1991) *Socialt arbete med sma barn*. Lund: Studentlitteratur.

Barnombudsmannen (1998) *Barnkonventionen i myndigheterna. En kartläggning av myndigheters arbete med FN:s konvention om barnets rättigheter* Stockholm: Barnombudsmannen.

Billquist, L. (1999) *Rummet, mötet och ritualerna En studie av socialbyran, klientarbetet och klientskapet* Göteborg: Institutionen för socialt arbete, Göteborgs Universitet.

Bronfenbrenner, U. (1979) *The Ecology of Human Development* Cambridge: Harvard University Press.

Brunnberg, E. (2000) *Barnperspektiv i socialt arbete* Göteborg: Göteborgs Universitet CEFOS.

Cederborg, A-C. (1998) 'Sma barns berättelse om sexuella övergrepp' *Socialvetenskaplig tidskrift*, 1 s 24–43.

Farmer, E. and Owen, M. (1995) *Child Protection Practice: Private Risks and Public Remedies*. London: HMSO.

Farmer, E. and Owen, M. (1998) Gender and the Child Protection Process. *British Journal of Social Work*, 28: 545–64.

Garbarino, J.and Eckenrode, J. (1997) *Understanding Abusive Families: An*

Ecological Approach to Theory and Practice. San Francisco, Jossey-Bass Publishers.

Granström, K. and Einarsson, C. (1995) *Forskning om liv och arbete i svenska klassrum* Stockholm:Liber förlag.

Hessle, S. (1996) 'Hur vet man när barn far illa?' i Andersson, G. (Ed.) *Barnet i den sociala barnavarden* Stockholm: Centrum för utvärdering av socialt arbete. Liber.

Holmberg, C. (1999) 'Det goda mötet eller en outtalad könskonflikt?' *Socionomen* , 1999: 4 s 65–9.

Hydén, M. (1994) 'Det upprepade valdet mot kvinnor i äktenskapet och fragan om manlig ansvarsbefrielse' *Socialvetenskaplig tidskrift* , 1994: 2–3 s 193–204.

Jergeby, U. (1999) *Att bedöma en social situation – Tillämpning av vinjettmetoden* Stockholm Socialstyrelsen Centrum för utvärdering av socialt arbete.

Kahl, I. (1995) *Socialarbetarkaren. Den lindansande Professionen* Sverige: Bokbox förlag.

Kullberg, C. (1994) *Socialt arbete som kommunikativ praktik* Linköping: Linköpings universitet, Tema Kommunikation.

Lundström, T. (1996) 'Den sociala barnavarden' i Andersson, G. (Ed.) *Barnet i den sociala barnavarden* Stockholm: Centrum för utvärdering av socialt arbete. Liber.

Sayer, A. (1999) *System, lifeworld and gender: associational versus counterfactual thinking* Paper presenterat vid Örebro universitet.

SFS 1980:620 *Socialtjänstlag* Rättsnätet:Rixlex. Lag 1998:409 Lag 1988:323 Lag 1997:313

SFS (1990:52) *Lag med särskilda bestämmelser om vard av unga* Rättsnätet:Rixlex Lag 1990:52.

Socialstyrlsen (1999) *Insatser för barn och unga* 1998.

Soydan, H. and Stal, R. (1994) How to Use the Vignette Technique in Cross-cultural Social Work Research. *Scandinavian Journal of Social Welfare*, 3, 75–80.

UD informerar 1993:6 *Mänskliga rättigheter Förenta Nationerna och kvinnans rättigheter.*

UD informerar 1996:2 *FN:s barnkonvention.*

Weinhall, K. (1997) *Att växa upp i valdets närhet Ungdomars berättelse om vald i hemmet* Umea: Umea universitet kademiska avhandlingar vid Pedagogiska institutionen Nr 45.